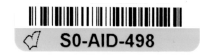

Diana

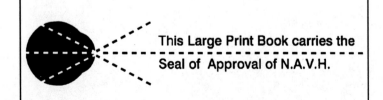

This Large Print Book carries the
Seal of Approval of N.A.V.H.

DIANA

HER TRUE STORY — IN HER OWN WORDS

ANDREW MORTON

THORNDIKE PRESS

A part of Gale, a Cengage Company

Farmington Hills, Mich • San Francisco • New York • Waterville, Maine
Meriden, Conn • Mason, Ohio • Chicago

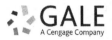

LIBRARY OF CONGRESS CATALOGING-IN-PUBLICATION DATA

Names: Morton, Andrew, 1953– author.
Title: Diana : her true story in her own words / by Andrew Morton.
Other titles: Diana, her true story in her own words
Description: Large print edition. | Waterville, Maine : Thorndike Press, part of Gale, a Cengage Company, 2017. | Series: Thorndike Press large print biographies and memoirs | Include bibliographical references
Identifiers: LCCN 2017027215| ISBN 9781432841164 (hardcover) | ISBN 1432841165 (hardcover)
Subjects: LCSH: Diana, Princess of Wales, 1961-1997. | Princesses—Great Britain—Biography. | Large type books.
Classification: LCC DA591.A45 M67 2017 | DDC 941.085092 [B] —dc23
LC record available at https://lccn.loc.gov/2017027215

Published in 2017 by arrangement with Simon & Schuster, Inc.

Printed in the United States of America
2 3 4 5 6 7 21 20 19 18 17

CONTENTS

ACKNOWLEDGEMENTS

This biography is unique in that the story contained in its pages would never have appeared had it not been for the wholehearted co-operation of Diana, the late Princess of Wales. The story is based on lengthy, tape-recorded interviews with Diana, supplemented by the testimony of her family and friends. Like Diana, they spoke with honesty and frankness in spite of the fact it meant laying aside the ingrained habits of discretion and loyalty which proximity to royalty invariably engenders. My thanks for their co-operation are therefore all the more heartfelt and sincere.

My grateful thanks, too, to the Princess of Wales's brother, the 9th Earl Spencer, for his insights and reminiscences, particularly about the Princess's childhood and teenage years.

My thanks also to the Baroness Falkender, Carolyn Bartholomew, Sue Beechey, Dr

James Colthurst, James Gilbey, Malcolm Groves, Lucinda Craig Harvey, Peter and Neil Hickling, Felix Lyle, Michael Nash, Delissa Needham, Adam Russell, Rory Scott, Angela Serota, now Baroness Bernstein of Craigweil, Muriel Stevens, Oonagh Toffolo and Stephen Twigg.

To Professor John Taylor and Dr Frank Prochaska, my thanks for your thoughts on legacy and the future of the monarchy.

There are others whose positions prevent me from officially acknowledging their assistance. Their unstinting guidance has been invaluable.

My thanks to my publisher, Michael O'Mara, for his guidance and support on the tortuous path from conception to the completion of the numerous editions that charted Diana's ultimately tragic journey.

FOREWORD

Even at a distance of 25 years, it is a scarcely believable story. Hollywood producers would dismiss the script as much too far-fetched; a beautiful but desperate princess, an unknown writer, an amateur go-between and a book that would change the Princess's life forever.

In 1991 Princess Diana was approaching 30. She had been in the limelight all of her adult life. Her marriage to Prince Charles in 1981 was described as a 'fairytale' by the Archbishop of Canterbury. In the popular imagination, the Prince and Princess, blessed with two young sons, Princes William and Harry, were the glamorous and sympathetic face of the House of Windsor. The very idea that their ten-year marriage was in dire trouble was unthinkable — even to the notoriously imaginative tabloid press. Commenting on a joint tour of Brazil that year, the *Sunday Mirror* described them as presenting a 'united front to the world', their closeness sending a 'shiver of excitement' around the massed media ranks.

Shortly afterwards I was to learn the unvarnished truth. The unlikely venue for these extraordinary revelations was a working man's café in the anonymous London suburb of Ruislip. As labourers noisily tucked into plates of egg, bacon and baked beans, I put on a pair of headphones, turned on a battered tape recorder and listened with mounting astonishment to the unmistakable voice of the Princess as she poured out a tale of woe in a rapid stream of consciousness. It was like being transported into a parallel universe, the Princess talking about her unhappiness, her sense of betrayal, her suicide attempts and two things I had never previously heard of: bulimia nervosa, an eating disorder, and a woman called Camilla.

I left the café reeling, scarcely able to believe what I had heard. It was as though I had been admitted into an underground club that was nursing a secret. A dangerous secret. On my way home that evening I kept well away from the edge of the Underground platform, my mind spinning with the same paranoia that infected the movie *All the President's Men,* about President Nixon, the

10

Watergate break-in and the subsequent investigation by Woodward and Bernstein.

For nearly ten years I had been writing about the royal family, and was part of the media circus chronicling their work as they toured the globe. It was, as the members of the so-called 'royal ratpack' used to say, the most fun you could have with your clothes on. I had met Prince Charles and Princess Diana on numerous occasions at press receptions which were held at the beginning of every tour. Conversations with the Princess were light, bright and trite, usually about my loud ties.

However, life as a royal reporter was not one long jolly. Behind the scenes of the royal theatre, there was a lot of hard work, cultivating contacts inside Buckingham Palace and Kensington Palace, where the Waleses occupied apartments eight and nine, in order to find out about royal life when the grease paint was removed. After writing books about life inside the various palaces, the royal family's wealth and a biography of the Duchess of York, as well as other works, I had got to know a number of friends and royal staff reasonably well and thought I had a fair idea of what was going on behind the wrought-iron royal gates. Nothing had prepared me for this.

My induction to the truth came courtesy of the man in charge of the tape recorder. I first met Dr James Colthurst in October 1986 on a routine royal visit when he escorted Diana after she opened a new CT scanner in his X-ray department at St Thomas' hospital in central London. Afterwards, over tea and biscuits, I questioned him about Diana's visit. It soon became clear that Colthurst, an Old Etonian and son of a baronet whose family have owned Blarney Castle in Ireland for more than a century, had known the Princess for years.

He could become, I thought, a useful contact. We became friendly, enjoying games of squash in the St Thomas' courts before sitting down to large lunches at a nearby Italian restaurant. Chatty but diffuse, James was happy to talk about any subject but the Princess. Certainly he had known her well enough to visit her when she was a bachelor girl living with her friends at Coleherne Court in Kensington and listen to her mooning about Prince Charles. They had even gone on a skiing holiday to France with a party of friends. Upon her elevation to the role of Princess of Wales, the easy familiarity that characterized her life was lost, Diana still speaking fondly of her 'Coleherne Court' but in the past tense.

It was only after she visited St Thomas' that Colthurst and the Princess renewed their friendship, meeting up for lunch every now and again. By degrees he too was admitted into her secret club and was given glimpses of the real life, rather than the fantasy, endured by the Princess. It was clear that her marriage had failed and that her husband was having an affair with Camilla Parker Bowles, the wife of his Army friend Andrew who held the curious title of Silver Stick in Waiting to the Queen. Mrs Parker Bowles, who lived near to Highgrove, the Waleses' country home, was so close to the Prince that she regularly hosted dinners and other gatherings for his friends at his Gloucestershire home.

While Colthurst felt he was being let in on a secret, he was not the only one. From the bodyguard who accompanied the Prince on his nocturnal visits to Camilla's home at Middlewick House, to the butler and chef ordered to prepare and serve a supper they knew the Prince would not be eating as he had gone to see his lover, and the valet who marked up programmes in the TV listings guide *Radio Times,* to give the impression the Prince had spent a quiet evening at home — all those working for the Prince and Princess were pulled, often against their will, into the deception. His valet Ken Stronach became ill with the daily deceit while their press officer Dickie Arbiter found himself in an 'impossible position', maintaining to the world the illusion of happy families while turning a blind eye to the private distance between them.

When Prince Charles broke his arm in a polo accident in June 1990 and was taken to Cirencester hospital, his staff listened intently to the police radios reporting on the progress of the Princess of Wales on her journey from London to the hospital. They were keenly aware that they had to usher out his first visitor — Camilla Parker Bowles — before Diana arrived.

Those in the know realized that the simmering cauldron of deceit, subterfuge and duplicity was going to boil over sooner or later. Every day they asked themselves how long the conspiracy to hoodwink the future queen could continue. Perhaps indefinitely. Or until the Princess was driven mad by those she trusted and admired, who told her, time after weary time, that Camilla was just a friend. Her suspicions, they reasoned, were misplaced, the imaginings, as the Queen Mother told her circle, of 'a silly girl'.

As Diana was to explain years later in her famous television interview on the BBC's

Panorama programme: 'Friends on my husband's side were indicating that I was again unstable, sick and should be put in a home of some sort in order to get better. I was almost an embarrassment.'

Far from being the ravings of a madwoman, Diana's suspicions were to prove correct, and the painful awareness of the way she had been routinely deceived, not just by her husband but by those inside the royal system, instilled in her an absolute and understandable distrust and contempt for the Establishment. They were attitudes that would shape her behaviour for the rest of her life.

So, as Colthurst tucked into his chicken kiev, he watched as Diana toyed with her wilted salad and spoke with a mixture of anger and sadness about her increasingly intolerable position. She was coming to realize that unless she took drastic action she faced a life sentence of unhappiness and dishonesty. Her first thought was to pack her bags and flee to Australia with her young boys. There were echoes here of the behaviour of her own mother, Frances Shand Kydd, who, following an acrimonious divorce from Diana's father, Earl Spencer, lived as a virtual recluse on the bleak island of Seil in north-west Scotland.

This attitude, however, was merely bravado and resolved nothing. The central issue remained: how to give the public an insight into her side of the story while untangling the legal, emotional and constitutional knots that kept her tethered to the monarchy. It was a genuine predicament. If she had just packed her bags and left, the public and media, who firmly believed in the fairytale, would have considered her behaviour irrational, hysterical and profoundly unbecoming. As far as she was concerned, she had done everything in her power to confront the issue. She had spoken with Charles and been dismissed. Then she had talked to the Queen but faced a blank wall.

Not only did she consider herself to be a prisoner trapped inside a bitterly unfulfilled marriage, she also felt shackled to a wholly unrealistic public image of her royal life and to an unsympathetic royal system which was ruled, in her phrase, by the 'men in grey suits'. She felt disempowered both as a woman and as a human being. Inside the palace she was treated with kindly condescension, seen as an attractive adornment to her questing husband. 'And meantime Her Royal Highness will continue doing very little, but doing it very well,' was the comment by one private secretary at a meeting to discuss future engagements.

Remember, this was the same woman who in 1987 had done more than anyone alive to remove the stigma surrounding the deadly Aids virus when she shook the hand of a terminally ill sufferer at London's Middlesex Hospital. While she was not able to fully articulate it, Diana had a humanitarian vision for herself that transcended the dull, dutiful round of traditional royal engagements.

As she looked out from her lonely prison, rarely a day passed by without the sound of another door slamming, another lock snapping shut as the fiction of the fairytale was further embellished in the public's mind. 'She felt the lid was closing in on her,' Colthurst later recalled. 'Unlike other women, she did not have the freedom to leave with her children.'

Like a prisoner condemned for a crime she did not commit, Diana had a crying need to tell the world the truth about her life, the distress she felt and the ambitions she nurtured. Her sense of injustice was profound. Quite simply, she wanted the liberty to speak her mind, the opportunity to tell people the whole story of her life and to let them judge her accordingly.

She felt somehow that if she was able to

explain her story to the people, her people, they could truly understand her before it was too late. 'Let them be my judge,' she said, confident that her public would not criticize her as harshly as the royal family or the mass media. However, her desire to explain what she saw as the truth of her case was matched by a nagging fear that at any moment her enemies in the Palace would have her classified as mentally ill and locked away. This was no idle fear — when her *Panorama* interview was screened in 1995, the then Armed Forces Minister, Nicholas Soames, a close friend and former equerry to Prince Charles, described her as displaying 'the advanced stages of paranoia'.

It gradually dawned on her and her intimate circle that unless the full story of her life was told, the public would never appreciate or understand the reasons behind any actions she decided upon. She chewed over a number of options, from commissioning a series of newspaper articles, to producing a television documentary and publishing a biography of her life. Diana knew her message; she was struggling to find a medium.

How then could she smuggle her message to the outside world? Reviewing Britain's social landscape she saw that there were few outlets for her story. The House of Windsor is the most influential family in the land, its tentacles wrapped tightly around the decision makers inside television and much of the press. Credible media outlets, the BBC, ITV and the so-called quality newspapers, would have had a collective attack of the vapours if she had signalled that she wanted them to publish the truth of her position. Again, if her story appeared in the tabloid press it would have been dismissed by the Establishment as so much exaggerated rubbish.

What to do? Within her small circle of intimate friends there was sufficient alarm at her current state of mind for several to fear for Diana's safety. It was known that she had made a number of half-hearted suicide attempts in the past and, as her desperation grew, there was genuine concern that she could take her own life; worries tempered by a balancing belief that ultimately her love for her children could never take her down that path.

At the time she knew that I was researching a biography of her and had been reasonably pleased with an earlier work, *Diana's Diary,* mainly because it irritated the Prince of Wales with its detailed description of the Highgrove interior. While researching that book, I had heard hints and rumours that all was not well inside the world of the Waleses. This gossip was but the bland hors d'œuvres before the barely digestible feast of information to come.

Without my fully knowing, Diana was gradually testing me out. She made it clear to Colthurst that she was not averse to him giving me titbits of information. In March 1991 he called me from a phone box on the southern tip of Ireland and told me that Prince Charles's private secretary Sir Christopher Airey had been sacked. The resulting article in the *Sunday Times* quietly thrilled Diana, knowing that she had secretly fired a salvo of her own in the direction of her husband. There were other tests which, though not on the scale of riddles posed by Puccini's Princess Turandot, had to be solved successfully.

She wanted to change her long-time hairdresser Richard Dalton and give another crimper a try. How best to dispense with his services tactfully and without his going to the newspapers to sell his story. Colthurst and I advised her to write him an honest letter, buy him an expensive present and send him on his way. The simple strategy worked.

At this time, what I completely failed to

understand was that, for a woman who was living in a system where every significant decision was made by someone else, these small choices and acts of defiance gave her a feeling of control. For her it was tremendously liberating.

At some point she asked Colthurst: 'Does Andrew want an interview?' It was by any standards, a mind-blowing suggestion. Princesses don't usually give interviews, especially when they are the most talked about and photographed princess of the age. These were the days before her *Panorama* confessional and before Prince Charles went on television to admit his adultery with Mrs Parker Bowles. It was simply unheard of.

Within days of Diana's suggestion, Colthurst summoned me to that working man's café in Ruislip to hear a sample of the story she had to tell. I expected it to be a few short sentences about her charity work and her thoughts about her humanitarian ambitions. Wrong again.

After jotting down notes on her suicide attempts, her eating disorders, her husband's adultery with this woman called Camilla, I hotfooted it to see my publisher, Michael O'Mara. Drawing on a pre-lunch cigar, he listened to a summary of my meet-

21

ing. Then, suspecting that Colthurst was a clever con man, he announced: 'If she is so unhappy why is she always smiling in the photographs?'

That went to the heart of the matter. If I was going to swim against the tide of public sentiment regarding the Princess of Wales and her husband, I needed some help. A few scratchy notes taken from a worn-out tape recorder wasn't going to cut it. What was needed was for the Princess to co-operate as far as she was able in a biography that told the story of her whole life, not just her royal career, thus placing her anxieties, her hopes and her dreams in context. To all intents and purposes the book that resulted from this co-operation, *Diana: Her True Story,* was her autobiography, the personal testament of a woman who saw herself at the time as voiceless and powerless.

Diana's initial commitment to the project was immediate and naïvely enthusiastic, as she wondered how many days it would take to publish the book. There was one major stumbling block: how to conduct the interviews with Diana. While I was keen to talk to the Princess directly, this was simply out of the question. At six-foot-four and as a writer known to palace staff, I would hardly be inconspicuous. As soon as it was known that a journalist was inside Kensington Palace — and at this time Prince Charles was nominally in residence — the balloon would go up and Diana would be constrained from any further indiscretions.

Just as Martin Bashir, the television journalist who later interviewed the Princess, was to discover, subterfuge was the only way to circumvent an ever-vigilant royal system. In November 1995, when Bashir conducted his interview, he smuggled his camera crew into Kensington Palace on a quiet Sunday when all her staff were absent.

For my part Diana was interviewed by proxy, James Colthurst the perfect agent to undertake this delicate and, as it turned out, historic mission. Armed with a list of questions I had prepared and his tape recorder, Colthurst set off on his sit-up-and-beg bicycle and pedalled nonchalantly up the drive of Kensington Palace. In May 1991 he conducted the first of six taped interviews that continued through the summer and into autumn, and would ultimately change the way the world saw the Princess and the royal family forever.

Colthurst vividly remembers that first session: 'We sat in her sitting room. Diana was dressed quite casually in jeans and a blue shirt. Before we began she took the phone off the hook and closed the door. Whenever we were interrupted by someone knocking she removed the body microphone and hid it in cushions on her sofa.

'For the first 20 minutes of that first interview she was very happy and laughing, especially when talking about incidents during her schooldays. When she got to the heavy issues, the suicide attempts, Camilla and her bulimia, there was an unmistakable sense of release, of unburdening.'

Early in their first conversation Colthurst said to her: 'Give me a shout if there is something you don't want me to touch on.' Her reply was telling: 'No, no, it's OK.' It was clear she wanted the world to know the whole truth, as she saw it.

At times she was annoyed and angered by the way she had been treated by her husband and the royal system, and yet in spite of her raw emotional state, what the Princess had to say was highly believable as many pieces of the jigsaw puzzle of her life began to fall into place. Deep-seated and intense feelings of abandonment and rejection which had dogged her for most of her life came to the surface. Though her childhood was privileged it was also unhappy, Diana describing a bleak emotional landscape where she recalled her guilt for not being born a boy in order to continue the family line, her divorced mother's tears, her father's lonely silences and her brother Charles sobbing himself to sleep at night.

While this long-distance interview technique was an imperfect method which gave no opportunity for immediate follow-ups, many questions were simply redundant as, once Diana started talking, she barely paused for breath, her story spilling out. It was a great release and a form of confessional. 'I was at the end of my tether. I was desperate,' Diana argued during her subsequent television interview. 'I think I was so fed up with being seen as someone who was a basket case because I am a very strong person and I know that causes complications in the system that I live in.'

The simple act of talking about her life aroused many memories for Diana, some cheerful, others almost too difficult to put into words. Like a gust of wind across a field of corn, her moods endlessly fluctuated. While she was candid, even whimsical, about her eating disorder, bulimia nervosa, and her half-hearted suicide attempts, she was at her lowest ebb when speaking about her early days inside the royal family; 'the dark ages', as she referred to them.

Time and again she emphasized her profound sense of destiny: a belief that she would never become Queen but that she had been singled out for a special role. She knew in her heart that it was her fate to travel along a road where the monarchy was secondary to her true vocation. With hindsight her words have a remarkable prescience.

At times she was amusingly animated, particularly when talking about her short life as a bachelor girl. She spoke wistfully about her romance with Prince Charles, sadly about her unhappy childhood and with some passion about the effect Camilla Parker Bowles had had on her life. Indeed, she was so anxious not to be seen as paranoid or foolish, as she had so often been told she was by her husband's friends, that she showed us several letters and postcards from Mrs Parker Bowles to Prince Charles to prove that she was not imagining their relationship.

These billets-doux, passionate, loving and full of suppressed longing, left my publisher and I in absolutely no doubt that Diana's suspicions were correct. It was quite evident that Camilla, who called Charles 'My most precious darling', was a woman whose love had remained undimmed in spite of the passage of time and the difficulties of pursuing the object of her devotion. 'I hate not being able to tell you how much I love you', she wrote, saying how much she longed to be with him and that she was his forever. I particularly remember one vivid passage that read: 'My heart and body both ache for you.'

Nevertheless, as we were informed by a leading libel lawyer, under strict British law, the fact that you know something to be true does not allow you to say it. Much to Diana's annoyance, and in spite of overwhelming evidence, I wasn't at the time able to write that Prince Charles and Camilla Parker Bowles were lovers. Instead I had to allude to a 'secret friendship' which had cast a long shadow over the royal marriage. Perhaps more importantly, Diana realized, after reading this cache of correspondence, that any hopes she might have harboured of saving her ten-year-old marriage were utterly doomed.

As much as she was engaged and enthusiastic about the project, the difficult unresolved issues under discussion, particularly her husband's relationship with Mrs Parker Bowles, would often leave her drained.

As I was working at one remove, I had to second-guess her moods and act accordingly. As a rule of thumb, mornings were times when she was at her most articulate and energetic, particularly if Prince Charles was absent. Those interview sessions were the most productive, Diana speaking with a breathless haste as she poured out her story. She could be unnervingly blithe even when discussing the most intimate and difficult periods of her life.

After she first talked about her suicide attempts, I naturally needed to know a great deal more about when and where they had occurred. I subsequently submitted a raft of specific questions on the subject. When they were presented to her, she treated it as a bit of a joke. 'He's pretty well written my obituary,' she told Colthurst.

On the other hand, if a session was arranged for the afternoon, when her energy was low, her conversation was less fruitful. This was particularly so if she had received some bad press or had a disagreement with her husband. Then it was usually sensible to focus on happy times, her memories of her bachelor days or her two children, Princes William and Harry. In spite of all these handicaps it was clear as the weeks passed that her excitement and involvement with the project was growing, particularly when a title for the book was decided upon. For example, if she knew I was interviewing a trusted friend she would do all she could to help by passing on a further scrap of information, a new anecdote or a correction relating to questions I had submitted earlier.

While she was desperate, almost to the point of imprudence, to see her words appear before a wider public, this mood was tempered by a fear that Buckingham Palace would discover her identity as the secret source, the 'Deep Throat', if you will, of my book. We realized that Diana must be given deniability, so that if the Princess was asked: 'Did you meet Andrew Morton?' she could answer with a resounding 'NO'. In fact the Princess was the last one to realize the importance of deniability, but once she knew that she would be kept firmly in the background she became much more enthusiastic.

The first line of deniability was her friends, who were used as cover to disguise her participation. In tandem with writing questions for the Princess, I sent out a number of letters to her circle of friends asking for an interview. They in turn contacted Diana to ask if they should or should not co-operate. It was a patchy process. With some she was encouraging, with others ambivalent, depending on how well she knew them.

Many of those who knew the real Diana truly believed that life couldn't get any worse for her, arguing that anything was better than her current situation. There was, too, a sense that the dam could burst at any moment, that the story could break early and if it came from the Prince of Wales' side it would certainly not favour Diana. In this febrile climate, her friends spoke with a frankness and honesty, bravely aware that their actions would bring an unwanted media spotlight upon themselves. Later on in the process, they were even prepared to sign statements confirming their involvement with the book in order to satisfy the doubts of the editor of the *Sunday Times,* Andrew Neil, who was due to publish extracts from the book. Diana later explained why her friends spoke out: 'A lot of people saw the distress that my life was in, and they felt it was a supportive thing to help in the way that they did.'

Her friend and astrologer, Debbie Frank, confirmed this mood when she spoke about Diana's life in the months before the book's publication. 'There were times when I would leave a meeting with Diana feeling anxious and concerned because I knew her way was blocked. When Andrew Morton's book was published I was relieved because the world was let into her secret.'

As my interviews progressed, her friends and other acquaintances confirmed that behind the public smiles and glamorous image was a lonely and unhappy young woman who endured a loveless marriage, was seen as an outsider by the Queen and the rest of the royal family, and was frequently at odds with the aims and objectives of the royal system. Yet one of the heartening aspects of the story was how Diana was striving, with mixed success, to come to terms with her life, transforming from a victim to a woman in control of her destiny. It was a process which the Princess continued until the very end.

After that first session with Dr Colthurst, Diana knew that she had crossed a personal Rubicon. She had thrown away the traditional map of royalty and was striking out on her own with only a hazy idea of the route. The reality was that she was talking by remote control to a man she barely knew, about subjects that, if mishandled, could ruin her reputation. It was by any standards a remarkably reckless and potentially foolhardy exercise. But it worked triumphantly.

During this extraordinary year of secrecy and subterfuge, O'Mara, myself and Colthurst found ourselves not only writing, researching and publishing what was to become a unique literary beast, an 'authorized unauthorized' biography, but we also became her shadow court, second-guessing her paid advisers. Everything from handling staff problems, dealing with media crises and even drafting her speeches came under our umbrella.

As Colthurst recalls: 'The speeches meant a lot to her. It was an area where she realized that she could put across her own message. It gave her a real sense of empowerment and achievement that an audience actually listened to what she had to say rather than just judged her clothes or her hairstyle. She used to ring up very excited if there had been coverage on TV and radio, delighted that she had received praise or even acknowledgement for her thoughts.'

It was an exhilarating and amusing time for us all, helping to shape the future of the world's most famous young woman right under the noses of Fleet Street and Buckingham Palace.

While it had its lighter moments, this was a high-stakes, winner-take-all game. I had been warned on two separate occasions by former Fleet Street colleagues that, after a series of accurate articles appeared in the *Sunday Times* about the war of the Waleses,

Buckingham Palace was looking hard for my mole. Shortly after one such warning, my office was burgled and files rifled through, but nothing of consequence, apart from a camera, was stolen. From then on, a scrambler telephone and local pay phones were the only sure way that Diana felt secure enough to speak openly. To be extra sure Diana had her sitting room at Kensington Palace 'swept' for listening devices — none were found — and routinely shredded every piece of paper that came across her desk. She trusted no one inside the royal system. Or for that matter outside the royal world.

Even with James Colthurst she was never entirely frank. While she raged against her husband's infidelity, she hid the fact that she had enjoyed a long if sporadic love affair with Major James Hewitt, a tank commander during the first Gulf War, as well as a brief dalliance with old friend James Gilbey. He was later exposed as the male voice on the notorious Squidgygate tapes, telephone conversations between Gilbey and the Princess illicitly recorded over New Year 1989–90. Nor did we have the faintest inkling of her infatuation with the married art dealer Oliver Hoare, who was the object of her love and devotion during the research and writing of *Diana: Her True Story.*

Looking back, her audacity was breathtaking and one is left wondering if Diana wanted to get her side of the story published first so that she would escape blame for the failure of the marriage. It is a question that will never be properly answered. In fact it was one of Diana's most enduring and probably intriguing qualities that no matter how close her friends thought they were to her she always held something back, keeping everyone in different compartments.

As the project gained momentum, with numerous phone calls between Colthurst and the Princess dealing with the quotidian details of her life, there was little time — or inclination — for considering her motivations. The priority was to produce a book that reflected her personality accurately, with sympathy and authenticity. Given the shocking nature of Diana's story, and the secrecy of her involvement, the book had to seem credible and believable.

My first acid test came when the Princess read the manuscript. It was delivered to her piecemeal at any and every opportunity. As with everything else to do with this book it was an amateur and haphazard operation. One such instance happened late one Saturday morning when I had to bicycle to the

Brazilian Embassy in Mayfair, where the Princess was having lunch with the Ambassador's wife, Lucia Flecha de Lima, so that I could pass on the latest offering.

Having been given the opportunity to write the story of the best-loved woman in the world I was obviously anxious to know that I had fairly and accurately interpreted her sentiments and her words. To my great relief she approved; on one occasion Diana was so moved by the poignancy of her own story that she confessed to weeping tears of sorrow.

She made a number of alterations, of fact and emphasis, but only one of any significance, a change which gives an insight into her respect for the Queen. During the interviews she had said that when she threw herself down the stairs at Sandringham while pregnant with Prince William, the Queen was the first on the scene. On the manuscript, Diana altered the text and inserted the Queen Mother's name, presumably out of deference to the Sovereign.

Other hurdles remained. While a number of Diana's close friends went on the record in order to underpin the authenticity of the text, the Princess accepted that the book needed a direct link with her own family in order to give it further legitimacy. After some discussion she agreed to supply the Spencer family photograph albums, which contained numerous delightful portraits of the growing Diana, many taken by her late father, Earl Spencer.

Shortly before he died, the Princess sent her father a short note explaining why she had co-operated in a book about her life.

I would like to ask you a special favour.

In particular I would like you to keep that as a secret between us. Please will you do that.

An author who has done me a particular favour is now writing a book on me as Diana, rather than PoW [Princess of Wales]. I trust him completely — and have every reason to do so. He has felt for a long time that the System has rather overshadowed my own life and would like to do a fuller book on me as a person.

It is a chance for my own self to surface a little rather than be lost in the system. I rather see it as a lifebelt against being drowned and it is terribly important to me — and this was brought home to me when I was showing the boys the albums — to remember these things which are *me.*

She then went on to ask her father to supply the family albums for the book and, hey presto, a few days later several large, red, gold-embossed family albums made their way to the South London offices of my publisher. A number of photographs were selected and duplicated, and the albums returned. The Princess herself helped to identify many of the people who appeared in the photographs with her, a process she greatly enjoyed as it brought back many happy memories, particularly of her teenage years.

She appreciated, too, that, in order to make the book truly distinctive, we had to have a previously unpublished jacket picture. As it was out of the question that she could attend a photo shoot, she personally chose and supplied the winsome Patrick Demarchelier cover photograph, which was one she kept in her study desk at Kensington Palace. This shot, and those of her and her children, which were used inside, were her particular favourites. We have chosen a hitherto unseen Demarchelier shot for the cover of this anniversary edition of *Diana: Her True Story — In Her Own Words*.

These were quiet interludes as the storm clouds gathered. The book was due to be published on 16 June 1992 and, as that date approached, the tension at Kensington

> Diana enjoyed herself enormously not least because it brought her
> sister down a peg or two. Yet it never entered her head for a
> moment to think that Prince Charles was remotely interested in
> romance. Certainly she never considered herself a match for the
> actress Susan George, who was his escort that evening. In any
> case life was much too fun to think about steady boyfriends. She
> had returned from her ill starred excursion to a Swiss finishing
> school desperate to begin an independent life in London. Her
> parents were not as enthusiastic. Her father, unhappy that she *just*
> had left West Heath before completing the extra year, was *some*
> disappointed when she dropped out of her finishing school as
> well. *did!*
>
> She had no paper qualifications, no special skills and no burning
> —ambitions bar a vague notion that she wanted to work with
> children. While Diana seemed destined for a life of unskilled,
> low paying jobs she was not that much out of the ordinary for
> girls of her class and background. Aristocratic families
> traditionally invest more thought and effort in educating boys
> than girls.

Diana made a number of alterations to the original manuscript in her own hand.

Palace became palpable. Her newly appointed private secretary, Patrick Jephson, described the atmosphere as 'like watching a slowly spreading pool of blood seeping from under a locked door'. In January 1992 she was warned that Buckingham Palace was aware of her co-operation with the book, even though at that stage they did not know its contents. Nonetheless she remained steadfast in her involvement with the venture. She knew that there was a cataclysm in the offing but had no doubts that she would survive it.

In a letter to James Colthurst some six months before the book's publication she wrote: 'Obviously we are preparing for the volcano to erupt and I do feel better equipped to cope with whatever comes our

As her father began his fight back to health, Diana's mother took a hand in guiding her career. She wrote to Miss Betty Vacani, the legendary dance teacher who has taught three generations of royal children, and asked if there was a vacancy for a student teacher. There was. Diana passed her interview and, in the spring term, began at the Vacani dance studio on the Brompton Road. It was not a particularly demanding job, basically playing Ring a Ring o' _Ballet_ Roses with a group of two-year-olds, but it did combine her love _Reached_ of children with her enjoyment of dance. Again she only lasted _cause_ three months. For once it wasn't her fault. _too._

In March her friend Mary-Anne Stewart-Richardson invited her to join her family on their skiing holiday in the French Alps. She fell badly on the slopes, tearing the tendons in her right ankle. For three months she was in and out of plaster as the tendons slowly heeled. It marked the end of her aspirations as a dance teacher.

What made it worse was that Prince Charles seemed less concerned about her predicament than that of his friend Camilla Parker-Bowles. When he called Diana on the phone he often spoke in sympathetic tones about the rough time Camilla was enjoying because there were three or four press outside her then home of Bolehyde Manor in Wiltshire. Diana bit her lip and said nothing, never mentioning the virtual seige she was living under. She didn't think that it was her place to do so nor did she want to appear to be a burden to the man she ~~longed to marry.~~ _was in love with_

As the romance gathered momentum, Diana began to harbour doubts about her new friend Camilla Parker-Bowles. She seemed to know everything that she and Charles had discussed in their rare moments of privacy and was full of advice on how best to handle Prince Charles. It was all very strange. Even Diana, an absolute

way! Thank you for your belief in me and for taking the trouble to understand this mind — it's such a relief not to be on my own any more and that it's _okay_ to be me.'

The volcano erupted on 7 June 1992 when the first extract appeared in the _Sunday Times_ under the banner headline: 'Diana driven to five suicide bids by "uncaring" Charles'. Underneath was the subheading: 'Marriage collapse led to illness; Princess says she will not be Queen.'

It is hard now, when the narrative of her unhappy life is conventional wisdom, as illustrated by the fact that Prince Charles and Camilla Parker Bowles have been happily married for 12 years, to convey the shock, disgust and astonishment that greeted the first instalment. Criticism was severe and unrelenting. The Archbishop of Canterbury warned about the damage to the boys, one Member of Parliament suggested I be imprisoned in the Tower of London, while the chairman of the Press Complaints Commission, Lord McGregor, accused the media of 'dabbling their fingers in the stuff of other people's souls'.

In the ensuing furore the book was condemned and banned by numerous major bookstores and supermarkets, in the process becoming Britain's most banned book of the 1990s. It is one of the ironies of this whole affair that a biography written and produced with the complete and enthusiastic co-operation of the subject should be piously boycotted on the suspicion that it was a false rendering of Diana's life.

As for the subject herself, she was relieved that at last her account was out, but desperately anxious that her cover story would hold water. She had to be able to deny involvement when she was put in the dock by the Palace.

It was a part she played with aplomb. The

author and TV star Clive James fondly recalled asking her over lunch whether she was behind the book. He wrote: 'At least once, however, she lied to me outright. "I really had nothing to do with that Andrew Morton book," she said. "But after my friends talked to him I had to stand by them." She looked me straight in the eye when she said this, so I could see how plausible she could be when she was telling a whopper.'

Certainly the first few days after the initial serialization tested Diana's resolve to the limit. Soon, though, she began to receive the kind of support that always meant so much to her, from her public. While the public's image of Diana underwent an astonishing transformation when her story was told, I don't think she ever truly thought through the consequences of her actions. When she was later asked that question, her response was hesitant: 'I don't know. Maybe people have a better understanding, maybe there's a lot of women out there who suffer on the same level but in a different environment who are unable to stand up for themselves because their self-esteem is cut in two.' Once again her instinct about the response was unerring. Thousands of women, many from America, expressed how, through reading about her life, they had discovered and explored something in their own lives. Letters came flooding in. Many came from people who had suffered with eating disorders and accepted their lot in silence. For me, one of the most touching instances came from a young bulimic woman in Perth in Western Australia, who could neither read nor write well but vowed to improve her education and her life, having been inspired by Diana's personal courage. It was an extraordinary response — and it meant so much to her.

Over the years there have been numerous suggestions that she regretted her part in the book, that it gave a sour snapshot at a difficult moment in her life. The truth is that she had put what she called 'the dark ages' of her life behind her and was anxious to move on to a more fulfilling future. As her friend film-maker Lord Puttnam recalled: 'She owned what she had done. She knew what she was doing and took a calculated risk even though she was scared shitless. But I never heard one word of regret, I promise you.'

In the months following that momentous event, the book not only altered the way the public viewed the monarchy and forced the Prince and Princess of Wales finally to address the ruins of their marriage, it also brought the one thing Diana had dreamed of — hope; the chance of fulfilment, of freedom and of a future where she was free at last to be a person in her own right.

In the last five years, and particularly the last few months, of her life, the world witnessed the flowering of Diana's humanitarian spirit, qualities which, I am sure, would have remained buried if she had not had the courage and determination to tell her public about the reality of her life. Diana achieved that aim, and the public's verdict can be gauged by the mountain of flowers outside Kensington Palace and elsewhere, and the outpouring of grief which convulsed not just her own country but the rest of the world when she died prematurely in a car crash in Paris on 31 August 1997.

She may now be gone, but her words are with us forever. The story contained in the pages of *Diana: Her True Story* came from her lips. There were no camera lights, rehearsals, second takes or glib sound bites. Her words came from the heart, outlining in graphic and, at times, agonizing detail the sorrow and loneliness felt by a woman admired and adored around the world. When I wrote *Diana: Her True Story* her testimony was used *sotto voce* throughout the text — in short, direct quotation or through third parties. One of the abiding sadnesses of her short life was that she never truly had the chance, as her brother said, to 'sing openly'. Following her death I was finally able to include a transcript of her unvarnished words in a new edition of the book. However, even then the limitations of the technology prevented us from being able to include as much as we would have liked. On one occasion, for instance, Colthurst had used the cover story of treating the Princess's painful shoulder to conduct an interview; unfortunately, the machine he was using came so close to the microphone that the noise interfered with the audio. Today, thanks to advances in modern technology, we've been able to extract her words and I can now share a more comprehensive account of her historic and truly unique interviews.

As you'll see, this volume is divided into three parts: the first is an edited transcript of the interviews Diana gave which formed the basis for the initial publication of *Diana: Her True Story;* the second is the biography itself; and the final part is an account of the aftermath, from the book's publication in 1992 to the present day.

If Diana had enjoyed a full life she would probably have written her own memoirs at some point. Sadly, that is no longer possible. The testimony which follows is her life story as she wanted to tell it. Her words are now all we have of her, her testament, the nearest we will now ever get to her autobiography. No one can deny her that.

DIANA, PRINCESS OF WALES IN HER OWN WORDS

Publisher's note: The following words are selected and edited from extensive taped interviews given by Diana, Princess of Wales in 1991–2 to Andrew Morton for publication in *Diana: Her True Story.*

Childhood

[My first memory] is really the smell of the inside of my pram. It was plastic and the smell of the hood. I was born at home, not in hospital.

The biggest disruption was when Mummy decided to leg it. That's the vivid memory we have — the four of us. We all have our own interpretations of what should have happened and what did happen. People took sides. Various people didn't speak to each other. For my brother and I it was a very wishy-washy and painful experience.

Charles [her brother] said to me the other day that he hadn't realized how much the divorce had affected him until he got married and started having a life of his own. But my other sisters — their growing up was done out of our sight. We saw them at holidays. I don't remember it being a big thing.

I idolized my eldest sister and I used to do all her washing when she came back from school. I packed her suitcase, ran her bath, made her bed — the whole lot. I did it all and I thought it was wonderful. I soon learned that doing that wasn't such a good idea. I always looked after my brother really. My two sisters were very independent.

We had so many changes of nannies, because Daddy was a very attractive divorcee and he was good bait for somebody. We tend to think they came for that rather than for looking after my brother and I. If we didn't like them we used to stick pins in their chair and throw their clothes out of the window. We always thought they were a threat because they tried to take mother's position. They were all very young and rather pretty. They were chosen by my father. It was terribly disruptive to come back from school one day to find a new nanny.

I always felt very different from everyone

else, very detached. I knew I was going somewhere different but had no idea where. I said to my father when I was aged 13, 'I know I'm going to marry someone in the public eye', thinking more of being an ambassador's wife — not the top one, very much so. It was a very unhappy childhood. Parents were busy sorting themselves out. Always seeing our mum crying. Daddy never spoke to us about it. We could never ask questions. Too many changes over nannies, very unstable, the whole thing. Generally unhappy and being very detached from everybody else.

At the age of 14 I just remember thinking that I wasn't very good at anything, that I was hopeless because my brother was always the one getting exams at school and I was the dropout. I couldn't understand why I was perhaps a nuisance to have around which, in later years, I've perceived as being part of the [whole question of the] son, the child who died before me was a son and both [parents] were crazy to have a son and heir and there comes a third daughter. What a bore, we're going to have to try again. I've recognized that now. I've been aware of it and now I recognize it and that's fine. I accept it.

I adored animals, guinea pigs and all that.

I had a mass of rabbits, guinea pigs and hamsters. Hamsters breed faster than most; I never got them sexed. They all had names, but I can't remember the first one. We just had endless animals. [When they died] the goldfish got flushed down the loo. [The rabbits were always buried] under a tree. They went off in a Clarks shoebox.

In my bed I'd have 20 stuffed animals and there would be a midget's space for me, and they would have to be in my bed every night.

They were all adored. They've got a Diana Spencer nametag on them from prep school — D. Spencer.

That was my family. I hated the dark and had an obsession about the dark, always had to have a light outside my door until I was at least ten. I used to hear my brother crying in his bed down at the other end of the house, crying for my mother and he was unhappy too, and my father right down the other end of the house and it was always very difficult. I never could pluck up courage to get out of bed. I remember it to this day.

I remember seeing my father slap my mother across the face. I was hiding behind the door and Mummy was crying. I remember Mummy crying an awful lot and every Saturday when we went up for weekends, every Saturday night, standard procedure, she would start crying. On Saturday we would both see her crying. 'What's the matter, Mummy?' 'Oh, I don't want you to leave tomorrow', which for a nine-year-old was devastating, you know. I remember the most agonizing decision I ever had to make. I was a bridesmaid to my first cousin and to go to the rehearsal I had to be smart and wear a dress and my mother gave me a green dress and my father had given me a white dress and they were both so smart, the dresses, and I can't remember to this day which one I got in but I remember being totally traumatized by it because it would show favouritism.

I remember there being a great discussion that a judge was going to come to me at Riddlesworth [Diana's preparatory school] and say who would I prefer to live with. The judge never turned up and then suddenly my stepfather [the late Peter Shand Kydd] arrived on the scene. Charles and I, my brother and I, went up to London and I said to Mummy, 'Where is he? Where is your new husband?' 'He's at the ticket barrier', and there was this very good-looking, handsome man and we were longing to love him and we accepted him and he was great to

51

us, spoiled us rotten. It was very nice being spoiled because [my] individual parents weren't attuned to that. [Peter] stood back [from the problems]. He was a bit of a manic — or *is* — a bit of a manic-depressive. His own worst enemy. So, when he had bad moods we just kept out the way. If he lost his temper, he lost his temper. It was never a problem.

Basically, we couldn't wait to be independent, Charles and I, in order to spread our wings and do our own thing. We had become horribly different at school because we had divorced parents and nobody else did at that time, but by the time we finished our five years at prep school everybody was. I was always different. I always had this thing inside me that I was different. I didn't know why. I couldn't even talk about it but in my mind it was there.

The divorce helped me to relate to anyone else who is upset in their family life, whether it be stepfather syndrome or mother or whatever, I understand it. Been there, done it.

I always got on very well with everybody. Whether it be the gardener, or the local police or whoever, I always went over to talk to them. My father always said: 'Treat everybody as an individual and never throw your weight around.'

My father used to sit us down every Christmas and birthday and we had to write our thank-you letters within 24 hours. And now if I don't, I get into a panic. If I come back from a dinner party or somewhere that needs a letter, at midnight I'll sit down and write it there and not wait until next morning because it would wrestle with my conscience. And William now does it — it's great. It's nice if other people appreciate it at the other end.

We were always shunted over to Sandringham [the Queen's Norfolk residence] for holidays. Used to go and see *Chitty Chitty Bang Bang,* the film. We hated it so much. I hated going over there. The atmosphere was always very strange when we went there and I used to kick and fight anyone who tried to make us go over there and Daddy was most insistent because it was rude. I said I didn't want to see *Chitty Chitty Bang Bang* for the third year running. Holidays were always very grim because, say we had a four-week holiday. Two weeks Mummy and two weeks Daddy and the trauma of going from one house to another and each individual parent trying to make it up in their area with material things rather than the actual tactile stuff, which is what we both craved for but

53

neither of us ever got. When I say neither of us my other two sisters were busy at prep school and were sort of out of the house whereas my brother and I were very much stuck together.

Birthdays were obviously a treat. My father once organized a dromedary to come along and give us rides around the lawn. He got it from Bristol [Zoo]. Birthdays were always a good time. Daddy loves parties. But there was still none of the arms round the shoulder, or hugging. It was always the other things.

I always wanted a pram for my birthday, and dolls. I was fiendish about the dolls and the prams. And I collected pieces of china. All sorts of fairytale things, and tiny little rabbits. I mean, anything that was small was wonderful as far as I was concerned.

Schooldays

Adored that [her preparatory school, Riddlesworth Hall]. I felt rejected, though, because I was busy looking after my father most of the time and then suddenly realized I was going to be away from him so I used to make threats like, 'If you love me you won't leave me here', which was jolly unkind to him at the time. Actually, I loved being at school. I was very naughty in the sense of always wanting to laugh and muck about rather than sit tight in the four walls of the schoolroom.

[I remember school plays] and the thrill of putting on make-up. It was one of those nativity plays. I was one of the twits who came and paid homage to the baby Jesus. In another I was a Dutch doll or something like that. My big moment. But I never put myself forward to speak in a play. I never read the lessons at school. I would go quietly. If I was asked to do it, my condition was I'd do it if I didn't have to speak.

[My first sporting cup] was for diving. I won it four years running, actually! I always won all the swimming and diving cups. I won all sorts of prizes for the best-kept guinea pig — maybe because mine was the only guinea pig in the guinea pig section. But in the academic department, you might as well forget about that!

At school we were only allowed one animal on the bed. I had a green hippo and painted his eyes luminous so that at night — I hated the dark — it looked as though he was looking at me!

I nearly got expelled because one night somebody said to me: 'Would you like to do a dare?' I thought: 'Why not? Life's so boring.' So they sent me out at 9 o'clock to the end of the drive which was half a mile long in pitch dark. I had to go and get some sweets at the gate from somebody called Polly Phillimore, I think she was called. I got there and there was nobody there.

I hid behind the gate as these police cars were coming in. I thought nothing more about it. I saw all the lights coming on in the school. I wandered back, terrified, to find that some twit in my bedroom said that she had appendicitis. Then they asked 'Where's Diana?' 'I don't know where she's gone.'

Both my parents were summoned — they were divorced then. Father was thrilled and my mother said: 'I didn't think you had it in you.' No telling off. Lots of girls had been doing it the previous nights as well — I think they'd been meeting boys or something — and they got expelled. There were all sorts of things that went on in the pack, and I just joined them for a bit of excitement. I must have been eleven or twelve.

I ate and ate and ate. It was always a great joke — let's get Diana to have three kippers at breakfast and six pieces of bread, and I did all that.

My sister [Jane] was a prefect at West

Heath School, and I was pretty ghastly for the first term. I was a bully because I thought it was so wonderful to have my sister as a prefect. I felt very important but the second term they all paid me back, all the people I was horrid to, and by the third term I was completely calm and sorted out.

I remember the food — terrible! The food was just gross. There was an enormous hall there which they had just built on. I used to sneak down at night when it was all dark and put on my music and do my ballet there in this enormous hall for hours on end and no one ever found me. All my friends knew where I was when I crept out and it always released tremendous tension in my head. I recognize it now but at the time it just seemed a good idea.

I liked all subjects. History fascinated me. Tudors and Stuarts, I adored them. To think that all these people lived x many years ago. I never anticipated I'd end up in the system, in the books. In English I loved *Far from the Madding Crowd* and *Pride and Prejudice*. But in O-levels you were so besieged with every single line that it became a chore rather than a pleasure. I took five — I got Ds for the lot. That's not even a pass. I remember when I wrote essays I wrote ten times more than I should have done. It just came out of the pen. On and on.

But I didn't think I'd end up in a place where I'd have to use all the information. I just thought it was part of the course, that you just learned it. If I could study a subject now it would be about people. The mind. Definitely the mind. I'd love to [study psychology].

[At school] I played the piano. I loved the piano. I did my tap dancing which I absolutely adored; tennis, I was captain of the netball team; hockey, you name it, because of my height. I was one of the tallest there. I adored being outdoors again, visited old people once a week, went to the local mental asylum once a week. I adored that. It was a sort of an introduction for bigger things. Then, by the time I got to the top of the school, all my friends had boyfriends but not me because I knew somehow that I had to keep myself very tidy for whatever was coming my way.

I had more girlfriends than boyfriends. I was always mucking about with girls rather than boys. But I didn't really have any friends that stuck.

I wasn't a good child, in the sense that I had horns in my ears. I was always looking for trouble. Yes, I was popular. I didn't shout out the answers in class because I didn't think I knew them. But I always knew how to behave. There was a time to be quiet and a time to be noisy. I could always tune in to which it should be. But I always felt that I was different, like I was in the wrong shell.

I had crushes, serious crushes on all sorts of people, especially my sisters' boyfriends. If they ever got chucked out from that department I used to try my way. I felt so sorry for them because they were so nice. That was purely it. Anyway, that was a dead miss.

Moving to Althorp

When I was 13 we moved to Althorp in Northampton and that was a terrible wrench, leaving Norfolk, because that's where everybody who I'd grown up with lived. We had to move because grandfather died and life took a very big turn because my stepmother, Raine, appeared on the scene, supposedly incognito. She used to sort of join us, accidentally find us in places and come and sit down and pour us with presents and we all hated her so much because we thought she was going to take Daddy away from us but actually she was suffering from the same thing.

She was very clever and she wanted to marry Daddy; that was her target and that was it. I've sat and boiled for years and years and two Septembers ago [1989] my brother got married and I told her what I thought about her and I've never known such anger in me. It's because my stepmother and my father were very rude to my mother at the rehearsal before [Charles'] wedding; they refused to speak to her, even sitting next to her on a pew. I thought that just for one day, for the sake of my brother, we could all be grown-up and get on with it. I just thought it was unbelievable. So I took it upon myself to air everyone's grievances in my family. And it was very difficult. My father didn't speak to me for six months. Raine doesn't speak to me now. But I stuck up for Mummy and my mother said that was the first time in 22 years anyone had ever stuck up for her. I said everything I possibly could. Raine said: 'You have no idea how much pain your mother has put your father through.' I said: 'Pain, Raine? That's one word you don't even know how to relate to. In my job and in my role I see people suffer like you've never seen, and you call that pain? You've got a lot to learn.' I remember really going for her gullet — I was so angry. I said: 'I hate you so much, if only you knew how much we all hated you for what you've done, you've ruined the house, you spend Daddy's money and what for?'

Diana's Father's Illness

And he had a haemorrhage, a brain haemorrhage. He suffered headaches, took Disprins, told nobody. I had a premonition that he was going to be ill whilst I was staying with some friends in Norfolk and they said: 'How's your father?' and I said: 'I've got this strange feeling that he's going to drop down and if he dies, he'll die immediately; otherwise he'll survive.' I heard myself say this — thought nothing more about it. Next day the telephone rang and I said to the lady, that will be about Daddy. It was. He'd collapsed. I was frightfully calm, went back up to London, went to the hospital saw Daddy was gravely ill. They said: 'He's going to die.' The brain had ruptured and we saw another side of Raine which we hadn't anticipated as she basically blocked us out of the hospital; she wouldn't let us see Daddy. My eldest sister took charge of that and went in sometimes to see him. Meanwhile, he couldn't talk because he had a tracheotomy so he wasn't able to ask where his other children were. Goodness knows what he was thinking because no one was telling him. Anyway, he got better and he basically changed character. He was one person before and he was certainly a different person after. He's remained estranged but adoring since. If he comes and sees me he comes and sees me, if he doesn't he doesn't. It's not my problem any more. It's his.

On Her Brother

I've always seen him as the brains in the family. I still see that. He's got S-levels and things like that. But if you're talking about how to deal with situations and how to deal with people — no. I think that my brother, being the youngest and the only boy, was quite precious because Althorp is a big place. Remember I was the girl who was supposed to be a boy. Being third in line was a very good position to be in — I got away with murder. I was my father's favourite, there's no doubt about that. Do you know he hasn't spoken to me since July? Incredible. And he hasn't given me a birthday present, nothing. He says he's going off to Paris to get one. He thinks by ringing me up saying he's going to Paris I'm going to get excited. I don't want a present from Paris. I just want to see him. Anyway. He's not the same since he's had that haemorrhage.

I longed to be as good as Charles in the schoolroom. I was never jealous of him. I so understand him. He's quite mature in some ways; he's quite immature in others. But that's to be expected, for God's sake, the boy's only [28]. He's very like me as opposed to my two sisters. I understand, he's a great one. He will always suffer, Charles, because he's like me. There's something in us that attracts that department. Whereas my two sisters are blissfully happy being detached from various situations.

Finishing School

I know that when I went to finishing school [the Institut Alpin Videmanette in Switzerland] I wrote something like 120 letters in the first month. I was so unhappy there — I just wrote and wrote and wrote. I felt out of place there. I learned how to ski but I wasn't very good with everybody else. It was just too claustrophobic for me, albeit it was in the mountains. I did one term there. When I found out how much it cost to send me there I told my parents it was a waste of their money. So they whipped me back.

My parents said: 'You can't come to London until you are 18, you can't have a flat until you are 18.' So I went and worked with a family in Headley, Bordon in Hampshire, Philippa and Jeremy Whitaker. I looked after their one daughter, Alexandra, and lived as part of their team. It was all right. I was itching to go to London because I thought the grass was greener on the other side.

Bachelor Girl in London

It was nice being in a flat with the girls. I loved that — it was great. I laughed my head off there. I kept myself to myself. I wasn't interested in having a full diary. I loved being on my own, as I do now — a great treat.

[On her nannying jobs] They were often pretty grim employers — velvet hairbands. I was sent out to all sorts of people from my sisters — their friends were producing rapidly. They sent me out the whole time — it was bliss. Solve Your Problems [employment agency] sent me on cleaning missions but nobody ever thanked me for it. But that was just a fill-in on Tuesdays and Thursdays, because Mondays, Wednesdays and Fridays I worked in a kindergarten. So I had two jobs, which was great.

I did a cookery course in Wimbledon with Mrs Russell. She's French. I quite liked it, but more velvet hairbands. I got terribly fat because my fingers were always in the saucepans, for which I got fined. It wasn't my idea of fun but my parents wanted me to do it. At the time it seemed a better alternative than being behind a typewriter — and I got a diploma!

Meeting the Prince of Wales

I've known her [the Queen] since I was tiny so it was no big deal. No interest in Andrew and Edward — never thought about Andrew. I kept thinking, 'Look at the life they have, how awful' so I remember him coming to Althorp to stay, my husband, and the first impact was 'God, what a sad man.' He came with his labrador [Harvey]. My sister was all over him like a bad rash and I thought: 'God, he must really hate that.' I kept out of the way. I remember being a fat, podgy, no make-up, unsmart lady but I made a lot of noise and he liked that and he came up to me after dinner and we had a big dance and he said: 'Will you show me the gallery?' and I was just about to show him the gallery and my sister Sarah comes up and tells me to push off and I said: 'At least, let me tell you where the switches are to the gallery because you won't know where they are', and I disappeared. And he was charm himself and when I stood next to him the next day, a 16-year-old, for someone like that to show you any attention — I was just so sort of amazed. 'Why would anyone like him be interested in me?' and it *was* interest. That was it for about two years. Saw him off and on with Sarah and Sarah got frightfully excited about the whole thing, then she saw something different happening which I hadn't twigged on to, i.e. when he had his 30th birthday dance I was asked too.

'Why is Diana coming as well?' [my] sister asked. I said: 'Well, I don't know but I'd like to come.' 'Oh, all right then', that sort of thing. Had a very nice time at the dance — fascinating. I wasn't at all intimidated by the surroundings [Buckingham Palace]. I thought, amazing place.

Then I was asked to stay at the de Passes in July 1980 by Philip de Pass, who is the son. 'Would you like to come and stay for a couple of nights down at Petworth because we've got the Prince of Wales staying. You're a young blood, you might amuse him.' So I said 'OK.' So I sat next to him and Charles came in. He was all over me again and it was very strange. I thought: 'Well, this isn't very cool.' I thought men were supposed not to be so obvious, I thought this was very odd. The first night we sat down on a bale at the barbecue at this house and he'd just finished with Anna Wallace. I said: 'You looked so sad when you walked up the aisle at Lord Mountbatten's funeral.' I said: 'It was the most tragic thing I've ever seen. My heart bled for you when I watched. I thought: "It's wrong, you're lonely — you should be with somebody to look after you." '

The next minute he leapt on me practically and I thought this was very strange, too, and I wasn't quite sure how to cope with all this. Anyway we talked about lots of things and anyway that was it. Frigid wasn't the word. Big F when it comes to that. He said: 'You must come to London with me tomorrow. I've got to work at Buckingham Palace, you must come to work with me.' I thought this was too much. I said: 'No, I can't.' I thought: 'How will I explain my presence at Buckingham Palace when I'm supposed to be staying with Philip?' Then he asked me to Cowes on *Britannia* and he had lots of older friends there and I was very intimidated but they were all over me like a bad rash. I felt very strange about the whole thing; obviously somebody was talking.

I came in and out, in and out, then I went to stay with my sister Jane at Balmoral where Robert [Fellowes, Jane's husband] was assistant private secretary [to the Queen]. I was shitting bricks, I was terrified, because I had never stayed at Balmoral and I wanted to get it right. The anticipation was worse than actually being there. You're all right once you get in through the front door. I had a normal single bed! I'm just telling you. I have a double bed now, but it works as a single. I have always done my own packing and unpacking. Now, obviously, I don't — I haven't got the time. But I was always appalled that [Prince] Charles takes 22 pieces of hand luggage with him. That's before all the other stuff. I always have four or five. I felt rather embarrassed.

I stayed back at the castle because of the press interest. They just considered it a good idea. Mr and Mrs Parker Bowles were there at all my visits. I was the youngest there by a long way. Charles used to ring me up and say: 'Would you like to come for a walk, come for a barbecue?' so I said: 'Yes, please.' I thought this was all wonderful.

Courtship
It sort of built up from there, then the press seized upon it. Then that became simply unbearable in our flat, but my three girls were wonderful, star performers; loyalty beyond belief. The feeling [in Sandringham]

was I wish Prince Charles would hurry up and get on with it. The Queen was fed up. He wrote to me from Klosters and then he rang me up and said: 'I've got something very important to ask you.' An instinct in a female tells you what it is. I sat up all night with my girls, saying: 'Christ, what am I going to do?'

By that time I'd realized there was somebody else around. I'd been staying at Bolehyde [Manor] with the Parker Bowleses an awful lot and I couldn't understand why she [Camilla] kept saying to me: 'Don't push him into doing this, don't do that.' She knew so much about what he was doing privately and about what we were doing privately . . . if we were going to stay at Broadlands, I couldn't understand it. Eventually I worked it all out and found the proof of the pudding and people were willing to talk to me.

Anyway, next day I went to Windsor and I arrived about 5 o'clock and he sat me down and said: 'I've missed you so much.' But there was never anything tactile about him. It was extraordinary, but I didn't have anything to go by because I had never had a boyfriend. I'd always kept them away, thought they were all trouble — and I couldn't handle it emotionally, I was very screwed up, I thought. Anyway, so he said: 'Will you marry me?' and I laughed. I remember thinking: 'This is a joke', and I said: 'Yeah, OK', and laughed. He was deadly serious. He said: 'You do realize that one day you will be Queen.' And a voice said to me inside: 'You won't be Queen but you'll have a tough role.' So I thought: 'OK', so I said: 'Yes.' I said: 'I love you so much, I love you so much.' He said: 'Whatever love means.' He said it then. So I thought that was great! I thought he meant that! And so he ran upstairs and rang his mother.

In my immaturity, which was enormous, I thought that he was very much in love with me, which he was, but he always had a sort of besotted look about him, looking back at it, but it wasn't the genuine sort. 'Who was this girl who was so different?' But he couldn't understand it because his immaturity was quite big in that department too. For me it was like a call of duty, really — to go and work with the people.

I came back [to the flat] and sat on my bed. 'Girls, guess what?' They said: 'He asked you. What did you say?' 'Yes please.' They screamed and howled and we went for a drive around London with our secret. I rang my parents the next morning. Daddy was thrilled. 'How wonderful.' Mummy was thrilled. I remember telling my brother and he said: 'Who to?'

I then went away two days later to Australia for three weeks to sort of settle down and to organize lists and things with my mother. That was a complete disaster because I pined for him but he never rang me up. I thought that was very strange and whenever I rang him he was out and he never rang me back. I thought: 'OK.' I was just being generous — 'He is being very busy, this, that and the other.' I come back from Australia, someone knocks on my door — someone from his office with a bunch of flowers and I knew that they hadn't come from Charles because there was no note. It was just somebody being very tactful in the office.

We fell in love gradually. It wasn't really dramatic. One blink and it would have gone.

Press Harassment
Then it all started to build up, sort of like the press were being unbearable following my every move. I understood they had a job, but people did not understand they had binoculars on me the whole time. They hired the opposite flat in Old Brompton

Road, which was a library which looked into my bedroom, and it wasn't fair on the girls. I couldn't put the telephone off the hook in case any of their family were ill in the night. The papers used to ring me up at 2 a.m. — they were just putting out another story — 'Could I confirm it or deny it?'

[On one occasion at Balmoral] I saw [the press], so I said to Charles: 'I must get out of the way, because you don't need any aggravation.' So I went up, up, up, up, up to the bank and sat behind a tree for a good half an hour while Charles was obviously complaining and fishing a lot. Instead of showing my face, I thought I'd bring my powder compact out [to take a look at them].

I failed once [her driving test] and then got it second time. With the media I always made sure that I was going through just as the light was turning red, so they were stuck. Sometimes I cycled. They'd chase me everywhere. We're talking about thirty of them — not two. Granny said: 'Would you like to borrow my car for a weekend. They keep following your metro.' So I borrowed her silver Golf.

I had to get out of Coleherne Court once to go to stay with him [Prince Charles] at Broadlands. So we took my sheets off the bed and I got out of the kitchen window, which is on the side street, with a suitcase. I did it that way round.

I was constantly polite, constantly civil. I was never rude. I never shouted. I cried like a baby to the four walls. I just couldn't cope with it. I cried because I got no support from Charles and no support from the Palace press office. They just said: 'You're on your own', so I thought: 'Fine.'

[Prince Charles] wasn't at all supportive. Whenever he rang me up he said: 'Poor Camilla Parker Bowles. I've had her on the telephone tonight and she says there's lots of press at Bolehyde. She's having a very rough time.' I never complained about the press to him because I didn't think it was my position to do so. I asked him: 'How many press are out there?' He said: 'At least four.' I thought: 'My God, there's 34 here!' and I never told him.

I was able to recognize an inner determination to survive. Anyway, thank God, it got announced [the engagement] and before I knew what happened, I was in Clarence House [the London residence of the Queen Mother]. Nobody there to welcome me. It was like going into a hotel. Then everyone said: 'Why are you at Clarence House?' and

I said I was told that I was expected to be at Clarence House. And I'd left my flat for the last time and suddenly I had a policeman. And my policeman the night before the engagement said to me: 'I just want you to know that this is your last night of freedom ever in the rest of your life, so make the most of it.' It was like a sword went in my heart. I thought: 'God', then I sort of giggled like an immature girl.

It was about three days before we went to the Palace [from Clarence House]. At Clarence House I remember being woken in the morning by a very sweet elderly lady who brought in all the papers about the engagement and put them on my bed.

Marrying into the Royal Family

My grandma [Ruth, the late Lady Fermoy] always said to me: 'Darling, you must understand that their sense of humour and their lifestyle are different and I don't think it will suit you.'

The Attractions of Becoming a Princess

You see, I had a very good lifestyle myself. I was Lady Diana Spencer. I was living in a big house, I had my own money. So it wasn't as though I was going into anything different.

Choosing the Engagement Ring

A briefcase comes along on the pretext that [Prince] Andrew is getting a signet ring for his 21st birthday and along come these sapphires. I mean *nuggets*! I suppose I chose it, we all chipped in. The Queen paid for it.

That Black Dress

I remember my first [royal] engagement so well. *So* excited. I got this black dress from the Emanuels and I thought it was OK because girls my age wore this dress. I hadn't appreciated that I was now seen as a royal lady, although I'd only got a ring on my finger as opposed to two rings. I remember walking into my husband-to-be's study, and him saying: 'You're not going in that dress, are you?' I replied: 'Yes, I am.' And he said: 'It's black! But only people in mourning wear black!' And I said: 'Yes, but I'm not part of your family yet.'

Black to me was the smartest colour you could possibly have at the age of 19. It was a real grown-up dress. I was quite big-chested then and they all got frightfully excited. I learned a lesson that night. I remember meeting Princess Grace and how wonderful and serene she was but there was troubled water under her, I saw that.

It was a horrendous occasion. I didn't know whether to go out of the door first. I didn't know whether your handbag should be in your left hand or your right hand. I was terrified really — at the time everything was all over the place. I remember that evening so well. I was terrified — nearly sick.

Engagement

It happened in the nursery at Windsor. I missed my girls so much I wanted to go back there and sit and giggle like we used to and borrow clothes and chat about silly things, just being in my safe shell again. One day you've got the King and Queen of Sweden coming to give you their wedding present of four brass candlesticks, the next minute you get the President of Somewhere Else coming to see. I was just pushed into the fire but I have to say my upbringing was able to handle that. It wasn't as though I was picked out like *My Fair Lady* and told to get on with it. I did know how to react.

Meeting Camilla

[I met her] very early on. I was introduced to the circle, but I was a threat. I was a very young girl but I was a threat.

We always had discussions about Camilla

though. I once heard him on the telephone in his bath on his hand-held set saying: 'Whatever happens, I will always love you.' I told him afterwards that I had listened at the door and we had a filthy row.

When I arrived at Clarence House there was a letter on my bed from Camilla, dated two days previously, saying: 'Such exciting news about the engagement. Do let's have lunch soon when the Prince of Wales goes to Australia and New Zealand. He's going to be away for three weeks. I'd love to see the ring, lots of love, Camilla' and that was 'Wow!' So I organized lunch. We had lunch and, bearing in mind that I was so immature, I didn't know about jealousy or depressions or anything like that. I had such a wonderful existence being a kindergarten teacher — you didn't suffer from anything like that, you got tired but that was it. There was no one around to give you grief. So we had lunch. Very tricky indeed. She said: 'You are not going to hunt are you?' I said: 'On what?' She said: 'Horse. You are not going to hunt when you go and live at Highgrove are you?' I said: 'No.' She said: 'I just wanted to know', and I thought as far as she was concerned that was her communication route. Still too immature to understand all the messages coming my way.

Anyway, somebody in his office told me that my husband had had a bracelet made for her which she wears to this day. It's a gold chain bracelet with a blue enamel disc. It's got 'G and F' entwined in it, 'Gladys' and 'Fred' — they were their nicknames. I walked into this man's office one day and said: 'Oh, what's in that parcel?' He said: 'Oh, you shouldn't look at that.' I said: 'Well, I'm going to look at it.' I opened it and there was a bracelet and I said: 'I know where this is going.' I was devastated. This was about two weeks before we got married. He said: 'Well, he's going to give it to her tonight.' So rage, rage, rage! 'Why can't you be honest with me?' But, no, he [Prince Charles] cut me absolutely dead. It's as if he had made his decision, and if it wasn't going to work, it wasn't going to work. He'd found the virgin, the sacrificial lamb, and in a way he was obsessed with me. But it was hot and cold, hot and cold. You never knew what mood it was going to be, up and down, up and down.

He took the bracelet, lunchtime on Monday, we got married on the Wednesday. I went to his policeman who was back in the office and said: 'John, where's Prince Charles?' and he said: 'Oh, he's gone out for lunch.' So I said: 'Why are you here?

Shouldn't you be with him?' 'Oh, I'm going to collect him later.'

So I went upstairs, had lunch with my sisters who were there and said: 'I can't marry him, I can't do this, this is absolutely unbelievable.' They were wonderful and said: 'Well, bad luck, Duch, your face is on the tea-towels so you're too late to chicken out.' So we made light of it.

[On impressions of Buckingham Palace] I couldn't believe how cold everyone was, how I thought one thing but actually another thing was going on. The lies and the deceit. The first thing that hit me was my husband sending Camilla Parker Bowles flowers when she had meningitis. 'To Gladys from Fred.'

I never dealt with that side of things. I just said to him: 'You must always be honest with me.' On our honeymoon, for instance, we were opening our diaries to discuss various things. Out come two pictures of Camilla. On our honeymoon we have our white-tie dinner for President Sadat [of Egypt]. Cufflinks arrive on his wrists — two 'C's entwined like the Chanel 'C's. Got it in one; knew exactly. 'Camilla gave you those didn't she?' He said: 'Yes, so what's wrong? They're a present from a friend.' And, boy, did we have a row. Jealousy, total jealousy — and it's such a good idea the two 'C's but it wasn't that clever in some ways.

I was the only one here [when planning the wedding] because he had pushed off to Australia and New Zealand on tour, and you may recall, of course, the picture of me sobbing in a red coat when he went off in the aeroplane. It had nothing to do with him going. The most awful thing had happened before he went. I was in his study talking to him, when the telephone rang. It was Camilla, just before he was going for five weeks. I thought: 'Shall I be nice or shall I just sit here?' So I thought I'd be nice so I left them to it. It just broke my heart that.

Highgrove House

He said he wanted to be in the Duchy [of Cornwall] vicinity but it's only 11 miles from her house. He chose the house and I came along afterwards. First went there after he bought it. He had painted all the walls white. He wanted me to do it up even though we were not engaged. I thought it was very improper but he liked my taste.

The Highgrove Set

[The Highgrove Set] appeared at various events, like the opera and going to Annabel's [nightclub] afterwards. The circuit then was Jeremy and Sue Phipps, Charlie and Patti Palmer-Tomkinson, Camilla and Andrew Parker Bowles, Emilie and Hugh van Cutsem, Simon and Annabel Elliot — Camilla's sister and brother-in-law. They were the big speakers. Then there were some on the outside, too.

I started to think: 'Gosh, they talk rather strangely to me.' I was very normal in the sense that I said what I thought because nobody ever told me to shut up. They were all oiling up, basically, kissing his feet, and I thought it was so bad for an individual to receive all that.

Now the circle has broadened. Other people have come in and they're not so much of a threat, they're actually terribly nice to me. I get on very well with them. But the ones who were there at the beginning are the ones that rumble a lot.

Emilie van Cutsem used to be my best friend. She told me about Camilla. She's very formidable, very outspoken.

Decorating Two New Homes

[Dudley Poplak] did up my mother's house ten years previously and had always been a friend of my mother's, so I said to her: 'What do you think?' She said: 'Well, use him, he's been marvellous, very loyal.' I chose the decorations and had a free hand to do that.

Choosing St Paul's or Westminster Abbey

[Prince] Charles said that people could see more and the acoustics were better [at St Paul's]. Great debate in the family about it, it had never happened before. 'I want it that way,' Charles said. Great confusion.

Wedding Presents

Charles and I went around the General Trading Company [a fashionable gift store frequented by the Establishment]. Looking back on it was quite a funny thing to do. And a lot of organizations offered us things, and Dudley [Poplak] went to see if the gifts were practical or if we could change them for something else. He was marvellous.

The Wedding

Great anticipation. Happiness because the crowds buoyed you up — I don't think I was happy. We got married on Wednesday and on the Monday we had gone to St Paul's for our last rehearsal and that's when the camera lights were on full and a sense of what the day was going to be. And I sobbed my eyes out. Absolutely collapsed and it was collapsing because of all sorts of things. The Camilla thing rearing its head the whole way through our engagement and I was desperately trying to be mature about the situation but I didn't have the foundations to do it and I couldn't talk to anyone about it.

I remember my husband being very tired — both of us were quite tired. Big day. He sent me a very nice signet ring the night before to Clarence House, with the Prince of Wales feathers on and a very nice card that said: 'I'm so proud of you and when you come up I'll be there at the altar for you tomorrow. Just look 'em in the eye and knock 'em dead.'

I had a very bad fit of bulimia the night before. I ate everything I could possibly find which amused my sister [Jane] because she was staying at Clarence House with me and nobody understood what was going on there. It was very hush-hush. I was sick as a parrot that night. It was such an indication of what was going on.

I was very calm the next morning when we were getting up at Clarence House. Must have been awake about 5 a.m. Interesting — they put me in a bedroom overlooking the Mall, which meant I didn't get any sleep. I was very, very calm, deathly calm. I felt I was a lamb to the slaughter. I knew it and couldn't do anything about it. My last night of freedom with Jane at Clarence House.

Father was so thrilled he waved himself stupid. We went past St Martin-in-the-Fields and he thought we were at St Paul's. He was ready to get out. It was wonderful, that.

As I walked up the aisle I was looking for her [Camilla]. I knew she was in there, of course. I looked for her. Anyway I got up to the top. I thought the whole thing was hysterical, getting married, in the sense that it was just like it was so grown up and here was Diana — a kindergarten teacher. The whole thing was ridiculous!

I cried a lot on the Monday when we had done the rehearsal because the tension had suddenly hit me. But by Wednesday I was fine and I had to get my father basically up the aisle and that's what I concentrated on and I remember being terribly worried about curtsying to the Queen. I remember being so in love with my husband that I couldn't take my eyes off him. I just absolutely thought I was the luckiest girl in the world. He was going to look after me. Well, was I wrong on that assumption?

So walking down the aisle I spotted Camilla, pale grey, veiled pillbox hat, saw it all, her son Tom standing on a chair. To this day you know — vivid memory. Well, there you are, that's it, let's hope that's all over with. Got out [of St Paul's], was a wonderful feeling, everybody hurraying, everybody happy because they thought we were happy and there was the big question mark in my mind. I realized I had taken on an enormous role but had no idea what I was going into — but *no* idea.

Back to Buckingham Palace, did all the photographs, nothing tactile, nothing. I was basically wandering around trying to find where I should be, clutching my long train with my bridesmaids and pages. Got out on the balcony, overwhelming what we saw, so humble-making, all these thousands and thousands of people happy. It was just wonderful. Sat next to him at the wedding breakfast, which was a lunch. Neither of us spoke to each other — we were so shattered. I was exhausted at the whole thing.

My mother let me down terribly with the wedding. She kept crying and being all valiant and saying that she couldn't cope with the pressure. I tended to think that I was the one under pressure, because I was the bride. So I didn't speak to her for three or four years afterwards. She drove me mad when I was engaged — mad, mad. It was me that was being strong and her sobbing the whole time. Gordon Honeycombe [TV broadcaster and writer] used to ring her up the whole time — with the book [on the royal wedding]. My mum was very good-looking and she loved the buzz. But when I didn't include her [in wedding preparations] she got hurt, so out came the Valium. She's been on Valium ever since.

Honeymoon

I never tried to call it off in the sense of really doing that but the worst moment was when we got to Broadlands. I thought, you know, it was just grim. I just had tremendous hope in me, which was slashed by day two. Went to Broadlands. Second night, out come the van der Post novels he hadn't read [Laurens van der Post, the South African philosopher and adventurer, was much admired by Prince Charles]. Seven of them — they came on our honeymoon. He read them and we had to analyse them over lunch every day. We had to entertain all the top people on *Britannia* every night so there was never any time on our own. Found that very difficult to accept. By then the bulimia was appalling, absolutely appalling. It was rife, four times a day on the yacht. Anything I could find I would gobble up and be sick two minutes later — very tired. So, of course, that slightly got the mood swings going in the sense that one minute one would be happy, next blubbing one's eyes out.

I remember crying my eyes out on our honeymoon. I was so tired, for all the wrong reasons totally.

We survived that all right. Then went off to Balmoral straight from the yacht; everyone was there to welcome us and then the realization set in. My dreams were appalling. At night I dreamt of Camilla the whole time. Charles got Laurens van der Post up to come and help me. Laurens didn't understand me. Everybody saw I was getting thinner and thinner and I was being sicker and sicker. Basically they thought I could adapt to being Princess of Wales overnight. Anyway, a godsend, William was conceived in October. Marvellous news, occupied my mind.

Obsessed by Camilla totally. Didn't trust him, thought every five minutes he was ringing her up asking how to handle his marriage. All the guests at Balmoral coming to stay just stared at me the whole time, treated me like glass. As far as I was concerned I was Diana, the only difference was people called me 'Ma'am' now, 'Your Royal Highness', and they curtsied. That was the only difference, but I treated everybody else exactly the same.

Charles used to want to go for long walks around Balmoral the whole time when we were on our honeymoon. His idea of enjoyment — this will make you laugh — would be to sit on top of the highest hill at Balmoral. It is beautiful up there. I completely understand; he would read Laurens van der Post or Jung to me, and bear in mind I hadn't a clue about psychic powers or anything, but I knew there was something in me that hadn't been awoken yet and I didn't think this was going to help! So anyway we read those and I did my tapestry and he was blissfully happy, and as far as he was happy that was fine.

He was in awe of his Mama, intimidated by his father, and I was always the third person in the room. It was never 'Darling, would you like a drink?' it was always 'Mummy, would you like a drink?' 'Granny, would you like a drink?' 'Diana, would you like a drink?' Fine, no problem. But I had to be told that that was normal because I always thought it was the wife first —

stupid thought!

I got terribly, terribly thin. People started commenting: 'Your bones are showing.' So that was the October and then we stayed up there [at Balmoral] from August to October. By October I was in a very bad way. I was so depressed, and I was trying to cut my wrists with razor blades. It rained and rained and rained and I came down early from Balmoral to seek treatment, not because I hated Balmoral but because I was in such a bad way. Anyway, came down here [London]. All the analysts and psychiatrists you could ever dream of came plodding in trying to sort me out. Put me on high doses of Valium and everything else. But the Diana that was still very much there had decided it was just time; patience and adapting were all that were needed. It was me telling them what I needed. They were telling me 'pills'! That was going to keep them happy — they could go to bed at night and sleep, knowing the Princess of Wales wasn't going to stab anyone.

In those days my greatest pleasure was that I was lucky enough to have a baby on the way. Got married in July, and William was on the way by October.

Pregnancy

Then I was told I was pregnant, fine, great excitement; then we went to Wales for three days to do our visit as Princess and Prince of Wales. Boy, oh boy, was that a culture shock in every sense of the word. Wrong clothes, wrong everything, wrong timing, feeling terribly sick, carrying this child, hadn't told the world I was pregnant but looking grey and gaunt and still being sick. Desperately trying to make him proud of me. Made a speech in Welsh. He was more nervous than I was. Never got any praise for it. I began to understand that that was absolutely normal. Sick as a parrot, rained the whole time round Wales. It wasn't easy, I cried a lot in the car, saying I couldn't get out, couldn't cope with the crowds. 'Why had they come to see us? Someone help me.' He said: 'You've just got to get out and do it.' I just got out. He tried his hardest and he did really well in that department, got me out and once I was out I was able to do my bit. But it cost me such a lot because I hadn't got the energy because I was being sick with my bulimia — so much; let alone the support for him or vice versa.

Couldn't sleep, didn't eat, whole world was collapsing around me. Very, very difficult pregnancy indeed. Sick the whole time, bulimia *and* morning sickness. People tried to put me on pills to stop me from being sick. I refused to risk the child becoming handicapped as a result. So sick, sick, sick, sick, sick. And this family's never had anybody who's had morning sickness before, so every time at Balmoral, Sandringham or Windsor in my evening dress I had to go out I either fainted or was sick. It was so embarrassing because I didn't know anything because I hadn't read my books, but I knew it was morning sickness because you just do. So I was 'a problem' and they registered Diana as 'a problem'. 'She's different, she's doing everything that we never did. Why? Poor Charles is having such a hard time.' Meanwhile, he decided he couldn't suggest too much.

I suppose I did [worry about William]; with Harry it wasn't so bad [the morning sickness]. With William it was appalling, almost every time I stood up I was sick. But that was a combination, I couldn't define which was which or what triggered it off but obviously I felt it was a nuisance to the set-up and I was made to feel it was a nuisance to the set-up. Suddenly in the middle of a black dress and black-tie do, I would go out to be sick and come back again and they'd say: 'Why didn't she go off to bed?' I felt it was my duty to sit at the table, duty was all over the shop. I didn't know which way to turn at all.

There was only ever one cancellation when I was carrying William, the visit to the Duchy of Cornwall's estate. And I was made to feel so guilty by my husband for that. Every time I got out of bed I was sick.

I threw myself down the stairs [at Sandringham]. Charles said I was crying wolf and I said I felt so desperate and I was crying my eyes out and he said: 'I'm not going to listen. You're always doing this to me. I'm going riding now.' So I threw myself down the stairs. The Queen comes out, absolutely horrified, shaking — she was so frightened. I knew I wasn't going to lose the baby; quite bruised around the stomach. Charles went out riding and when he came back, you know, it was just dismissal, total dismissal. He just carried on out of the door.

Birth of William

When we had William we had to find a date in the diary that suited him and his polo. William had to be induced because I couldn't handle the press pressure any longer, it was becoming unbearable. It was as if everybody was monitoring every day for me. Anyway we went in very early. I was sick as a parrot the whole way through the labour, very bad labour. They wanted a Caesarean, no one told me this until afterwards. Anyway, the boy arrived, great excitement. Thrilled, everyone absolutely high as a kite — we had found a date where Charles could get off his polo pony for me to give birth. That was very nice, felt very grateful about that! [When the Queen came to see William in hospital after Diana had given birth] She looked in the incubator and said: 'Thank goodness he hasn't got ears like his father.' Came home and then postnatal depression hit me hard and it wasn't so much the baby that had produced it, it was the baby that triggered off all else that was going on in my mind. Boy, was I troubled. If he didn't come home when he said he was coming home I thought something dreadful had happened to him. Tears, panic, all the rest of it. He didn't see the panic because I would sit there quietly.

[At William's christening] I was treated like nobody else's business on 4 August [1982]. Nobody asked me when it was suitable for William — 11 o'clock couldn't have been worse. Endless pictures of the Queen, Queen Mother, Charles and William. I was excluded totally that day. I felt desperate, because I had literally just given birth — William was only six weeks old. And it was all decided around me. Hence the ghastly pictures. Everything was out of control, everything. I wasn't very well and I just blubbed my eyes out. William started crying too. Well, he just sensed that I wasn't exactly hunky-dory.

Royal Life

When I first arrived on the scene I'd always put my head down. Now that I interpret it, that did look sulky. I've never sulked. I've been terrified out of my tiny little mind. I never sulked as a child, it's just not in me. I was just so frightened of the attention I was getting; it took me six years to get comfortable in this skin and now I'm ready to go forward.

One minute I was nobody, the next minute I was Princess of Wales, mother, media toy, member of this family, you name it, and it was too much for one person at that time.

Basically my husband's office got in a turmoil because one minute there was one and the next minute there were two and the presents coming in from the wedding were so phenomenal — from a swimming pool, to a desk set, to a photograph frame to six dining-room chairs. Chaos! I ended up writing my own thank-you letters. Eventually we sorted out something and I had Oliver Everett [former Assistant Private Secretary to Prince Charles], who used to work for my husband, come back to help me. I drove him quite potty because he pushed me into a corner that didn't suit. There were basically lots of tears. From me!

Edward Adeane [Prince Charles's private secretary from 1979–85] was wonderful — we got on so well. Very much the bachelor and I was always trying to find him the ideal woman but I didn't succeed at all. He was sweet. He said: 'I know some nice ladies who might be ladies-in-waiting. Will you come and see them and meet them?' So I said 'Yes' to them all, even though I didn't really know them and one or two have gone by the wayside but the others have remained very strong and I've gathered a few on the way as well.

[On organizing her diary] What I can remember is that I didn't want to do anything on my own. I was too frightened. The thought of me doing anything on my own sent tremors, so I stuck with whatever Charles did. If that included a wife I went with him all the way — wherever. But the pace was phenomenal. I knew I couldn't do engagements as well as get married, plus doing up two houses.

[On Grace of Monaco's Funeral] When Grace died, I said to Charles: 'I feel I'd very much like to represent your mama at the funeral', and he said, 'Well, we'll have to ask her but I doubt she'll let you go.' And I said: 'Well, I think it's important because she was an outsider who married into a big family and I've done the same, so it would [feel] right.' I went to her private secretary, who was then Philip Moore, who said he didn't think it would be possible because I'd only been in the job, three or four months. And I said I could do it perfectly standing on my head. There was no worry about that. I knew exactly how to behave etcetera etcetera and I wanted to be a part of her funeral because I admired her so much; she was so sweet to me.

So I went to the Queen and I said: 'You know, I'd like to do this', and she said: 'I don't see why not, if you want to do this you can.' And I said: 'That would be marvellous, thank you.' I went there, did my bit, came back and everyone was all over me like a bad rash. 'Oh, you did so well!' and I thought: 'Well, interesting.'

Building Up Her Wardrobe

On the day we got engaged I literally had one long dress, one silk shirt, one smart pair of shoes and that was it. Suddenly my mother and I had to go and buy six of everything. We bought as much as we thought we needed but we still didn't have enough. Bear in mind you have to change four times a day and suddenly your wardrobe expands to something unbelievable. Hence, probably, the criticism when I first arrived on the scene of having new clothes all the time. Three seasons and I had to deck myself out from January to December overnight with hats, gloves, the lot. After that I asked Anna Harvey from *Vogue,* where both my sisters had worked, to come and help me out with the basic things like two of this, three of this, one of that. But after that I was on my own. Once I got established names like Victor Edelstein and Catherine Walker I could do it myself, ring them up and talk to them. But, before then, Anna definitely helped out for the first year. I had to find a niche where I was happy with the designer and what I required. I couldn't have fashionable clothes because it wouldn't have been practical for the job but I had to have clothes that had to last all day long, sensible colours and sensible neckline and skirt length. I never knew a thing about having weights in hems [to prevent skirts from blowing up in the wind]. I found it all out in my own time. No one helped with that.

First Royal Engagements

[One of] the very first royal ones was with Elizabeth Taylor. It was a play at the Victoria [Palace] theatre called *The Little Foxes.* I remember I turned up in a fake white fur coat and all the antis came out against me for evermore. So that went back into the cupboard, never to be seen again. I was pregnant with William and it was agonizing because I didn't find Elizabeth Taylor very easy to talk to. I thought she was stuck-up. I'd hoped she'd help me out because she'd been on the stage, in inverted commas, more than I had. I remember getting through that evening feeling amazed.

[On switching on the Regent Street Christmas lights] I remember wearing a pair of navy blue culottes with a pink shirt and I felt so sick. I couldn't do them up because I was pregnant but I didn't have anything else to wear. And I was so nervous. I had to make a speech in front of the whole of Regent Street. I was shit scared.

It didn't get easier — I just got used to what people required from the Princess of

Wales. What Diana thought wasn't going to come into it — yet. I hadn't got enough background on what the Princess of Wales was supposed to do. I could adapt but it took some time. [Although] I've never been over-awed by anything that's come my way.

I went to Hereford [SAS headquarters] and did a driving course. Bombs were being thrown at me. It was terrifying. Graham Smith was my first policeman; he came from Princess Anne. He'd been with her a few years. I remember asking him as a first question: 'Do you like horses?' He said: 'No.' I said: 'Good', because at the time I wasn't interested in horses. He was sweet but it took a long time to get used to having a policeman — God, suddenly to have this man in your car, music had to be turned down, I had to make sure he was fed, all those things which you don't have to do, but I was brought up to look after others.

I have [held a gun] now. I know how to shoot an air gun, but only because I asked.

The First Overseas Tour

Then it was make-or-break time for me. We went to [Australia and] New Zealand, [beginning at] Alice Springs. This was the real hard crunch, the hard end of being the Princess of Wales. There were thousands of press following us. We were away six weeks and the first day we went to this school in Alice Springs. It was hot, I was jet-lagged, being sick. I was too thin. The whole world was focusing on me every day. I was in the front of the papers. I thought that this was just so appalling, I hadn't done something specific like climb Everest or done something wonderful like that. However, I came back from this engagement and I went to my lady-in-waiting, cried my eyes out and said: 'Anne [Anne Beckwith-Smith], I've got to go home, I can't cope with this.' She was devastated, too, because it was her first job. So that first week was such a traumatic week for me, I learned to be royal, in inverted commas, in one week. I was thrown into the deep end. Now I prefer it that way. Nobody ever helped me *at all.* They'd be there to criticize me, but never there to say: 'Well done.'

When we came back from our six-week tour I was a different person. I was more grown up, more mature, but not anything like the process I was going to go through in the next four or five years. Basically our tour was a great success. Everybody always said when we were in the car: 'Oh, we're in the wrong side, we want to see her, we don't want to see him', and that's all we could hear when we went down these crowds and obviously he wasn't used to that and nor was I. He took it out on me. He was jealous; I understood the jealousy but I couldn't explain that I didn't ask for it. I kept saying you've married someone and whoever you'd have married would have been of interest for the clothes, how she handles this, that and the other, and you build the building block for your wife to stand on to make her own building block. He didn't see that at all.

The first foreign trip we took William to was Australia and New Zealand. That was for six weeks. That was great — we were a family unit and everything was fine. It was very tricky, mentally, for me, because the crowds were just something to be believed. My husband had never seen crowds like it and I sure as hell hadn't and everyone kept saying it will all quieten down when you've had your first baby, and it never quietened down, never.

We never had a fight [about taking Prince William on tour]. The person who never got any credit was Malcolm Fraser who was then Prime Minister [but wasn't by the time of the tour]. He wrote to us out of the blue. All ready to leave William. I accepted that as part of duty, albeit it wasn't going to be easy. He wrote to me and said: 'It seems to me that you being such a young family would you like to bring your child out?' And Charles said: 'What do you think about this?' I said: 'Oh, it would be absolutely wonderful.' He said: 'Then we can do six weeks instead of four and we can cover New Zealand as well so it would be perfect.'

I said: 'Wonderful.' It was always reputed that I had had an argument with the Queen. We never even asked her, we just did it. It was very nice. We didn't see very much of him [William] but at least we were under the same sky, so to speak. That was a great fulfilment for me because everyone wanted to know about his progress.

Other Foreign Trips

President and Mrs Göncz of Hungary, I had an instant rapport with them. I got out of the aeroplane and we held hands. Extraordinary, it felt so normal me doing it. It was on the front of all the papers at home. I remember thinking: 'What's so odd about that?' It all got very intense after that with the public. Sudden shifts but I couldn't understand it. I had no one to talk to about that with. I just thought I was growing up. Put it down to experience.

I thought that was rather wonderful, very special [an audience with Pope John Paul II]. I was totally overwhelmed. I was so intimidated by the set-up. When you're sat there with this man in a white frock, it was quite strange. I said one thing to him. I plucked up courage and said: 'How are your wounds?' He had recently been shot. He thought I was talking about my womb! So he thought I was having a baby! So after that mistake I went very quietly.

In Spain I wasn't well at all, tiredness, exhaustion, bone tired. I told everybody I was tired but it was the bulimia taking a grip of me. Portugal was the last time we were close as man and wife. That's going back six or seven years ago now. Then Majorca [on holiday with the King and Queen of Spain], the first trip I spent my whole time with my head down the loo. I hated it so much. Because they were all so busy thinking Charles was the most wonderful creature there's ever been and who was this girl coming along? And I knew there was something inside me that wasn't coming out and I didn't know how to use it, in the sense of letting them see it. I didn't feel at all comfortable in that situation.

No one has ever taught me how to talk to people. And sometimes you have an interpreter, depending on how complicated their English is. A brief comes from the Foreign Office, but you know what not to broach.

Christmas at Sandringham

It was highly fraught. I know I gave, but I can't remember being a receiver [of Christmas presents]. Isn't that awful? I do all the presents and [Prince] Charles signs the cards. [It was] terrifying and so disappointing. No boisterous behaviour, lots of tension, silly behaviour, silly jokes that outsiders would find odd but insiders understood. I sure was [an outsider].

Trooping the Colour

Everybody mingles around. And everybody who wants to avoid each other avoids each other, and those who want to talk to each other talk to each other. There are too many of us.

The Birth of Harry

Then between William and Harry being born it is total darkness. I can't remember much, I've blotted it out, it was such pain. However, Harry appeared by a miracle. We were very, very close to each other the six weeks before Harry was born, the closest we've ever, ever been and ever will be. Then suddenly as Harry was born it just went bang, our marriage, the whole thing went down the drain. I knew Harry was going to be a boy because I saw on the scan. Charles always wanted a girl. He wanted two children and he wanted a girl. I knew Harry was a boy and I didn't tell him. Harry arrived, Harry had red hair, Harry was a boy. First comment was: 'Oh God, it's a boy', second comment: 'and he's even got red hair'. Something inside me closed off. By then I knew he had gone back to his lady but somehow we'd managed to have Harry. Harry was a complete joy and is actually closer to his father than perhaps William at the moment.

[Prince] Charles went to talk to my mother at Harry's christening and said: 'We were so disappointed — we thought it would be a girl.' Mummy snapped his head off, saying: 'You should realize how lucky you are to have a child that's normal.' Ever since that day the shutters have come down and that's what he does when he gets somebody answering back at him.

[I chose the names William and Harry because] the alternative was Arthur and Albert. No thank you. There weren't fights over it. It was just a fait accompli.

Relations with the Royal Family:
The Queen

The relationship certainly changed when we got engaged because I was a threat, wasn't I? I admire her. I long to get inside her mind and talk to her and I will. I've always said to her: 'I'll never let you down but I cannot say the same for your son.' She took it quite well. She does relax with me. She indicated to me that the reason why our marriage had gone downhill was because Prince Charles was having such a difficult time with my bulimia. She told me that. She hung her coat on the hook, so to speak. And it made me realize that they all saw that as the *cause* of the marriage problems and not one of the symptoms. I kept myself to myself. I didn't knock on her door and ask her advice, because I knew the answers myself.

I get on very well with them [her parents-in-law] but I don't go out of my way to go and have tea with them.

Prince Charles

[I was] accused very early on of stopping him shooting and hunting — that was total rubbish. He suddenly went all vegetarian and wouldn't kill. His family thought he had gone mad, and he was ostracized within the family. They couldn't understand it and they were fearful of the future — all the estates have things that need to be shot on them. So if the heir wasn't going to take an interest, panic was going to set in. It was an influence well before me, but it all came back eventually in his own time. He does that — he has these crazes and then he drops them.

I never wanted to get rid of anyone [in Charles's group of friends]. I just wanted to keep my head above water. It was Charles's choice when we first got married not to run around with the PTs [Palmer-Tomkinsons], with the PBs [Parker Bowleses] and everything. It was his decision; he wanted to try and have a home life of some sort, but he didn't know how to do it because he's never been taught. So the whole thing just evaporated.

Stephen Barry [Prince Charles's valet] was very good to me. We got on terribly well. On our honeymoon, Stephen and I were standing outside looking out at Egypt and he said to me: 'Now the boss is married, it's time for me to move on. And I can see he's in good hands now, and I'd like to move on.'

[Charles's clothes] He had an awful lot

but he had very little. For instance, he had ghastly Aertex pyjamas that were honestly, simply hideous, so I bought him a silk pair, that sort of thing — and shoes. Yes, they were well received. He was absolutely thrilled.

[Charles as a father] He loved the nursery life and couldn't wait to get back and do the bottle and everything. He was very good, he always came back and fed the baby. I [breast] fed William for three weeks and Harry for eleven weeks.

[Charles's attitude to Diana] Once, we were in the swimming pool at Highgrove and I was telling him [William] off, and he turned around to me and said: 'You're the most selfish woman I've ever met. All you do is think of yourself.' And I was so stunned. I mean, this is seven years ago. I said: 'Where did you hear that?' 'Oh, I've often heard Papa saying it.' The one thing I've always prided myself on — if I may be so bold — is that I've never been a selfish person. But Charles was always telling me I was being selfish, and I sort of believed it.

[When Diana danced on stage with Wayne Sleep at the Royal Opera House at an event for the Friends of Covent Garden] he was horrified. He said I was too thin.

[On sleeping separately] The snoring

could be heard through two doors. Four times a night I'd be woken up. And then it became a habit. He just got fed up and went into his dressing room.

Queen Mother
[The Queen Mother's 90th birthday] Quite grim and stilted. All her household are anti me. My grandmother [Ruth, Lady Fermoy] has done a good hatchet job on me.

Prince Philip and Prince Charles
Very tricky, very tricky. Prince Charles longs to be patted on the head by his father while his father longs to be asked advice instead of listening to Prince Charles giving advice. After all, it was my father-in-law who started off the environmental thing, but it was Charles who got listened to.

Prince Andrew
Andrew was very, very noisy and loud. It occurred to me that there was something troubling him. He wasn't for me. Andrew was very happy to sit in front of the television all day watching cartoons and videos because he's not a goer. He doesn't like taking exercise — he loves his golf and it's rather touching. But he gets squashed by his family the whole time. He's dismissed as

an idiot but actually there's a lot more that hasn't arisen yet. He's very shrewd, believe it or not, and very astute.

The big brother [Charles] was very jealous of [Andrew going to the Falklands war] because he wanted to go out and do something.

Sweet Koo [Kathleen Dee-Anne Stark, an American film actress] adored him. She was terribly good to have around. Very gentle and looked after him. All her energies were directed at him. Very quiet. They suited each other so well. Met her lots of times.

[On Andrew and Fergie] I only know two single girls who are from 'good breeding' stock: Susie Fenwick, who's now married, was one, and Fergie was the other. I didn't actually notice anything going on, but then Andrew would ask if he could bring Sarah to come and stay at Highgrove. Things like that happened. They were all over each other. I didn't advise them. I just said that I was there if they needed me.

Princess Anne
We're always supposed to have had this tricky relationship. I admire her enormously. I keep out of her way but when she's there I don't rattle her cage and she's never rattled mine and the fuss about her being god-

mother to Harry was never even thought about. I thought to myself: 'There's no point having anyone in the family as godparents as they are either aunts or uncles.' I said: 'The press will go for that', and Charles said: 'So what?' They had this great thing about she and I not getting on. We get on incredibly well, but in our own way. I wouldn't ring her up if I had a problem, nor would I go and have lunch with her but when I see her it's very nice to see her. Her mind stimulates me, she fascinates me, she's very independent and she's gone her own way.

Other Royals

I've always adored Margo [the late Princess Margaret], as I call her. I love her to bits and she's been wonderful to me from day one. Everyone keeps themselves to themselves. The Gloucesters — they are a very shy couple anyway. Feel sorry for her [the Duchess of Kent]. Would look after her if I had to.

Diana's Mother and Grandmother and the Royal Family

Mummy was quite special to look at when I was younger. She's dynamite. Not unlike Princess Grace, in a funny sort of way.

My mother and grandmother never got on. They clashed violently. Mummy sticks up for me, whereas my grandmother goes out to lacerate me at any opportunity. She feeds the royal family with hideous comments about my mother, about her running away and leaving the children. Whenever I mention my mother's name within the royal family, which I barely do, they come on me like a ton of bricks. So I can never do anything in that department. They're convinced she's the baddie and that poor Johnnie [her father] had a very rough time. Now, I know it takes two to get in a situation like that. The four of us never knew what happened and we don't actually want to know. But Mummy's come off very badly because Granny's done a real hatchet job on her. And my husband won't even talk to her.

[On Diana's mother's relationship with Peter Shand Kydd] She wanted him out the house, so he went. He was a bit of a manic-depressive and a drinker. And when Mummy heard that he'd fallen in love with another lady she went spare. It was like a teenage crush. I used to ring her up and she'd cry down the telephone. I'd tell her:

'You know, Mummy, you've had two goes at marriage, and if you can't get it right you've got to look at yourself. I'm stuck in this one, and I'm worse off than you.' She didn't like that. 'You must let me cry, you must let me cry.' So I said: 'You can cry as much as you like, it's very good to cry, but you're not getting any sympathy from me.'

The Media

[The press attention] was like Marilyn Monroe publicity. She only had to click her heels and the whole world was at her feet. It was very odd. I'm never comfortable in it. Never ever. I was absolutely mesmerized by the whole thing. I couldn't believe it. [The royal family] all thought: 'Oh she's got lots of press, she must be doing all right.'

One of the worst things that ever happened was when we went to Wales after the flooding [in 1987]. There'd been a tremendous amount of press about Charles and I being apart, and we got into the jet and I burst into tears. He said: 'Oh God, what's the matter?' And I said: 'I've had a very bad time with the press.' Because they'd literally hunted me. And he said: 'Well if you were in the right place none of this would happen', indicating that I should be up in Scotland. But I said: 'I choose to work, because that's my role in life.' And it was terrible, he completely ignored me.

It was a real cry for help. I wasn't blubbing because I'd just turned the taps on. It was just desperation. And it showed in all the photographs.

[On avoiding appearing on *It's a Royal Knockout*] I said to Charles: 'Why aren't we being involved? Why aren't we doing this?' He said: 'You must be joking! Neither of us are doing it.' Thank God we didn't, we were so appalled when we saw it. But leading up to it, I didn't want to be left out.

[On the interview with TV broadcaster Alastair Burnet in 1985] I was basically bribed to do that. First of all, American Network was going to do it and I said I didn't want to do it. And Charles said: 'Okay, I'll do it.' They came back and said: 'No, no — we want both of you, or we don't want any of you.' So I said no, so they dropped Charles and then ITN picked it up and said: 'If your wife does it with you, we'll pay you such and such money.' So there was the bribe — into the charities' trusts, not to us individually. So that's how that happened. He [Alastair Burnet] followed us around for eighteen months. [It was] very strange.

When it actually came to being interviewed by Alastair, I remember thinking:

'Gosh, I'm not flapping my arms about. I'm sitting here quite calmly. But if only the man would be more receptive to what I'm saying.' Every time he asked a question he'd then look at the next bit of paper. There was no eye contact. I thought it was hopeless. But my father-in-law said to Charles how impressed he was that I'd come across so calmly, which I hadn't appreciated at the time. It was very nice that he said that.

[On Lynda Lee-Potter, columnist at the *Daily Mail*] I always admire her because she always hits the nerve on the head about me. She seems to know me so well. I met her earlier this year at the Women of the Year launch and I asked if someone could fish her out. And I said to her: 'I'm sorry to dig you out of the masses, but I just did want to say thank you very much for all your support.' And she was very sweet and just said nothing, but understood everything. It meant so much.

[On Patrick Demarchelier] Very nice. I much prefer to be photographed by him than anyone else. Because he's a) so professional and b) he understands what it's like to be at the other end of the lens. Which means he brings one alive. He knows when you're tired so he lets you have a rest. He doesn't punish you.

Diana's Charity Work

[On the first patronages] I didn't have any choice. It was thought: 'You're interested in children, let's go with the children aspect.' One or two I could have done without now. But the ones I have — I have over a hundred now — I choose myself. They're usually to do with the terminally ill. I haven't got the courage to stop any yet.

[On the idea of a Princess's Trust] It won't be going ahead. My husband won't allow it.

[On working with the dying] It doesn't frighten me when people die, like Adrian [Ward-Jackson, Diana's friend who died from Aids-related illnesses], it doesn't frighten me at all. He says he wants me to be there at the end — it's a privilege. I'm not so gripped by those who are getting better. Just the ones on their way out that I feel a deep need to be with.

Years of Suffering

I think an awful lot of people tried to help me because they saw something going wrong but I never leant on anyone. None of my family knew about this at all. Jane, my sister, after five years of being married, came to check on me.

I had a V-neck on and shorts. She said: 'Duch [Diana's childhood nickname], what's that marking on your chest?' I said: 'Oh, it's nothing.' She said: 'What is it?' And the night before I wanted to talk to Charles about something. He wouldn't listen to me, he said I was crying wolf. So I picked up his penknife off his dressing table and scratched myself heavily down my chest and both thighs. There was a lot of blood and he hadn't made any reaction whatsoever. Jane just went for me. She said: 'You mustn't let the side down.' And I turned on her, and said: 'Give me some credit that I haven't troubled any of the family in five years about this.' Their perception is very different now. They're annoyed by the lack of support from my husband.

[On other suicide attempts] I was running around with a lemon knife, one with the serrated edges. I was just so desperate. I knew what was wrong with me but nobody else around me understood me. I needed rest and to be looked after inside my house and for people to understand the torment and anguish going on in my head. It was a desperate cry for help. I'm not spoiled — I just needed to be allowed to adapt to my new position.

I don't know what my husband fed her [the Queen]. He definitely told her about my bulimia and she told everybody that was the reason why our marriage had cracked up because of Diana's eating and it must be so difficult for Charles.

It was at the Expo [in Canada] where I passed out. I remember I had never fainted before in my life. We'd been walking round for four hours, we hadn't had any food and presumably I hadn't eaten for days beforehand. When I say that, I mean food staying down. I remember walking round feeling really ghastly. I didn't dare tell anyone I felt ghastly because I thought they'd think I was whinging. I put my arm on my husband's shoulder and said: 'Darling, I think I'm about to disappear', and slid down the side of him. Whereupon David Roycroft and Anne Beckwith-Smith [royal aides] who were with us at the time took me to a room. My husband told me off. He said I could have passed out quietly somewhere else, behind a door. It was all very embarrassing. My argument was I didn't know anything about fainting. Everyone was very concerned. I fainted in the American section. While Anne and David were bringing me round, Charles went on around the exhibition. He left me to it. I got back to the hotel in Vancouver and blubbed my eyes out. Basically I was overtired, exhausted and on my knees because I hadn't got any food inside me. Everyone was saying: 'She can't go out tonight, she must have some sleep.' Charles said: 'She must go out tonight otherwise there's going to be a sense of terrific drama and they are going to think there's something really awful wrong with her.' Inside me I knew there was something wrong with me but I was too immature to voice it. A doctor came and saw me. I told him I was being sick. He didn't know what to say because the issue was too big for him to handle. He just gave me a pill and shut me up.

It was all very strange, I just felt miserable. I knew the bulimia started the week after we got engaged. My husband put his hand on my waistline and said: 'Oh, a bit chubby here, aren't we?' and that triggered off something in me — and the Camilla thing, I was desperate, desperate.

I remember the first time I made myself sick. I was so thrilled because I thought this was the release of tension. The first time I was measured for my wedding dress I was 29 inches around the waist. The day I got married I was 23 1/2 inches. I had shrunk into nothing from February to July. I had shrunk to nothing.

[On people trying to help] but they were coming from Charles's side, such as the odd lady-in-waiting. They weren't coming from my side. I shut my friends out because I didn't want to pull them in on it. My mother tried to give me Valium. Someone else tried to take me off it. I never actually took it. But it was all very strange. There were so many forces pulling me and I didn't have a clue which way to turn.

I didn't get any choice over the people I met [for therapy]. I didn't take to either [doctor]. One of them drove me mad. He seemed to be the one who needed help, not me. The other would ring me at 6 o'clock and I'd have to explain to him the conversations I'd had with my husband throughout the day. There weren't many conversations, more tears than anything else.

On the outside, people were saying I gave my husband a hard time, that I was acting like a spoiled child, but I knew I just needed rest and patience and time to adapt to all the roles that were required of me overnight. By then there was immense jealousy because every single day I was on the front of the newspapers. I read two newspapers, albeit I was always supposed to have read them all. I did take criticism hard because I tried so hard to show them that I wasn't going to let them down, but obviously that didn't come across strongly enough at that point. We had a few trying to cut wrists, throwing things out of windows, breaking glass. I threw myself downstairs when I was four months pregnant with William, trying to get my husband's attention, for him to listen to me.

But he just said: 'You're crying wolf.'

I gave everybody a fright. I couldn't sleep, I just never slept. I went for three nights without any sleep at all. I had no fuel to sleep on. I thought my bulimia was secret but quite a few of the people in the house recognized it was going on, though nobody mentioned it. They all thought it was quite amusing that I ate so much but never put any weight on.

I always kept my breakfast down. I don't know what the hell it was. I didn't take any vitamin pills or anything. I just got help from somewhere — I don't know where it came from. I swam every day, I never went out at night, I didn't burn candles at both ends. I got up very early in the morning, on my own, to be on my own, and at night-time went to bed early, so it wasn't as though I was being a masochist — I was to my system but not to my energy level. I always had terrific energy — I've always had.

It went on and on. Only a year and a half

ago I suddenly woke up and realized that I was on the way down fast. I just cried at every opportunity, which thrilled people in a way because when you're crying in this system you are weak and 'We can handle her.' But when you bounce up again, 'What the hell has happened?' questions again.

The public side was very different from the private side. The public side, they wanted a fairy princess to come and touch them and everything will turn into gold and all their worries would be forgotten. Little did they realize that the individual was crucifying herself inside, because she didn't think she was good enough. 'Why me, why all this publicity?' My husband started to get very jealous and anxious by then, too. Inside the system I was treated very differently, as though I was an oddball and I felt I was an oddball, and so I thought I wasn't good enough. But now I think it's good to be the oddball, thank God, thank God, thank God!

I had so many dreams as a young girl that I wanted, and hoped this that and the other, that my husband would look after me. He would be a father figure and he'd support me, encourage me, say: 'Well done', or 'No, it wasn't good enough', but I didn't get any of that. I couldn't believe it, I got none of

122

that, it was role reversal.

He [Prince Charles] ignores me everywhere. Ignored everywhere and have been for a long time but if people choose to see that now, they are a bit late in the day. He just dismisses me.

[The worst day of my life] was realizing that Charles had gone back to Camilla.

[On her feelings of isolation] Definitely separation from friends. I would be too embarrassed to ask them to come in for lunch. I couldn't cope with that. I would be apologizing the whole way through lunch.

Fergie

I met Fergie when Charles was getting near me and she kept rearing her head for some reason and she seemed to know all about the royal set-up, things like that. She just sort of encouraged it. I don't know, she just suddenly appeared and she sat in the front pew of our wedding — and everything like that. She came to lunch at Buckingham Palace and didn't seem daunted by it all.

I wasn't quite sure how to take it. Suddenly everybody said: 'Oh, isn't she marvellous, a breath of fresh air, thank God she's more fun than Diana.' So Diana was listening and reading every line. I felt terribly insecure. I thought maybe I ought to be like Fergie and my husband said: 'I wish you would be like Fergie — all jolly. Why are you always so miserable? Why can't you be like Grannie?' I'm quite glad I'm not Grannie now. I made so many balls-ups trying to be like Fergie. I went to a pop concert, Spider concert, David Bowie, with David Waterhouse and David Linley. I went in leather trousers, which I thought was the right thing to do, completely putting out of mind that I was the future Queen and future Queens don't wear leather like that in public. So I thought that was frightfully 'with it', frightfully pleased to act my own age. Slapped hands. The same summer at Ascot I put somebody's umbrella up somebody's backside. In my astrological chart Penny Thornton always said to me: 'Everything you will do this summer you will pay for.' I did, definitely. I learned a lot.

I got terribly jealous [of Fergie] and she got terribly jealous of me. She kept saying to me: 'You mustn't worry, Duch, everything is going to be fine, let me do this, let me do that.' I couldn't understand it, she was actually enjoying being where she was, whereas I was fighting to survive. I couldn't understand how she could find it so easy. I thought she would be like me and put her head down and be shy. No, a different kettle of fish altogether and she wooed everybody in this family and did it so well. She left me looking like dirt. Another dark age.

But up in Scotland she used to do everything that I never did. So I thought: 'This can't last; the energy of this creature is unbelievable.' Meanwhile everybody looking at me — 'It's a pity Diana has gone so introverted and quiet, she was so busy dieting and trying to sort herself out', and then this holocaust arrived. I knew eventually she would turn round and say: 'Duch, how on earth have you survived all these years?' She's said it now for the last two years. I never explain. I just say it's just happened.

It's fascinating watching Fergie trying to make her way. I'm in the wings just watching her do it — it's very clever. But it's not recognized, it's effort. They think: 'Oh, isn't it nice Sarah's doing that!' But it's not, you don't get ten points for doing it. You don't get one point.

Philip Dunne and Major David Waterhouse
Fergie was asked by Charles to find two single men for our ski holiday in Klosters. It was the year before Hugh Lindsay was killed. And both these young men came in and they were great fun, particularly David

[Waterhouse]. I took an enormous shine to him, unfortunately. And he made me laugh very much. Philip [Dunne] was very sweet, but he didn't have the charisma that David had. And we went off skiing, the four of us, Catherine Soames, David, Philip and I.

When we came back [home] I saw a lot of David, sometimes with or without Philip. Then that weekend, when we went to stay at Gatley Park [the Herefordshire home of Dunne's parents, Thomas and Henrietta]. [The press] got so excited, [even though] there must have been about fifteen of us in the house. Philip was there, obviously, and David, as well. A lovely weekend, and then the press picked up on Philip. They knew it was one of them, but I think they just went for Philip because he was the better-looking. And that's how everybody got excited [hinting at an affair].

[I was] totally shocked by the attention. [David was] laughing about it, thinking it was all funny, whereas I didn't. When I went to the David Bowie concert, David Waterhouse, who I shouldn't have taken anyway, came and sat on my right and that's how the picture arose. One ran on every front page on Monday morning.

I was in tears. I was hysterical. I was horrified, mortified, cross with myself. I rang David up in the [Household Cavalry] to apologize, and I got such a strange reply back. 'Oh it's fine, it's all right. I can cope with it.' And I thought: 'Wait a minute, he's enjoying this.' I was so naïve. He enjoyed the whole thing. And I absolutely loathed it.

But it was a foot on the outside, [to have] someone who said they actually liked being with me. And that to me meant everything.

Jacob Rothschild

Jacob's very clever, *very clever.* I admire him enormously. He's fascinating. And he's got a very nice wife too. I go and have lunch with him and his partner. And there's so much to learn from that man, I just drink it all up. He's a terrific gossip — I have to be very careful what I say to him. For instance, he wants a painting of me to go into Spencer House, as one of the three Spencer daughters.

He kept ringing me up [when he was refurbishing Spencer House] asking if I'd like to come round and talk to the builders, which I did very happily. As I felt more comfortable with him [I'd be able to ask] penetrating questions rather than saying: 'Gosh, Jacob, you're marvellous to have done this house. Isn't it lovely!'

I don't know if it's a crush, I can't quite work that out yet. But I'm bubbling along because Jacob's fascinating and I just learn from him. I don't see myself falling in love with him. Oh no. No, no, no, no.

The Turning Point [in Klosters, Switzerland, in 1988]

We went off skiing. I had flu, I had been in bed for two days. Third day in bed. Fergie came back in the afternoon at 2.30 p.m. She was carrying Beatrice then, she was four to five months pregnant. She landed upside-down in a ditch and had come back shaken, pale and exhausted. I put her to bed and both of us were in the chalet and we heard this helicopter go up. I said to her: 'There's been an avalanche', and she said: 'Something's gone wrong.'

We heard Philip Mackie [royal aide] come into the chalet. He didn't know that the two girls were upstairs. We heard him say: 'There's been an accident', so I shouted down: 'Philip, what's going on?' 'Oh, nothing at all, nothing at all, we'll tell you soon.' I said: 'Tell us now.' He said: 'There's been an accident and one of the party is dead.' So we sat there, we just sat on top of the stairs, Fergie and I, and we didn't know who it was.

Half an hour later it came through that it was a man and then three-quarters of an hour later Charles rang up Fergie to tell her that it wasn't him, that it was Hugh [Major Hugh Lindsay, a former equerry to the Queen]. That really turned me inside out. So everyone started shaking. They didn't know what to do next. I said to Fergie: 'Right, we must go upstairs and pack Hugh's suitcase and do it now while we don't know what's hit us. We must take the passport out and give it to the police.' And we went upstairs and packed everything. I took the suitcase downstairs and said to Tony [Prince Charles's bodyguard]: 'I've put the suitcase under your bed. It's there when you need it but we'd like Hugh's belongings back so we can give them to Sarah [Major Lindsay's wife], his signet ring, his watch.' And then it all went haywire. My husband was very much the centre of attention — how he coped with it, and whether he was going to crack up. Charlie Palmer-Tomkinson comes in and says: 'Patricia's having a second operation on her legs.' So we, as a party, think: well why isn't he with her? 'Oh, I'll see her in the morning,' he said. The coroner came and told us quite a strange story about how it was because the snow had been dangerous. To this day I think it was the two men — my husband and Charlie's — sense of danger that took someone's life. And when [the press] said my husband suffered, okay, he suffered but nothing like Sarah suffered. [She was then heavily pregnant with her first child, Alice]. When I went to talk to my husband about Sarah Lindsay and how she felt about Hugh being taken, he always said to me: 'I don't understand why she's angry.'

I felt terribly in charge of the whole thing. I said to my husband: 'We're going home, to take the body home to Sarah; we owe it to Sarah to take the body home. And we're not going skiing tomorrow.' Charlie said: 'It's not a case of falling off a horse and getting back on the next day to get rid of the nerves; it doesn't work like that. We must take Hugh back.' Anyway, there were tremendous arguments about that. So, eventually, we had to use the words 'selfish' and 'Sarah a widow' and it worked. I got my policeman to get Hugh's body out of the hospital and [we] took him home.

Anyway, so we came back from Klosters and everyone said: 'Poor Charles, poor this, poor that.' We arrived back at Northolt and we had Hugh's coffin in the bottom of the aeroplane and Sarah was waiting at Northolt, six months pregnant and it was a ghastly sight, just chilling. We had to watch the coffin come out and I said to Sarah: 'You'll never guess what we packed in Hugh's suitcase — his black curly wig.' And she laughed at that. And I thought: 'My God, you don't know what you're going to go through in the next few days.' Then Sarah came to stay with me at Highgrove when I was on my own and she cried from dawn to dusk and my sister came and every time we mentioned the name of Hugh, there were tears, tears, but I thought it was good to mention his name because she had to cleanse herself of it, and her grief went long and hard, because he was killed in a foreign country, she wasn't out there with him, they'd only been married eight months, she was expecting a baby. The whole thing was ghastly and what a nice person he was. Out of all the people who went it should never have been him.

Fergie and I were closer to Hugh than Charles ever was. Hugh just felt sorry for Charles. He was very good with all the members of my husband's family, he always was a star trouper.

I took charge there. I was practically bossy.

I woke up to the fact that I can cope with a drama. My husband made me feel so inadequate in every possible way that each time I came up for air he pushed me down again and when my bulimia finished two years [ago] I felt so much stronger mentally and physically so was able to soldier on in the world. Even if I ate a lot of dinner Charles would say: 'Is that going to reappear later? What a waste.' He talked to my sister about it and said: 'I'm worried about Di, she's not sleeping, she's being sick, can't you talk to her?' I suppose he's worked it out.

Long Road to Recovery

I think the bulimia actually woke me up. I suddenly realized what I was going to lose if I let go and was it worth it? Carolyn Bartholomew rang me up one night and said: 'Do you realize that if you sick up potassium and magnesium you get these hideous depressions?' I said: 'No.' 'Well, presumably that's what you suffer from, have you told anyone?' I said: 'No.' 'You must tell a doctor.' I said: 'I can't.' She said: 'You must; I'll give you one hour to ring up your doctor and if you don't I'm going to tell the world.' She was so angry with me, so that's how I got involved with the shrink called Maurice Lipsedge. He came along, a sweetheart, very nice. He walked in and said: 'How many times have you tried to do yourself in?' I thought: 'I don't believe this question', so I heard myself say: 'Four or five times.' He asked all these questions and I was able to be completely honest with him and I spent a couple of hours with him and he said: 'I'm going to come and see you once a week for an hour and we're just going to talk it through.' He said: 'There's nothing wrong with you; it's your husband.' And when he said that, I thought: 'Maybe it's not me.' He helped me get back my self-esteem and he gave me books to read. I kept thinking: 'This is me, this is me, I'm not the only person.'

Dr Lipsedge said: 'In six months' time you won't recognize yourself. If you can keep your food down you will change completely.' I must say it's like being born again since then, just odd bursts, lots of odd bursts, especially at Balmoral (very bad at Balmoral) and Sandringham and Windsor. Sick the whole time. Last year I was all right, it was once every three weeks whereas it used to be four times a day; and it was a big 'hooray' on my part. My skin never suffered from it nor my teeth. When you think of all the acid! I was amazed at my hair.

From my point of view, I thought because the public saw a smiling picture on the front of the *Daily Mail* they'd think I was all right. But I guess they did wonder, but nobody voiced it. The dressmakers noticed, but it's like doctors who say: 'Oh you've lost a bit', or 'you've put on a bit' or 'What's happened here? You must look after yourself.' But that was the extent anyone ever went into it.

I hated myself so much I didn't think I was good enough, I thought I wasn't good enough for Charles, I wasn't a good enough mother — I mean doubts as long as one's leg.

I've got what my mother's got. However bloody you're feeling you can put on the most amazing show of happiness. My mother is an expert at that. I've picked it up, kept the wolves from the door, but what I couldn't cope with in those dark ages was people saying: 'It's her fault.' I got that from everywhere, everywhere, the system, and the media started to say it was my fault — 'I was the Marilyn Monroe of the 1980s and that I was adoring it.' I've never *ever* sat down and said: 'Hooray, how wonderful', never, because the day I do that we're in trouble in this set-up. I am performing a duty as the Princess of Wales as my time is allocated. And if I go somewhere else, I go somewhere else. If life changes, it changes, but at least when I finish, as I see it, my 12 to 15 years as Princess of Wales . . . I don't see it any longer, funnily enough.

From day one, I always knew I would never be the next Queen. No one said that to me — I just knew it. I got an astrologist in six years ago. Fergie introduced me to Penny Thornton. I said: 'I've got to get out, I can't bear it any longer', and she said to me: 'One day you will be allowed out but you will be allowed out as opposed to divorcing or something like that.' It always sat in my mind; she told me that in 1984, so I've known it for some time.

I'd be dressed up to go for dinner and he [Charles] would say: 'Oh, not that dress again', or something like that, but one of the bravest moments of my entire ten years was when we went to this ghastly party for Camilla's sister's 40th birthday. Nobody expected me to turn up but again a voice inside me said: 'Go for the hell of it.' So I psyched myself up something awful. I decided I'm not going to kiss Camilla hello any more, I was going to shake hands with her instead. This was my big step. And I was feeling frightfully brave and bold and basically Diana's going to come away having done her bit. He needled me the whole way down to Ham Common where the party was. 'Oh, why are you coming tonight?' — needle, needle, needle, the whole way down. I didn't bite but I was very, very on edge.

Anyway, I walk into the house and stick my hand out to Camilla for the first time and think: 'Phew, I've got over that.' There were about forty of us there and we all sat down and, bearing in mind they were all my husband's age, I was a total fish out of water but I decided I am going to try my hardest. I was going to make an impact.

And then after dinner we were all upstairs and I was chatting away and suddenly noticed there was no Camilla and no Charles upstairs. So this disturbed me, so I make my way to go downstairs. I know what I'm going to confront myself with. They tried to stop me from going downstairs. 'Oh, Diana, don't go down there.' 'I'm just going to find my husband, I would like to see him.' I had been upstairs about an hour and a half so I was entitled to go down and find him. I go downstairs and there is a very happy little threesome going on downstairs — Camilla, Charles and another man chatting away. So I thought: 'Right, this is your moment', and joined in the conversation as if we were all best friends and the other man said: 'I think we ought to go upstairs now.' So we stood up and I said: 'Camilla, I'd love to have a word with you if it's possible', and she looked really uncomfortable and put her head down, and I said to the men: 'Okay boys, I'm just going to have a quick word with Camilla', and 'I'll be up in a minute', and they shot upstairs like chickens with no heads, and I could feel upstairs all hell breaking loose. 'What's she going to do?'

I said to Camilla: 'Would you like to sit down?' So we sat down and I was utterly terrified of her and I said: 'Camilla, I would just like you to know that I know exactly what is going on.' She said: 'I don't know what you're talking about!' And I said: 'I know what's going on between you and Charles, and I just want you to know that.' And she said: 'Oh, it's not a cloak-and-dagger situation.' I said: 'I think it is.' I wasn't as strong as I'd have liked, but at least I got the conversation going. She told me: 'You never let him see the children when he's up in Scotland.' I told her: 'Camilla, the children are either at High-grove or in London.' That's Charles's biggest fault: he never sees the children. But I never take them away. The other day, for instance, William said: 'Papa, will you play with us.' 'Oh, I don't know if I have time.' Famous quote — always happens. So, he can't gripe about that.

Anyway; going back to Camilla. She said to me: 'You've got everything you ever wanted. You've got all the men in the world falling in love with you, and you've got two beautiful children. What more could you want?' I didn't believe her, so I said: 'I want my husband.'

Someone came down to relieve us, obviously. 'For God's sake, go down there, they're having a fight.' It wasn't a fight — calm, deathly calm, and I said to Camilla: 'I'm sorry I'm in the way, I obviously am in the way and it must be hell for both of you, but I do know what is going on. Don't treat me like an idiot.' So I went upstairs and people began to disperse. In the car on the way back my husband was over me like a bad rash and I cried like I have never cried before — it was anger, it was seven years' pent-up anger coming out. I cried and cried and cried and I didn't sleep that night. And the next morning when I woke up I felt a tremendous shift. I'd done something, said what I felt, still the old jealousy and anger swilling around, but it wasn't so deathly as before, and I said to him at the weekend three days later: 'Darling, I'm sure you'll want to know what I said to Camilla. There's no secret. You may ask her. I just said I loved you — there's nothing wrong in that.' He said: 'I don't believe it.' I said: 'That's what I said to her. I've got nothing to hide, I'm your wife and the mother of your children.' That always makes him slightly twitch, when I say 'mother of your children'. He hates being made aware of it.

That was it, really. It was a big step for me.

I was desperate to know what she said to him — no idea of course! He told a lot of people the reason why the marriage was so wobbly was because I was being sick the whole time. They never questioned what it was doing to me.

[Diana's sister] Jane's wonderfully solid. If you ring up with a drama, she says: 'Golly, gosh, Duch, how awful, how sad' and gets angry. But she doesn't do anything about it. Whereas my sister Sarah swears about it behind my back and says: 'Poor Duch, such a shitty thing to happen.' But she won't say it to my face. My father says: 'Just remember we always love you', and does nothing. And my mother just writes letters when she feels like it.

But that summer [1988] when I made so

many cock-ups I sat myself down in the autumn, when I was in Scotland, and I remember saying to myself: 'Right, Diana, it's no good, you've got to change it right round, this publicity; you've got to grow up and be responsible. You've got to understand that you can't do what other 26- and 27-year-olds are doing. You've been chosen to do a position so you must adapt to the position and stop fighting it.' I remember my conversation so well, sitting by water. I always sit by water when contemplating.

Stephen Twigg [a therapist] used to teach me affirmations about myself. But I could never believe them. It's one thing to say them, it's another to believe. He said if I wanted to get better I could. He said once: 'Whatever anybody else thinks of you is none of your business.' That sat with me. Then once someone said to me, when I said I've got to go up to Balmoral: 'Well, you've got to put up with them but they've also got to put up with you.' This myth about me hating Balmoral — I love Scotland but just the atmosphere drains me to nothing. I go up 'strong Diana'. I come away depleted of everything because they just suck me dry, because I tune in to all their moods and, boy, are there some undercurrents there! Instead of having a holiday, it's the most stressful time of the year. It's very close quarters. I love being out all day. I love the stalking.

I panic a lot when I go up to Balmoral. It's my worst time, and I think: 'How the hell am I going to get out of this?' The first couple of days I'm frightfully chirpy when I get up there and everything's wonderful. By the third day they're sapping me again. There are so many negative atmospheres. That house sucks one dry. But I come back down to London to see someone, and I'll go back the same day. And it will be like an injection, a replenishment coming into my set-up. I say to myself: 'I am normal, it's okay to be me, it's all right, you're going back to work soon, going to be back in your own home; you go back up there again and try and perform.' It's exhausting.

I'm much happier now. I'm not blissful but much more content than I've ever been. I've really gone down deep, scraped the bottom a couple of times and come up again, and it's very nice meeting people now and talking about tai chi and people say: 'Tai chi — what do you know about tai chi?' and I say: 'An energy flow', and all this and they look at me and they say: 'She's the girl who's supposed to like shopping and clothes the whole time. She's not supposed to know about spiritual things.'

At the Aids hospice last week [July 1991] with Mrs Bush was another stepping stone for me. I had always wanted to hug people in hospital beds. This particular man who was so ill started crying when I sat on his bed and he held my hand and I thought: 'Diana, do it, just do it', and I gave him an enormous hug and it was just so touching because he clung to me and he cried. It was wonderful! It made him laugh, and I thought: 'That's all right.'

On the other side of the room, a very young man, who I can only describe as beautiful, lying in his bed, told me he was going to die about Christmas, and his lover, a man sitting in a chair, much older than him, was crying his eyes out so I put my hand out to him and said: 'It's not supposed to be easy, all this. You've got a lot of anger in you, haven't you?' He said: 'Yes. Why him not me?' I said: 'Isn't it extraordinary, wherever I go it's always those like you, sitting in a chair, who have to go through such hell, whereas those who accept they are going to die are calm?' He said: 'I didn't know that happened', and I said: 'Well, it does, you're not the only one. It's wonderful that you're actually by his bed. You'll learn so much from watching your friend.' He was crying his eyes out and clung on to my hand and I felt so comfortable in there. I just hated being taken away.

All sorts of people have come into my life — elderly people, spiritual people, acupuncturists, all these people came in after I finished my bulimia.

When I go into the Palace for a garden party or summit meeting dinner I am a very different person. I conform to what's expected of me. They can't find fault with me when I'm in their presence. I do as I'm expected. What they say behind my back is none of my business, but I come back here and I know when I turn my light off at night I did my best.

New Age Values

She [the late Countess Spencer, Diana's paternal grandmother] looks after me in the spirit world. I know that for a fact. Used to stay at Park House with us. She was sweet and wonderful and special. Divine really.

I've got a lot to learn. I've got 101 books sitting by my bedside, which I'm going to read in the next two weeks. And I'm going to be amused by people's reaction to their titles. I'm absolutely gripped.

I'd never discuss it with anyone, they

would all think I'm, you know? I used the word 'psychic' to my policemen a couple of times and they have freaked out.

I've got a lot of that [*déjà vu*]. Places I think I've been before, people I've met.

[On reincarnation] I've had various rooms around the world where I feel I've been before. One just feels 'Goodness, oh!' But I don't go and talk to anyone about it. I'm just aware that it's *déjà vu;* it's very strong.

I have an awful lot of dreams about things, if someone's troubled. I knew Adrian wasn't very well this weekend, and I couldn't get through. But something told me something was wrong, and he had a very, very bad weekend. Instinct. I'll walk into a room and straight into them.

I recall sitting in a Land Rover with my policeman and watching [Prince Charles's] horse [Alibar] coming along and rearing its head back. I said: 'That horse is going to have a heart attack and die.' And it did. It had a heart attack then and there.

I've known her [Debbie Frank, her astrologer] for about three years. She's very sweet. She does astrology and counselling. She doesn't advise, she just tells me from her angle and, with astrology, I listen to it but I don't believe it totally. It's a direction and a suggestion rather than it's definitely going to happen. She's been sweet, particularly when I was going through a rough patch two years ago. She just said you've got to hang on because things will get brighter but she never forced me with information at all.

[On a visit to her clairvoyant] My grandmother came in first, very strong, then my uncle and then Barry [Mannakee, her former police protection officer]. I hesitated about asking her questions about Barry because — well, I don't know — I just hesitated, but I've always had a question mark about his death and I've been given an answer and that's the end of that.

The Princess and the People
I hope they know that I love children and little people but I suppose it comes across. I'm just demented [about my own children] and it's mutual. There's terrific understanding.

Top of the Pops, Coronation Street, all the soap operas. You name it, I've watched it. The reason why I watch them so much now is not so much out of interest but if I go out and about, whether it be to Birmingham, Liverpool or Dorset, I can always pick up on a TV programme and you are on the same level. That I decided for myself. It works so well. Everybody watches it and I say: 'Did you see so and so? Wasn't it funny when this happened or that happened?' and you are immediately on the same level. You are not the princess and they the general public — it's the same level.

[On her work life] I still like to do what I call my 'Awaydays' once a week. I do Birmingham, Liverpool, Manchester so no one can say to me she never goes out of London. It would be much more convenient to stay put. It's a real effort to go away but it's worth it. I'd change a few things in that I would go around hospices, Aids, cancer. I'd do that full time. I don't find it exhausting.

[On how the public relate to Diana] Well, from a female's point of view, all the ladies ever want to do is see what colour I'm in and what I'm wearing and how the boys are. From a male point of view, I don't know. When I first started the job there used to be just a certain age group — my age group — and now there's everything from two-year-olds to ninety-five-year-olds. It's very interesting to see the thirty-five-year-olds to forty-five-year-olds because that's not a particular area I relate to very well. [I relate better to] the very old. I suppose also the thirty-year-olds, now I'm [that age] myself.

But I couldn't understand why they were always hanging around me. I always used to think people just looked at my clothes and I was desperate for the other side to come out and be dealt with and didn't know how to do it.

I'd change the Queen's broadcast for Christmas — top of the list. It makes me cringe so much, that; it upsets me to such a degree, there's no relating. What else would I change? I'd have garden parties for all the handicapped and wheelchairs — which we did just before we got married — people who've never seen Buckingham Palace let alone been on the grass. But they are not allowed too many wheelchairs because it ruins the grass.

The size of the crowds — if that doesn't make me seem like a pop star; people thanking me for bringing happiness in their lives; little sentences that put together make a very wonderful, very special day. Thank you for coming; thank you for making the effort; thank you for being you and all those things, never used to believe. Now I'm more comfortable receiving that sort of information whether or not it's true. I can now digest that sort of thing whereas I used to throw it back. No one has ever said to me: 'Well done.' Because I had a smile on my face everybody thought I was having a wonderful time. That's what they chose to think — it made them happier thinking that.

Princes William and Harry

Harry was supposed to be a girl. [Charles] was absolutely amazed and he adores him. But I know we had two boys for a reason. We were the only people in the family to have two boys. The rest of the family had a boy and a girl and we were the first to change and I know fate played a hand there — Harry's a 'backup' in the nicest possible way. William is going to be in his position much earlier than people think now.

When Beatrice or Eugenie are running around I'll say to Charles: 'There you are, you missed that one.' 'What do you mean?' And I'll say: 'Well, you could have had a daughter.' 'No, we'd have had a third boy.' And I'd say: 'No, not necessarily.' And sometimes we get the albums out, of the boys, and he'll tell me: 'Oh, you were so good with them in the nursery, you were marvellous.'

I want to bring them up with security, not to anticipate things, because they will be disappointed. That's made my own life so much easier. I hug my children to death. I get into bed with them at night, hug them and say: 'Who loves them most in the whole world?' and they always say: 'Mummy'. I always feed them love and affection — it's so important.

[Preparing Prince William] I am altering it for him but in a subtle way; people aren't aware of it but I am. I would never rattle their cage, the monarchy, because when I think the mother-in-law has been doing it for 40 years who am I to come along and change it just like that? But through William learning what I do, and his father to a certain extent, he has got an insight into what's coming his way. He's not hidden upstairs with the governess.

I've chosen all the schools so far, and there was never any argument. It was just Charles wanted them to be governessed here and I said no, they've got to go out if they're going to survive when they're adults.

[On William being treated differently because he's the future monarch] He's appallingly embarrassed by the whole thing. He's very uncomfortable about that.

The Future
I think I'm going to cut a very different path from everyone else. I'm going to break away from this set-up and go and help the man on the street. I hate saying 'man on the

street' — it sounds so condescending. I don't know yet but I'm being pushed more and more that way. I don't like the glamorous occasions any more — I feel uncomfortable with them. I would much rather be doing something with sick people — I'm more comfortable there.

I have been positive about the future for some time but obviously there's endless question marks, especially when my space is crowded around me — oh, then I see my friends having a good time and I never . . .

I always felt so different — I felt I was in the wrong shell. I knew my life was going to be a winding road.

What I do now since I've learned to be assertive, I let a silence follow while I'm ticking away and then I say I'd like to think about that, I'll give you an answer later on in the day; that's if I'm not sure, but if I am sure, a gut instinct tells me I'm sure, I say: 'No thank you' and nobody comes back at me.

If I was able to write my own script I'd say that I would hope that my husband would go off, go away with his lady and sort that out and leave me and the children to carry the Wales name through to the time William ascends the throne. And I'd be behind them all the way and I can do this job so much better on my own; I don't feel trapped.

I would love to go to the opera — that would be a great treat — or ballet or a film. I like it as normal as possible. Walking along the pavement gives me a tremendous thrill.

I'm not bitter about that but it would be quite nice to go and do things like a weekend in Paris, but it's not for me at the moment. But I know one day if I play the rules of life — the game of life — I will be able to have those things I've always pined for and they will be that much more special because I will be that much older and I'll be able to appreciate them that much more.

I don't want my friends to be hurt and think I've dropped them but I haven't got time to sit and gossip, I've got things to do and time is precious.

I love the countryside and I live in London because I'm all secure, but I see myself one day living abroad. I don't know why I think that and I think of either Italy or France, which is rather unnerving; not yet. Last August a friend said to me that I'm going to marry somebody who's foreign, or who has got a lot of foreign blood in them. I

thought it was always interesting. I do know
I'm going to remarry or live with someone.

DIANA: HER TRUE STORY

1
'I Was Supposed to Be a Boy'

It was a memory indelibly engraved upon her soul. Diana Spencer sat quietly at the bottom of the cold stone stairs at her Norfolk home, clutching the wrought-iron banisters while all around her there was a determined bustle. She could hear her father loading suitcases into the boot of a car, then Frances, her mother, crunching across the gravel forecourt, the clunk of the car door being shut and the sound of a car engine revving and then slowly fading as her mother drove through the gates of Park House and out of her life. Diana was six years old. A quarter of a century later, it was a moment she could still picture in her mind's eye and she could still summon up the painful feelings of rejection, breach of trust and isolation that the break-up of her parents' marriage signified to her.

It may have happened differently but that was the picture Diana carried with her.

There were many other snapshots of her childhood which crowded her memory. Her mother's tears, her father's lonely silences, the numerous nannies she resented, the endless shuttling between parents, the sound of her brother Charles sobbing himself to sleep, the feelings of guilt that she hadn't been born a boy and the firmly fixed idea that somehow she was a 'nuisance' to have around. She craved cuddles and kisses; she was given a catalogue from Hamleys toyshop. It was a childhood where she wanted for nothing materially but everything emotionally. 'She comes from a privileged background but she had a childhood that was very hard,' said her astrologer Felix Lyle.

The Honourable Diana Spencer was born late on the afternoon of 1 July 1961, the third daughter of Viscount Althorp, then aged 37, and Viscountess Althorp, 12 years his junior. She weighed 7lb 12oz and while her father expressed his delight at a 'perfect physical specimen' there was no hiding the sense of anticlimax, if not downright disappointment, in the family that the new arrival was not the longed-for male heir who would carry on the Spencer name. Such was the anticipation of a boy that the couple hadn't considered any girls' names. A week later they settled on 'Diana Frances', after a Spencer ancestress and the baby's mother.

While Viscount Althorp, the late Earl Spencer, may have been proud of his new daughter — Diana was very much the apple of his eye — his remarks about her health could have been chosen more diplomatically. Just 18 months previously Diana's mother had given birth to John, a baby so badly deformed and sickly that he survived for only ten hours. It was a harrowing time for the couple and there was much pressure from older members of the family to see 'what was wrong with the mother'. They wanted to know why she kept producing girls. Lady Althorp, the late Frances Shand Kydd, then still only 23, was sent to various Harley Street clinics in London for intimate tests. For Diana's mother, fiercely proud, combative and tough-minded, it was a humiliating and unjust experience, all the more so in retrospect as nowadays it is known that the sex of the baby is determined by the man. As her son Charles, the present Earl Spencer, observed: 'It was a dreadful time for my parents and probably the root of their divorce because I don't think they ever got over it.'

While she was too young to understand, Diana certainly caught the pitch of the family's frustration, and, believing that she was 'a nuisance', she accepted a corresponding load of guilt — and failure for disappointing her parents and family, feelings she learned later to accept and recognize.

Three years after Diana's birth the longed-for son arrived. Unlike Diana, who was christened in Sandringham church and had well-to-do commoners for godparents, baby brother Charles was christened in style at Westminster Abbey with the Queen as principal godparent. The infant was heir to a rapidly diminishing but still substantial fortune accumulated in the 15th century when the Spencers were among the wealthiest sheep traders in Europe. With their fortune they collected an earldom from Charles I, built Althorp House in Northamptonshire, acquired a coat of arms and motto — 'God defend the right' — and amassed a fine collection of art, antiques, books and *objets d'art.*

For the next three centuries Spencers were at home in the palaces of Kensington, Buckingham and Westminster as they occupied various offices of State and Court. If a Spencer never quite reached the commanding heights, they certainly walked confidently along the corridors of power. Spencers became Knights of the Garter, Privy

Councillors, ambassadors and a First Lord of the Admiralty, while the third Earl Spencer was considered as a possible Prime Minister. They were linked by blood to Charles II, the Dukes of Marlborough, Devonshire and Abercorn and, through a quirk of history, to seven American presidents, including Franklin D. Roosevelt, and to the actor Humphrey Bogart and, it is said, the gangster Al Capone.

The Spencer qualities of quiet public service, the values of *noblesse oblige* were well expressed in their service to the Sovereign. Generations of Spencer men and women have fulfilled the functions of Lord Chamberlain, equerry, lady-in-waiting and other positions at Court. Diana's paternal grandmother, Countess Spencer, was a Lady of the Bedchamber to Queen Elizabeth, the Queen Mother, while her maternal grandmother, Ruth, Lady Fermoy, was one of her Women of the Bedchamber for nearly 30 years. Diana's father served as equerry to both King George VI and the present Queen.

However, it was the family of Diana's mother, the Fermoys, with their roots in Ireland and connections in the United States, who were responsible for the acquisition of Park House, her childhood home in

Norfolk. As a mark of friendship with his second son, the Duke of York (later George VI), King George V granted Diana's grandfather, Maurice, the 4th Baron Fermoy, the lease of Park House, a spacious property originally built to accommodate the overflow of guests and staff from nearby Sandringham House.

The Fermoys certainly made a mark on the area. Maurice Fermoy became the Conservative Member of Parliament for King's Lynn, while his Scottish wife, who gave up a promising career as a concert pianist to marry, founded the King's Lynn Festival for Arts and Music which, since its inception in 1951, has attracted world-renowned musicians such as Sir John Barbirolli and Yehudi Menuhin.

For the young Diana Spencer, this long noble heritage was not so much impressive as terrifying. She never relished visits to the ancestral home of Althorp. There were too many creepy corners and badly lit corridors peopled with portraits of long-dead ancestors whose eyes followed her unnervingly. As her brother recalled: 'It was like an old man's club with masses of clocks ticking away. For an impressionable child it was a nightmarish place. We never looked forward to going there.'

This sense of foreboding was hardly helped by the bad-tempered relationship which existed between her gruff grandfather Jack, the 7th Earl, and his son Johnnie Althorp. For many years they were barely on grunting, let alone speaking terms. Abrupt to the point of rudeness yet fiercely protective of Althorp, Diana's grandfather earned the nickname of 'the curator earl' because he knew the history of every picture and piece of furniture in his stately home. He was so proud of his domain that he often followed visitors around with a duster and once, in the library, snatched a cigar from out of Winston Churchill's mouth. Beneath this irascible veneer was a man of cultivation and taste, whose priorities contrasted sharply with his son's *laissez-faire* approach to life and amiable enjoyment of the traditional outdoor pursuits of an English country gentleman.

While Diana was in awe of her grandfather, she adored her grandmother, Countess Spencer. 'She was sweet, wonderful and very special. Divine really,' said the Princess. The Countess was known locally for her frequent visits to the sick and the infirm and was never at a loss for a generous word or gesture. While Diana inherited her mother's sparky, strong-willed nature she was also blessed with her paternal grandmother's qualities of thoughtfulness and compassion.

In contrast to the eerie splendours of Althorp, Diana's rambling ten-bedroomed home, Park House, was positively cosy, notwithstanding the staff cottages, extensive garages, outdoor swimming pool, tennis court and cricket pitch in the grounds, as well as the six full-time staff who included a cook, a butler and a governess.

Screened from the road by trees and shrubs, the house is substantial but its dirty, sand-brick exterior makes it appear rather bleak and lonely. In spite of its forbidding appearance, the Spencer children loved the rambling pile. When they moved to Althorp in 1975 on the death of their grandfather, the 7th Earl, Charles said goodbye to every room. The house was later turned into a Cheshire Home holiday hotel for the disabled; during visits to Sandringham Diana would occasionally visit it.

Park House was a home of atmosphere and great character. On the ground floor was the stone-flagged kitchen, the dark-green laundry room, domain of Diana's foul-tempered ginger cat called Marmalade, and the schoolroom where their governess, Miss Gertrude Allen — known as 'Ally' —

taught the girls the rudiments of reading and writing. Next door was what the children called 'The Beatle Room', a room devoted entirely to psychedelic posters, pictures and other memorabilia of Sixties pop stars. It was a rare concession to the postwar era. Elsewhere the house was a snapshot of upper-class English life, decorated with formal family portraits and regimental pictures, as well as the plaques, photographs and certificates which were testimony to a lifetime spent in good works.

From her pretty cream bedroom in the first-floor nursery, Diana enjoyed a pleasant prospect of grazing cattle, a patchwork of open fields and parkland interspersed with copses of pine, silver birch and yew. Rabbits, foxes and other woodland creatures were regularly seen on the lawns while the frequent sea frets which softly curled around her sash windows were evidence that the Norfolk coast was only six miles away.

It was a heavenly place for growing children. They fed trout in the lake at Sandringham House, slid down the banisters, took Jill, their springer spaniel, for long rambles, played hide-and-seek in the garden, listened to the wind whistling through the trees and hunted for pigeons' eggs. In summer they swam in the heated outdoor swimming pool, looked for frogs and newts, picnicked on the beach near their private hut at Brancaster and played in their very own tree house. And, as in Enid Blyton's *Famous Five* children's books, there were always 'lashings of ginger beer' and the smell of something appetizing baking in the kitchen.

Like her elder sisters, Diana was on horseback aged three and soon developed a passion for animals, the smaller the better. She had pet hamsters, rabbits, guinea pigs, her cat Marmalade, which Charles and Jane loathed, and, as her mother recalls, 'anything in a small cage'. When one of her menagerie died, Diana dutifully performed a burial ceremony. While goldfish were flushed down the lavatory, she normally placed her other dead pets in a cardboard shoe box, dug a hole beneath the spreading cedar tree on the lawn and laid them to rest. Finally, she placed a makeshift cross above their grave.

Graveyards held a sombre fascination. Charles and Diana frequently visited their brother John's lichen-covered grave in the Sandringham churchyard and mused about what he would have been like and whether they would have been born if he had lived. Charles felt that his parents would have completed their family with Diana while the

Princess herself felt that she would not have been born. It was a matter for endless unresolved conjecture. In Diana's young mind her brother's gravestone, with its simple 'In Loving Memory' epitaph, was a permanent reminder that, as she later recalled: 'I was the girl who was supposed to be a boy.'

Just as her childhood amusements could have originated from the pages of a 1930s children's book, so Diana's upbringing reflected the values of a bygone age. She had a nanny, Kent-born Judith Parnell, who took the infant Diana for walks around the grounds in a well-used, highly sprung perambulator. Indeed, Diana's first memory was 'the smell of the warm plastic' of her pram hood. The growing girl did not see as much of her mother as she would have wished, and less of her father. Her sisters, Sarah and Jane, her seniors by six and four years respectively, were already spending mornings in the downstairs classroom when she was born and by the time Diana was ready to join them they were packing their bags for boarding school.

Mealtimes were spent with nanny. Simple fare was the order of the day. Cereals at breakfast, mince and vegetables for lunch and fish every Friday. Her parents were a benign though distant presence and it wasn't until Charles was seven that he actually sat down to a meal with his father in the downstairs dining room. There was a formality and restraint to their childhood, a reflection of the way Diana's parents had been raised. As Charles recalled: 'It was a privileged upbringing out of a different age, a distant way of living from your parents. I don't know anyone who brings up children like that any more. It certainly lacked a mother figure.'

Privileged yes, snobbish no. At a very early age the Spencer children had impressed upon them the value of good manners, honesty and accepting people for what they were, not for their position in life. Charles said: 'We never understood the whole title business. I didn't even know I had any kind of title until I went to prep school when I started to get these letters saying: "The Honourable Charles". Then I started to wonder what it was all about. We had no idea that we were privileged. As children we accepted our circumstances as normal.'

Their royal next-door neighbours simply fitted in to a social landscape of friends and acquaintances who included the children of the Queen's land agent, Charles and Alexandra Loyd, the local vicar's daughter

Penelope Ashton, and William and Annabel Fox, whose mother, Carol, was Diana's godmother. Social relations with the royal family were sporadic, especially as they only spent a small part of the year on their 20,000-acre Sandringham estate. A royal visit to Park House was such a rare event that when Princess Anne said she would call round after church one Sunday there was consternation in the Spencer household. Diana's father didn't drink and staff frantically searched through the cupboards looking for a bottle of something suitable to offer their royal guest. Finally they found a cheap bottle of sherry, which had been won in a church bazaar, lying forgotten in a drawer.

Occasionally Princess Margaret's son, Viscount Linley, and the Princes Andrew and Edward might come to play for the afternoon but there certainly weren't the comings and goings many have assumed. In fact the Spencer children viewed their invitations to the Queen's winter home with trepidation. After watching a screening of the Walt Disney film *Chitty Chitty Bang Bang* in the private cinema, Charles had nightmares about a character called the Child Catcher. For Diana it was the 'strange' atmosphere of Sandringham itself which she hated. On one occasion she refused to go. She kicked and screamed her defiance until her father told her that it would be considered very bad manners if she didn't join the other children. If anyone had told her then that one day she would join the royal family she would have run a mile.

If the atmosphere at Sandringham was uncomfortable, at Park House it became unbearable as Diana's little world fell apart at the seams. In September 1967 Sarah and Jane went to boarding school at West Heath in Kent, a move which coincided with the collapse of the Althorps' 14-year marriage.

That summer they decided on a trial separation, a decision which came as a 'thunderbolt, a terrible shock' to Charles, horrified both families and shocked the county set. Even for a family with a penchant for turning a drama into a crisis, this was an exceptional event. They remembered how their marriage in 1954 was trumpeted as 'the society wedding of the year', their union endorsed by the presence of the Queen and Queen Mother. Certainly in his bachelor days Johnnie Spencer was the catch of the county. Not only was he heir to the Spencer estates, he also served with distinction as a captain in the Royal Scots Greys during World War Two and, as equerry to the Queen, he had accompanied her and Prince Philip on their historic tour of Australia shortly before his marriage.

The sophistication exuded by a man 12 years her senior was no doubt part of the attraction for the Honourable Frances Roche, the younger daughter of the 4th Baron Fermoy, who was an 18-year-old debutante when they first met. With her trim figure, vivacious personality and love of sports Frances caught the eye of many young men that season, among them Major Ronald Ferguson, father of Sarah, Duchess of York. However, it was Johnnie Spencer who won her heart and, after a short courtship, they married at Westminster Abbey in June 1954.

They obviously took the words of the Bishop of Norwich to heart. Just nine months after he had declared at their wedding: 'You are making an addition to the home life of your country on which, above all others, our national life depends', their first daughter Sarah was born. They settled for a country life; Johnnie studied at the Royal Agricultural College in Cirencester and, following an uneasy spell on the Althorp estate, they moved to Park House. Over the next few years they built up a 650-acre farm, a sizeable chunk of which was bought with £20,000 of Frances's inheritance.

Tensions soon simmered beneath the impression of domestic harmony and marital bliss. The pressure to produce a male heir was ever-present and there was Frances's growing realization that a lifestyle which had seemed urbane to her in her youth was, on mature reflection, dull and uninspiring. The late Earl Spencer said: 'How many of those 14 years were happy? I thought all of them, until the moment we parted. I was wrong. We hadn't fallen apart, we'd drifted apart.'

As cracks appeared in the façade of unity, the atmosphere at Park House soured. In public the couple were all smiles, in private it was a different story. While the freezing silences, heated exchanges and bitter words can only be imagined, the traumatic effect on the children was only too evident. Diana clearly remembered witnessing a particularly violent argument between her mother and father as she peeked from her hiding place behind the drawing-room door.

The catalyst which provoked that indignation was the appearance in their lives of a wealthy businessman, the late Peter Shand Kydd, who had recently returned to Britain after selling a sheep farm in Australia. The

Althorps first met the extrovert, university-educated entrepreneur and his artist wife, Janet Munro Kerr, at a dinner party in London. A subsequent arrangement to go on a skiing holiday in Switzerland together proved a fatal turning point in their lives. Peter, an amusing *bon viveur* with an attractive bohemian streak, seemed to possess all the qualities Johnnie lacked. In the exhilaration of their affair Lady Althorp, 11 years his junior, did not notice his bouts of depression and black moods. That would come later.

On their return from holiday Peter, then aged 42, moved out of his London home leaving behind his wife and three children. At the same time he began to see Frances secretly at an address in South Kensington in central London.

When the Althorps agreed to a trial separation, Diana's mother moved out of Park House into a rented apartment in Cadogan Place, Belgravia. It was then that the myth of 'the bolter' was born, that Frances had left her husband and deserted her four children for the love of another man. She was cast as the selfish villainess of the drama, her husband the innocent injured party. In fact when she left home Lady Althorp had already made arrangements for

Charles and Diana to live with her in London. Diana was enrolled at a girls' day school, Charles at a nearby kindergarten.

When Frances arrived at her new home, to be followed weeks later by her children and their nanny, she had every hope that the children would be relatively unaffected by her marital breakdown, especially as Sarah and Jane were away at boarding school. During term-time the younger children returned to Park House at weekends while their father, Viscount Althorp, stayed with them in Belgravia when he visited London. They were bleak meetings. Charles's earliest memory is playing quietly on the floor with a train set while his mother sat sobbing on the edge of the bed, his father smiling weakly at him in a forlorn attempt to reassure his son that everything was all right. The family was reunited at Park House for half-term and again during the Christmas holidays. But, as Mrs Shand Kydd later stated: 'It was my last Christmas there for by now it had become apparent that the marriage had completely broken down.'

That fateful visit was marked by a distinct absence of seasonal goodwill or tidings of joy for the future. Viscount Althorp insisted, in spite of his wife's fierce objections, that the children return permanently to Park House and continue their education at Silfield School in King's Lynn. 'He refused to let them return in the New Year to London,' she said.

As the legal machinery for divorce ground into action, the children became pawns in a bitter and acrimonious battle which turned mother against daughter and husband against wife. Lady Althorp sued for custody of the children, an action started with every hope of success as the mother usually wins — unless the father is a nobleman. His rank and title give him prior claims.

The case, which was heard in June 1968, wasn't helped by the fact that two months earlier Lady Althorp had been named as the 'other woman' in the Shand Kydds' divorce while, most galling of all, her own mother, Ruth, Lady Fermoy, sided against her. It was to be the greatest betrayal of her life and one she never forgave. The Althorps' divorce went through in April 1969 and a month later, on 2 May, Peter Shand Kydd and Lady Althorp married in a quiet register office ceremony and bought a house on the West Sussex coast where Peter could indulge his love of sailing.

It was not just the adults who were scarred by this vicious legal battle. However much their parents and the family tried to muffle the blow, the impact on the children was still profound. Subsequently, family friends and biographers have tried to minimize the effect. They have claimed that Sarah and Jane were barely troubled by the divorce as they were away at school, that Charles, aged four, was too young to understand while Diana, then seven, reacted to the break-up with 'the unthinking resilience of her age' or even regarded it as 'fresh excitement' in her young life.

The reality was more traumatic than many have realized. It is significant that at one time in their lives both Sarah and Diana have suffered from debilitating eating disorders, anorexia nervosa and bulimia respectively. These conditions were rooted in a complex web of relations between parents and daughters, food and anxiety and, to use the jargon, 'malfunctioning' family life. As Diana said: 'Parents were busy sorting themselves out. Always seeing my mother crying. Daddy never spoke to us about it. We never asked questions. Too many changes over nannies, very unstable, the whole thing.'

To the casual visitor Diana seemed happy enough. She was always a busy, tidy little girl, going around the house at night making sure all the curtains were drawn and tucking up the zoo of small furry animals which crowded her bed — she kept them all her life. She raced around the driveway on her blue tricycle, took her dolls for walks in her pram — she always asked for a new doll as a birthday present — and helped to dress her smaller brother. The warm, maternal, caring streak which characterized her adult life was becoming evident in her daily life. There were more frequent visits to grandparents and other relations. Countess Spencer often stayed at Park House while Ruth, Lady Fermoy, taught the children card games. In her elegant home, described as 'a little corner of Belgravia in Norfolk', she explained the intricacies of mah-jong and bridge. However, there was no disguising the bewilderment Diana felt.

Night-times were worst. As children, Diana and Charles were afraid of the dark and they insisted that the landing light was left on or a candle lit in their rooms. With the wind whistling in the trees outside their window and the night-time cries of owls and other creatures, Park House could be a creepy place for a child. One evening when their father casually mentioned that a murderer was on the loose in the vicinity, the children were too terrified to sleep, listening anxiously to every rattle, creak and squeak in the darkened house. Diana daubed luminous paint on the eyes of her cuddly green hippo so that at night it seemed as though he was keeping watch and looking after her.

Every night as she lay in her bed, surrounded by her cuddly toys, she could hear her brother sobbing, crying for his mother. Sometimes she went to him, sometimes her fear of the dark overcame her maternal instincts and she stayed in her room listening as Charles wailed: 'I want my mummy, I want my mummy.' Then she too would bury her head in the pillow and weep. 'I just couldn't bear it,' she later recalled. 'I could never pluck up enough courage to get out of bed. I remember it to this day.'

Nor did she have much confidence in many of the nannies who now worked at Park House. They changed with alarming frequency and ranged from the sweet to the sadistic. One nanny was sacked on the spot when Diana's mother discovered that her employee was lacing her elder daughters' food with laxatives as a punishment. She wondered why they constantly complained of stomach pains until she caught the woman red-handed.

Another nanny beat Diana on the head

with a wooden spoon if she was naughty, or alternatively banged Charles and Diana's heads together. Charles recalled kicking a hole in his bedroom door when he was sent to his room for no good reason. 'Children have a natural sense of justice and if we felt they were unjust we would rebel,' he explained. Other nannies, such as Sally Percival, were kind and sympathetic and received Christmas cards from the 'children' long after they had left their employ.

However, the task of a new nanny was made all the more difficult because the children, bewildered and unhappy, felt that the nannies had come to take the place of their mother. The prettier they were, the more suspicious Diana was of them. The children put pins in their chairs, threw their clothes out of the window and locked them in the bathroom. In fact Charles's childhood experiences confirmed him in his decision not to employ a nanny for his own children.

Their father sometimes joined the children for tea in the nursery but, as their former nanny Mary Clarke recalled, 'It was very hard going. In those early days he wasn't very relaxed with them.' Johnnie buried himself in his work for Northamptonshire County Council, the National Association of Boys' Clubs and his cattle farm. Charles recalled: 'He was really miserable after the divorce, basically shell-shocked. He used to sit in his study the whole time. I remember occasionally, very occasionally, he used to play cricket with me on the lawn. That was a great treat.'

School simply cast the problem in another mould. Charles and Diana were 'different' and knew it. They were the only pupils at Silfield School whose parents were divorced. It set them apart from the start, a point emphasized by her former form captain, Delissa Needham: 'She was the only girl I knew whose parents were divorced. Those things just didn't happen then.'

The school itself was welcoming and friendly enough. Run by headmistress Jean Lowe, who gave evidence on Lord Althorp's behalf during the divorce case, it had a real family atmosphere. Classes were small and teachers were generous with house points and gold stars for achievements in reading, writing or drawing. Outside was a tennis court, a sandpit, a lawn for playing netball and rounders as well as a garden for weekly 'scavenger hunts'. Diana, unused to the hurly-burly of school life, was quiet and shy although she did have her friend Alexandra Loyd to keep her company.

While her handwriting was clear and she read fluently, Diana found the scholarly side rather confusing. Miss Lowe remembered her kindness to the smaller children, her love of animals and general helpfulness, but not her academic potential. She was good at art as well, but her friends couldn't explain why she burst into tears for no apparent reason during a painting class one sunny afternoon. They remember that she dedicated all her pictures to 'Mummy and Daddy'.

As she muddled through her 'tables' and *Janet and John* books, Diana became increasingly envious of her younger brother, who was remembered as a 'solemn' but well-behaved little boy. 'I longed to be as good as him in the schoolroom,' she said. As with all siblings there were fights which Diana, being bigger and stronger, invariably won. As she pinched, Charles complained. Soon he realized that he could wound with words, teasing his sister mercilessly. Both parents ordered him to stop calling his sister 'Brian', a nickname derived from a slow and rather dull-witted snail who featured in a popular children's TV show, *The Magic Roundabout*.

He had sweet revenge with the unexpected help of the local vicar's wife. Charles recalled, with relish: 'I don't know whether a pyschologist would say it was the trauma of the divorce but she had real difficulty telling the truth purely because she liked to embellish things. On the school run one day the vicar's wife stopped the car and said: "Diana Spencer, if you tell one more lie like that I am going to make you walk home." Of course I was triumphant because she had been rumbled.'

While the sibling competition was an inevitable part of growing up, far less bearable was the growing parental rivalry, conscious or not, as Frances and Johnnie vied with each other to win the love of their children. Yet while they showered their offspring with expensive presents this wasn't accompanied by the affectionate cuddles and kisses that the children craved. Diana's father, who already had a reputation locally for organizing splendid fireworks displays on Guy Fawkes Night, laid on a wonderful party for her seventh birthday. He borrowed a dromedary called Bert from Dudley Zoo for the afternoon and watched with evident delight as the surprised children were taken for rides around the lawn.

Christmas was simply an exercise in extravagance. Before the big day Charles and Diana were given the catalogue for

Hamleys, a large toyshop in London's West End, and told to tick what presents they wanted Father Christmas to bring. Lo and behold, on Christmas Day their wishes came true, the stockings on the end of their beds bulging with goodies. 'It makes you very materialistic,' said Charles. There was one present which gave Diana the most agonizing decision of her young life. In 1970 she was a guest at the wedding of her cousin Elizabeth Wake-Walker to Anthony Duckworth-Chad held at St James's Piccadilly. For the rehearsal her father gave her a smart white dress and her mother an equally smart green dress. 'I can't remember to this day which one I got in but I remember being totally traumatized by it because it would show favouritism.'

That tightrope was walked every weekend when Charles and Diana took the train with their nanny from Norfolk to Liverpool Street station in London where their mother met them. Shortly after they reached her apartment in Belgravia the standard procedure was for their mother to burst into tears. 'What's the matter, Mummy?' they would chorus, to which she invariably answered: 'I don't want you to go tomorrow.' It was a ritual which resulted in the children feeling guilty and confused.

Holidays, split between parents, were just as grim.

In 1969 life became more relaxed and carefree when Peter Shand Kydd was officially introduced into their lives. They first met him on the platform at Liverpool Street station during one of their regular Friday shuttles between Norfolk and London. Handsome, smiling and smartly suited, he was an immediate hit, all the more so when their mother told them that they had been married that morning.

Peter, who had made his fortune in the family wallpaper business, was a generous, demonstrative and easy-going stepfather. After a brief time in Buckinghamshire, the newly-weds moved into an unassuming suburban house called Appleshore in Itchenor on the West Sussex coast, where Peter, a Royal Navy veteran, took the children sailing. He allowed Charles to wear an admiral's hat and so his nickname 'The Admiral' was born. Diana he dubbed 'The Duchess', a nickname her friends still use. As Charles observed: 'If you want an insight into why Diana was not just some sort of spoiled toff it is because we had very contrasting lifestyles. It wasn't all stately homes and butlers. My mother's home was an ordinary set-up and every holiday we spent half the holiday with our mother so we were in an environment of relative normality for much of our time.'

Three years later in 1972 the Shand Kydds bought a 1,000-acre farm on the Isle of Seil, south of Oban in Argyllshire, where Mrs Shand Kydd lived until her death in June 2004. When the children came for summer holidays they enjoyed a 'Swallows and Amazons' idyll, spending their days mackerel fishing, lobster potting and sailing and, on fine days, having barbecues on the beach. Diana even had her own Shetland pony called Soufflé.

It was on horseback that she suffered a broken arm which made her anxious about riding afterwards. She was galloping on her pony, Romilly, in the grounds of Sandringham Park when the horse stumbled and she fell off. Although she was in pain, there was no evidence that the arm was broken and so two days later she went skiing to Switzerland. During the holiday her arm felt so lifeless that she went to a local hospital for an X-ray. She was diagnosed as suffering from a 'greenstick' fracture, a condition in which children's bones are so flexible they bend, rather than break. A doctor strapped the arm but when she later tried to go riding again she lost her nerve and dismounted.

She continued to ride in adult life but preferred to exercise by swimming or playing tennis, sports which were better suited to life in central London.

Swimming and dancing were also activities at which she excelled. They stood her in good stead when her father enrolled her at her next school, Riddlesworth Hall, two hours' drive from Park House. She learned to love the school, which tried to be a home away from home to the 120 girls. However, her first feelings when she was sent there were of betrayal and resentment. Diana was nine and felt the wrench from her father keenly. In her motherly, concerned way, she was cosseting him as he tried to pick up the pieces of his life. His decision to send her away from her home and brother into an alien world was interpreted as rejection. She made threats such as: 'If you love me, you won't leave me here' as her father gently explained the benefits of attending a school which offered ballet, swimming, riding and a place to keep her beloved Peanuts, her guinea pig. She had won the Fur and Feather Section with him at the Sandringham Show — 'Maybe that was because he was the only entry,' she observed drily — and later won the Palmer Cup for Pets' Corner at her new school.

Her father also told her that she would be among friends. Alexandra Loyd, her cousin Diana Wake-Walker and Claire Pratt, the daughter of her godmother Sarah Pratt, were also at the all-girls boarding school near Diss in Norfolk. None the less, as he left her behind with her trunk labelled 'D. Spencer' and clutching her favourite green hippo — girls were only allowed one cuddly toy in bed — and Peanuts, he felt a deep sense of loss. 'That was a dreadful day,' he said, 'dreadful losing her.'

An excellent amateur cameraman, he took a photograph of Diana before she left home. It shows a sweet-faced girl, shy, yet with a sunny, open disposition, dressed in the school uniform which consisted of a dark red jacket and grey pleated skirt. He saved too the note she sent requesting 'Big choc. cake, ginger biscuits, Twiglets', just as he kept the clipping she sent him from the *Daily Telegraph* about academic failures who become gifted and successful later in life.

Although quiet and demure in her first term she was no goody-goody. She preferred laughter and high jinks to solid endeavour, but while she could be noisy she shied away from being the centre of attention. Diana would never shout out answers in class or volunteer to read the lessons at assembly.

Far from it. In one of her first school plays where she played a Dutch doll, she only agreed to take the part if she could remain silent.

Noisy with her friends in the dormitory, she was quiet in class. She was a popular pupil but somehow she always felt that she was set apart. Diana no longer felt so different because of her parents' divorce but because a voice inside her told her that she would be separate from the herd. That intuition told her that her life was, as she said, 'going to be a winding road. I always felt very detached from everyone else. I knew I was going somewhere different, that I was in the wrong shell.'

However, she joined in the school's activities with gusto. She represented her house, Nightingale, at swimming and netball and developed her lifelong passion for dance. When the annual nativity play came around she enjoyed the thrill of putting on make-up and dressing up. 'I was one of [those people] who came and paid homage to Jesus,' she recalled with amusement. At home she loved donning her sisters' clothes. An early picture shows her in a wide-brimmed black hat and white dress owned by Sarah.

While she respected Jane, the sensible member of the foursome, she hero-worshipped her eldest sister. When Sarah returned home from West Heath School, Diana was a willing servant, unpacking her suitcases, running her bath and tidying her room. Her loving domesticity was noticed not only by Viscount Althorp's butler, Albert Betts, who recalled how she ironed her own jeans and performed other household duties, but also by her headmistress at Riddlesworth, Elizabeth Ridsdale — Riddy to pupils — who awarded her the Legatt Cup for helpfulness.

That achievement was greeted with satisfaction by her grandmother, Countess Spencer, who had kept an affectionate eye on Diana since the divorce. The feeling was mutual and when, in the autumn of 1972, the Countess died of a brain tumour, Diana was heartbroken. She attended her memorial service along with the Queen Mother and Princess Margaret at the Chapel Royal in St James's Palace. Countess Spencer held a very special place in Diana's heart and she sincerely believed that her grandmother looked after her in the spirit world.

These otherworldly concerns gave way to more earthly considerations when Diana took the Common Entrance exam to enable her to follow in the footsteps of her sisters, Sarah and Jane, at West Heath boarding school, set in 32 acres of parkland and woods outside Sevenoaks in Kent. The school, which closed in 1997, was founded in 1865 on religious lines, and emphasized the value of 'character and confidence' as much as academic ability. Her sister Sarah had, however, shown a touch too much character for the liking of the headmistress, Ruth Rudge.

A competitor *par excellence,* Sarah passed six O-levels, rode for the school team at Hickstead, starred in amateur dramatic productions and swam for the school team. Her strong competitive streak also meant that she had to be the most outrageous, the most rebellious and the most undisciplined girl in school. 'She had to be the best at everything,' recalled a contemporary. While her grandmother, Ruth, Lady Fermoy, forgave her when the exuberant redhead rode her horse into Park House when she was visiting, Miss Rudge could not excuse other instances of her colourful behaviour. Sarah complained that she was 'bored' and so Miss Rudge told her to pack her bags and leave for a term.

Jane, who captained the school lacrosse team, was a complete contrast to Sarah. Highly intelligent, she gained a hatful of O- and A-levels and, eminently sensible and dependable, she was a prefect in the sixth form when Diana arrived.

Doubtless there was discussion in the teachers' common room about which sister the latest Spencer recruit to Poplar class would emulate, Sarah or Jane. It was a close-run thing. Diana was in awe of her eldest sister but it wasn't until later in life that she forged a close relationship with Jane. During their youth Jane was more likely to put her weight and invective behind brother Charles than her kid sister. Diana's inevitable inclination was to imitate Sarah. During her first weeks she was noisy and disruptive in class. In an attempt to copy her sister Sarah's exploits she accepted a challenge which nearly got her expelled.

One evening her friends, reviewing the dwindling stocks of sweets in their tuck boxes, asked Diana to rendezvous with another girl at the end of the school drive and collect more supplies from her. It was a dare she accepted. As she walked down the tree-lined road in the pitch black she managed to suppress her fear of the dark. When she reached the school gate she discovered that there was no one there. She waited. And she waited. When two police cars raced in through the school gates, presumably called by teachers worried as to her whereabouts, she hid behind a wall.

Then she noticed the lights going on all over the school but thought no more about it. Finally she returned to her dormitory, terrified not so much at the prospect of getting caught but because she had come back empty-handed. As luck would have it a fellow pupil in Diana's dormitory complained that she had appendicitis. As she was being examined, Diana's teacher noticed the empty bed. The game was up. It was not just Diana who had to face the music but her parents as well. They were summoned to see Miss Rudge, who took a dim view of the episode. Secretly Diana's parents were amused that their dutiful but docile daughter had displayed such spirit. 'I didn't think you had it in you,' said her mother afterwards.

While the incident curbed her wilder high jinks, Diana was always game for a dare. Food was a favourite challenge. 'It was always a great joke: let's get Diana to eat three kippers and six slices of bread for breakfast,' Diana recalled. 'And she did.' Her reputation as a glutton meant that while she often visited the matron with digestive problems, these escapades did little harm to her popularity. On one birthday her friends clubbed together to buy her a necklace decorated with a 'D' for Diana. Carolyn Pride, now Carolyn Bartholomew, who had the next bed in Diana's dormitory and later shared her London flat, remembers her as a 'strong character, buoyant and noisy'.

She added: 'Jane was very popular, nice, unassuming but uncontroversial. Diana, by contrast, was much more full of life, a bubbly character.' Carolyn and Diana were drawn to each other from the start because they were among the only pupils whose parents were divorced. 'It wasn't a great trial to us and we didn't sit sobbing in a corner about it,' she says, although other pupils remember Diana as a 'private and controlled' teenager who did not wear her emotions on her sleeve. It was noticeable that the two pictures which took pride of place on Diana's bedside dressing table were not of her family but of her favourite hamsters, Little Black Muff and Little Black Puff.

However, she did fret constantly about her average academic abilities. Her sisters proved to be a hard act to follow while her brother, then at Maidwell Hall in Northamptonshire, was displaying the scholastic skills which later won him a place at Oxford University. The gawky teenager, who tended to stoop to disguise her height, longed to be as good as her brother in the classroom. She was jealous and saw herself as a failure. 'I wasn't any good at anything. I felt hopeless, a dropout,' she said.

While she muddled through at maths and science she was more at home with subjects involving people. History, particularly the Tudors and Stuarts, fascinated her while in English she loved books like *Pride and Prejudice* and *Far from the Madding Crowd.* That didn't stop her from reading slushy romantic fiction by Barbara Cartland, soon to be her step-grandmother. In essays she wrote endlessly, her distinctive, well-rounded hand covering the pages. 'It just came out of the pen, on and on and on,' she said. Yet when it came to the silence of the examination hall, Diana froze. The five O-levels she took in English literature and language, history, geography and art resulted in 'D' grades which were classed as fails.

The success which eluded her in the classroom did arrive, but from an unexpected quarter. West Heath encouraged 'good citizenship' in the girls, these ideas expressed in visits to the old, the sick and those with special needs. Every week Diana and another girl saw an old lady in Sevenoaks. They chatted to her over tea and biscuits, tidied her house and did the odd spot of shopping. At the same time the local Voluntary Service Unit organized trips to Darenth Park, a large psychiatric hospital that was situated near Dartford. Dozens of teenage volunteers were bussed in on Tuesday evening for a dance with the patients.

Other youngsters helped with hyperactive teenagers who were so severely disturbed that to encourage a patient to smile was a major success story. 'That's where she learned to go down on her hands and knees to meet people because most of the interaction was crawling with the patients,' says Muriel Stevens, who helped organize the visits. Many new school volunteers were apprehensive about visiting the hospital, anxieties fed by their fear of the unknown. However, Diana discovered that she had a natural aptitude for this work. She formed an instinctive rapport with many patients, her efforts giving her a real sense of achievement. It worked wonders for her sense of self-esteem.

At the same time she was a good all-round athlete. She won swimming and diving cups four years running. Her 'Spencer Special', where she dived into the pool leaving barely a ripple, always attracted an audience. She was netball captain and played a creditable game of tennis. But she lived in the shadow of her sporty sisters and her mother, who was 'captain of everything' when she was at school and would have played at Junior Wimbledon but for an attack of appendicitis.

When Diana started to learn piano, any progress she made was always dwarfed by the achievements of her grandmother, Lady Fermoy, who had performed at the Royal Albert Hall in front of the Queen Mother, and her sister Sarah, who studied piano at a conservatoire in Vienna following her abrupt departure from West Heath. By contrast her community work was something she had achieved on her own without looking over her shoulder at the rest of her family. It was a satisfying first.

Dance gave her a further chance to shine. She loved her ballet and tap-dancing sessions and longed to be a ballet dancer but, at 5ft 10 1/2 inches, was too tall. A favourite ballet was *Swan Lake* which she saw at least four times when school parties travelled to the Coliseum or Sadler's Wells theatres in London. As she danced she could lose herself in the movement. Often she crept out of her bed in the dead of night and sneaked into the new school hall to practise. With music from a record player providing the background, Diana practised ballet for hours on end. 'It always released tremendous tension in my head,' she said. This extra effort paid dividends when she won the school dancing competition at the end of the spring term in 1976. Little wonder then that during the build-up to her wedding she invited her former teacher Wendy Mitchell and pianist Lily Snipp to Buckingham Palace so that she could have dancing lessons. For Diana it was an hour away from the stresses and strains of her new-found position.

When the family moved to Althorp in 1975 she had the perfect stage. On summer days she would practise her arabesques on the sandstone balustrades of the house and when the visitors had gone she danced in the black-and-white marble entrance hall, known officially as Wootton Hall, beneath portraits of her distinguished ancestors. They were not her only audience. While she refused to dance in public, her brother and staff took turns to look through the keyhole. 'We were all very impressed,' he said.

The family moved to Althorp following the death of her grandfather, the 7th Earl Spencer, on 9 June 1975. Although 83 he was still sprightly and his death from pneumonia following a short hospital stay came as a shock. It meant considerable upheaval. The girls all became Ladies, Charles, then aged 11, became Viscount Althorp while their father became the 8th Earl and inherited Althorp. With 13,000 acres of rolling Northamptonshire farmland, more than 100 tied cottages, a valuable collection of paintings, several by Sir Joshua Reynolds, rare books, and 17th-century porcelain, furniture and silver, including the Marlborough Collection, Althorp was more than just a stately home — it was a way of life.

The new Earl also inherited a £2.25 million bill for death duties as well as £80,000-a-year running costs. This did not prevent him paying for the installation of a swimming pool to amuse his children who roamed around their new domain during the holidays. Diana spent her days swimming, walking around the grounds, driving in Charles's blue beach buggy and, of course, dancing. The staff adored her; they found her friendly and unassuming with something of a passion for chocolates, sweets and the sugary romances of Barbara Cartland.

She eagerly awaited the days when Sarah arrived from London bringing with her a crowd of her sophisticated friends. Witty and sharp, Sarah was seen by her contemporaries as the queen of the season, especially after her father had organized a splendid coming-of-age party in 1973 at Castle Rising, a Norman castle in Norfolk. Guests arrived by horse-drawn carriages and the path to the castle was lit by blazing torches. The lavish party is still talked about today. Her escorts matched her status. Everyone expected her relationship with Gerald Grosvenor, the Duke of Westminster and Britain's wealthiest aristocrat, to end in marriage. She was as surprised as anyone when he looked elsewhere.

Diana was happy to bask in her sister's glory. Lucinda Craig Harvey, who shared a house in London with Sarah and later employed Diana as a cleaner for £1 an hour, first met her prospective charlady during a cricket match at Althorp. First impressions were not flattering. Diana struck her as 'a rather large girl who wore terrifying Laura Ashley maternity dresses'. She said: 'She was very shy, blushed easily and was very much the younger sister. Terribly unsophisticated, she certainly wasn't anything to look at.' None the less, Diana joined in the parties, the barbecues and the regular cricket matches with enthusiasm. These sporting contests between the house and the village ended with the arrival of a character who could have been dreamed up by Central Casting.

As a cryptic entry in the visitors' book noted: 'Raine stopped play.' The late Raine Spencer, who went on to assume the title of Comtesse de Chambrun, was not so much a person as a phenomenon. With her bouffant hairdo, elaborate plumage, gushing charm and bright smile she was a caricature of a countess. The daughter of the outspoken romantic novelist Barbara Cartland, she already had a half-page entry in *Who's Who* before she met Johnnie Spencer. As Lady Lewisham and later, after 1962, as the Countess of Dartmouth, she was a controversial figure in London politics where she served as a councillor on the London County Council. Her colourful opinions soon gave her a wider platform and she became a familiar face in the gossip columns.

During the 1960s she became notorious as a parody of the 'pearls and twinset' Tory councillor with views as rigid as her hairdos. 'I always know when I visit Conservative houses because they wash their milk bottles before they put them out,' was one howler which contributed to her being booed off the stage when she addressed students at the London School of Economics.

However, her outspoken opinions masked an iron determination matched by a formidable charm and a sharp turn of phrase. She and Earl Spencer worked on a book for the Greater London Council called *What is Our Heritage?* and soon found they had much in common. Raine was then 46 years old and had been married to the Earl of Dartmouth for 28 years. They had four children, William, Rupert, Charlotte and Henry. During their schooldays at Eton, Johnnie Spencer and the Earl of Dartmouth had been good friends.

Raine wielded her overwhelming charm on both father and son, effecting something of a reconciliation between Earl Spencer and her lover during the Earl's final years. The old Earl adored her, especially as for every birthday and Christmas she bought him a walking stick to add to his collection.

The children were less impressed. Like a galleon in full sail, she first hove into view during the early 1970s. Indeed, her presence at Sarah's 18th-birthday party at Castle Rising was the source of much muttering among the Norfolk gentry. A 'sticky' dinner at the Duke's Head hotel in King's Lynn was the first real opportunity Charles and Diana had of assessing the new woman in their father's life. Ostensibly the dinner was organized to celebrate a tax plan which would save the family fortune. In reality it was a chance for Charles and Diana to get to know their prospective stepmother. 'We didn't like her one bit,' said Charles. They told their father that if he did marry her they would wash their hands of them. In 1976 Charles, then 12 years old, spelled out his feelings by sending Raine a 'vile' letter while Diana encouraged a schoolfriend to write her prospective stepmother a poison pen letter. The incident which prompted their behaviour was the discovery, shortly before the death of Diana's grandfather, of a letter which Raine had sent to their father discussing her plans for Althorp. Her private opinions of the incumbent Earl did not match the way Diana and Charles saw her behave in public towards their grandfather.

With the family adamantly opposed to the match, Raine and Johnnie married quietly at Caxton Hall register office on 14 July 1977, shortly after he had been named in divorce proceedings by the Earl of Dartmouth. None of the children were told about the wedding in advance and the first Charles knew of his new stepmother was when the headmaster of his prep school informed him.

Immediately a whirlwind of change ripped

through Althorp as the new mistress endeavoured to turn the family home into a paying proposition so that the awesome debts the new Earl had taken on could be paid off. The staff were pared to the bone and in order to open the house to paying visitors the stable block was turned into a tea room and gift shop. Over the years numerous paintings, antiques and other *objets d'art* were sold and often, claimed the children, at rock bottom prices while they described in disdainful terms the way the house was 'restored'. Earl Spencer always stoutly defended his wife's robust management of the estate and said: 'The cost of restoration has been immense.'

However there was no disguising the sour relations that existed during this period between Raine and his children. She publicly commented on the rift when she spoke to newspaper columnist Jean Rook: 'I'm absolutely sick of the "Wicked Stepmother" lark. You're never going to make me sound like a human being, because people like to think I'm Dracula's mother but I did have a rotten time at the start and it's only just getting better. Sarah resented me, even my place at the head of the table, and gave orders to the servants over my head. Jane didn't speak to me for two years, even if we bumped in a passageway. Diana was sweet, always did her own thing.'

In fact, Diana's indignation at Raine simmered for years until finally it boiled over in 1989 at the church rehearsal for her brother's wedding to Victoria Lockwood, a successful model. Raine refused to speak to Diana's mother in church even though they were seated together in the same pew. Diana vented all the grievances which had been welling up inside her for more than ten years. As Diana challenged her Raine replied: 'You have no idea how much pain your mother put your father through.' Diana, who later admitted that she had never felt such fury, rounded on her stepmother. 'Pain, Raine, that's one word you don't even know how to relate to. In my job and in my role I see people suffer like you've never seen, and you call that pain. You've got a lot to learn.' There was much more in the same vein. Afterwards her mother said that was the first time anyone in the family had defended her.

However, in the early days of her tenure at Althorp, the children simply treated Raine as a joke. They played upon her penchant for pigeonholing house guests into their appropriate social categories. When Charles arrived from Eton, where he was then at school, he had primed his friends beforehand to give false names. So one boy said that he was 'James Rothschild', implying that he was a member of the famous banking family. Raine brightened. 'Oh, are you Hannah's son?' she asked. Charles's schoolfriend said that he didn't know before compounding his folly by spelling the surname incorrectly in the visitors' book.

At a weekend barbecue one of Sarah's friends wagered £100 that Charles couldn't throw his stepmother into the swimming pool. Raine, who appeared at this shorts and T-shirts party in a ballgown, agreed to Charles's request for a dance by the pool. As he tensed for a judo throw, she realized what was going on and slipped away. Christmas at Althorp with Raine Spencer in charge was a bizarre comedy, a sharp contrast to the extravagances of Park House. She presided over the present-opening like an officious timekeeper. The children were only allowed to open the present she indicated and only after she had looked at her watch to give the go-ahead to tear the paper off. 'It was completely mad,' said Charles.

The only bright spot was when Diana decided to give one of her presents away to a rather irascible night-watchman. While he had a fearsome reputation, Diana instinctively felt that he was just lonely. She and her brother went to see him and he was so touched by her gesture that he burst into tears. It was an early example of her sensitivity to the needs of others, a quality noticed by her headmistress, Miss Rudge, who awarded her the Miss Clark Lawrence Award for service to the school in her last term in 1977.

Diana was now growing in self-confidence, a quality recognized by her elevation to school prefect. When she left West Heath, Diana followed in sister Sarah's footsteps by enrolling at the Institut Alpin Videmanette, an expensive finishing school near Gstaad in Switzerland, where Diana took classes in domestic science, dressmaking and cookery. She was supposed to speak nothing but French all day. In fact she and her friend Sophie Kimball spoke English all the time and the only thing she cultivated was her skiing. Unhappy and stifled by school routine, Diana was desperate to escape. She wrote scores of letters pleading with her parents to bring her home. Finally they relented when she argued that they were simply wasting their money.

With her schooldays behind her, Diana felt as if some great weight had been lifted from her shoulders. She visibly blossomed, becoming jollier, livelier and prettier. Diana was now more mature and relaxed and her sisters' friends looked at her with new eyes. Still shy and overweight, she was nevertheless developing into a popular character. 'She was great fun, charming and kind,' said a friend.

However, the blooming of Diana was viewed with jealous misgivings by Sarah. London was her kingdom and she didn't want her sister taking the spotlight away from her. The crunch came on one of the last of the old-style weekends at Althorp. Diana asked her sister for a lift to London. Sarah refused saying that it would cost too much in petrol to have an extra person in the car. Her friends ridiculed her, seeing for the first time how the balance in their relationship had shifted in favour of adorable Diana.

Diana had been the Cinderella of her family for long enough. She had felt her spirit suppressed by school routine and her character cramped by her minor position in the family. Diana was eager to spread her wings and start her own life in London. The thrill of independence beckoned. As her brother Charles said: 'Suddenly the insignificant ugly duckling was obviously going to be a swan.'

2
'JUST CALL ME "SIR" '

By any standards it was an unusual romance. It was not until Lady Diana Spencer was formally engaged to His Royal
Highness the Prince of Wales that she was
given permission to call him 'Charles'. Until
then she had demurely addressed him as
'Sir'. He called her Diana. In Prince
Charles's circle this was considered the
norm. When Diana's sister Sarah enjoyed a
nine-month-long relationship with the
Prince of Wales she had been as formal. 'It
just seemed natural,' she recalls. 'It was
obviously right to do so because I was never
corrected.'

It was during her sister's romance that Diana first came into the path of the man
considered then to be the world's most
eligible bachelor. That historic meeting in
November 1977 was hardly auspicious. Diana, on weekend leave from West Heath
School, was introduced to the Prince in the

middle of a ploughed field near Nobottle Wood on the Althorp estate during a day's shooting. The Prince, who brought along his faithful labrador, Sandringham Harvey, is considered to be one of the finest shots in the country so he was more intent on sport than small talk on that bleak afternoon. Diana cut a nondescript figure in her checked shirt, her sister's anorak, cords and wellington boots. She kept in the background, realizing that she had only been brought along to make up numbers. It was very much her sister's show and Sarah was perhaps being rather mischievous when she said later that she 'played Cupid' between her kid sister and the Prince.

If Charles's first memories of Diana on that fateful weekend are of 'a very jolly and amusing and attractive 16-year-old — full of fun', then it was certainly no thanks to her elder sister. As far as Sarah was concerned Charles was her domain at that time and trespassers were not welcomed by the sparky redhead who applied her competitive instincts to the men in her life. In any case Diana was not overly impressed by Sarah's royal boyfriend. 'What a sad man,' she remembered thinking. The Spencers held a dance that weekend in his honour and it was noticeable that Sarah was enthusiastic in her attentions. Diana later told friends: 'I kept out of the way. I remember being a fat, podgy, no make-up, unsmart lady but I made a lot of noise and he liked that.'

When dinner was over he liked Diana enough to ask her to show him the 115-foot-long picture gallery which then housed one of the finest private collections of art in Europe. Sarah wanted to be the guide to the family's 'etchings'. Diana took the hint and left them to it.

While Sarah's behaviour was hardly that of a would-be Cupid, Charles's interest in her younger sister left Diana with much food for thought. He was, after all, her sister's boyfriend. Charles and Sarah had met at Ascot in June 1977 when Sarah was licking her wounds after her romance with the Duke of Westminster had ended. At that time she was suffering from anorexia nervosa, which friends believe was triggered by the collapse of her love affair. As one friend noted: 'Sarah always had to be the best at everything. The best car, the wittiest put-down, and the best dress. Dieting was part of her competitive nature, to be thinner than everybody else.'

Sarah has kept a picture of herself in her underwear when she was literally skin and bone. At that time, during the mid-1970s, she thought she was fat. Now she realizes how unwell she was. Her family, worried about her health, used every method possible to encourage her to eat. For example she would be allowed to speak to Prince Charles on the telephone if she put on 2 lbs in weight. In 1977 she elected to go to a nursing home in Regent's Park in central London where she was treated by Dr Maurice Lipsedge, a psychiatrist who, by pure coincidence, cared for Diana a decade later when she resolved to fight her bulimia.

As she tried to overcome her condition, Sarah frequently saw Prince Charles. During the summer of 1977 she watched him play polo at Smith's Lawn, Windsor, and when, in February 1978, he invited her to join him on a skiing party in Klosters, Switzerland, there was much speculation that she might be the future queen of England. However, Sarah's enjoyment of publicity overcame the circumspection a royal girlfriend is expected to display. She gave a magazine interview which considerably dented Prince Charles's image as a charming Casanova. 'Our relationship is totally platonic,' she stated. 'I think of him as the big brother I never had.' For good measure she added: 'I wouldn't marry a man I didn't love, whether it was a dustman or the King of England. If he asked me I would turn him down.'

While their romance cooled off, Charles still asked Sarah to attend his 30th birthday party at Buckingham Palace in November 1978. Much to Sarah's surprise, Diana was also invited. Cinderella was going to the ball.

Diana enjoyed herself enormously at the birthday party not least because it brought her sister down a peg or two. Yet it never entered her head for a moment to think that Prince Charles was remotely interested in romance. Certainly she never considered herself competition to the actress Susan George, who was his escort that evening. In any case, life was much too enjoyable to think about steady boyfriends. She had returned from her ill-starred excursion to the Swiss finishing school desperate to begin an independent life in London. Her parents were not as enthusiastic.

She had no paper qualifications, no special skills and only a vague notion that she wanted to work with children. While Diana seemed destined for a life of unskilled, low-paid jobs, she was not that much out of the ordinary for girls of her class and background. Aristocratic families traditionally invested more thought and effort in educating boys than girls. There was a tacit assumption that, after rounding off their formal education with a cookery or arts course, daughters would join their well-bred friends on the marriage market. At the start of the Queen's reign this feature of the London season was still formalized in the presentation of debutantes at Buckingham Palace which was followed by a series of coming-out balls. Indeed Diana's parents had met at her mother's coming-out ball in April 1953, while in her day Raine Spencer was voted 'Deb of the Year'.

Marriage was very much in Diana's mind when she returned from Switzerland. Her sister Jane had asked her to be chief bridesmaid at her wedding to Robert Fellowes, the son of the Queen's land agent at Sandringham and subsequently her private secretary, which was held in the Guards Chapel in April 1978. While there was no pressure from her family to embark on a structured career, there was considerable reluctance about allowing her to live on her own in London. As her Swiss headmistress, Madame Yersin, commented: 'She was rather young for a sixteen-year-old.' If she was an innocent abroad, her parents considered that a life cocooned in an all-girls school was hardly adequate preparation for the bright lights of the big city. They told her that she couldn't have her own flat until she was 18 years old.

Instead she was farmed out to family friends, Major Jeremy Whitaker, a photographer, and his wife, Philippa, who lived in Headley, near Bordon in Hampshire. She stayed with them for three months and as well as looking after their daughter Alexandra she cleaned and cooked. Yet she was itching to move to the metropolis and bombarded her parents with subtle and not so subtle requests. Finally a compromise was reached. Her mother allowed her to stay at her flat in Cadogan Square. As Mrs Shand Kydd spent most of the year in Scotland it was as good as her own place. It was to be her home for a year, sharing it initially with Laura Greig, an old school chum and later one of her ladies-in-waiting, and Sophie Kimball, the daughter of a Conservative Member of Parliament, Marcus Kimball.

In order to earn her keep Diana joined the ranks of what she would later dismissively refer to as the 'velvet hairband' brigade, the upper-class ladies who fitted a loose template of values, fashions, breeding and attitudes and who were commonly known as 'Sloane Rangers'. She signed up for two employment agencies, Solve Your Problems and Knightsbridge Nannies, and worked as a waitress at private parties and as a charlady. In between driving lessons — she passed her test at the second attempt — she was much in demand as a babysitter by her sisters' married friends while Sarah used her to make up numbers at her frequent dinner parties. Her London life was sedate, almost mundane. She didn't smoke and never drank, preferring to spend her free time reading, watching television, visiting friends or going out for supper in modest bistros. Noisy nightclubs, wild parties or smoky pubs were never her scene. 'Disco Di' has only ever existed in the minds of headline writers with an appreciation for alliteration. In reality Diana was a loner by inclination and habit.

Weekends were spent in the country, at Althorp with her father, at her sister Jane's cottage on the estate or at a house party organized by one of her growing circle of friends. Her friends from Norfolk and West Heath, Alexandra Loyd, Caroline Harbord-Hammond, the daughter of Lord Suffield, Theresa Mowbray, her mother's goddaughter, and Mary-Ann Stewart-Richardson, were all now living in London and formed the nucleus of her set.

It was while she was staying with Caroline one weekend in September 1978 at her parents' Norfolk home that she had a disturbing premonition. When she was politely asked about her father's health her reply startled the assembled company. She found herself saying that she felt her father was going to 'drop down' in some way. 'If he dies, he will die immediately, otherwise he'll survive,' she said. The following day the telephone rang. Diana knew it was about her father. It was. Earl Spencer had collapsed in the courtyard at Althorp suffering from a massive cerebral haemorrhage and had been rushed to Northampton General Hospital. Diana packed her bags and joined her sisters and brother Charles who had been driven from Eton by his brother-in-law, Robert Fellowes.

The medical prognosis was bleak. Earl Spencer was not expected to survive the night. According to his son, Charles, the Countess was matter-of-fact. He remembers her telling his brother-in-law: 'I'll be out of Althorp first thing in the morning.' The reign of Raine seemed to be over. For two days the children camped out in the hospital waiting-room as their father clung on to life. When doctors announced that there was a glimmer of hope, Raine organized a private ambulance to take him to the National Hospital for Nervous Diseases in Queen Square, Central London, where for several months he lay in a coma. As the family kept vigil, the children saw at close quarters the stubborn determination of their stepmother. She tried to stop the children visiting their critically ill father. Nurses were instructed to prevent them from seeing Earl Spencer as he lay helpless in his private room. As Raine said afterwards: 'I'm a survivor and people forget that at their peril. There's pure steel up my backbone. Nobody destroys me, and nobody was going to destroy Johnnie so long as I could sit by his bed — some of his family tried to stop me — and will my life force into him.'

During this critical time the ill feeling between Raine and the children boiled over into a series of vicious exchanges. There was iron too in the Spencer soul and numerous hospital corridors rang to the sound of the redoubtable Countess and the fiery Lady Sarah Spencer hissing at each other like a pair of angry geese.

In November Earl Spencer suffered a relapse and was moved to the Brompton Hospital in South Kensington. Once again his life hung in the balance. When his doctors were at their most pessimistic, Raine's will-power won through. She had heard of a German drug called Azlocillin which she thought could help and so she pulled every string to find a supply. It was unlicensed in Britain but that didn't stop her. The wonder drug was duly acquired and miraculously did the trick. One afternoon she was maintaining her usual bedside vigil when, with the strains of *Madam Butterfly* playing in the background, he opened his eyes 'and was back'. In January 1979 when he was finally released from hospital he and Raine booked into the Dorchester Hotel in Park Lane for an expensive month-long convalescence.

Throughout this episode the strain on the family was intense. Sarah, who lived near to the Brompton Hospital, visited her father regularly although Raine's hostility complicated an already fraught situation. When she was absent sympathetic nurses allowed Diana and Jane to see him but with Earl Spencer drifting in and out of consciousness he was never aware of the presence of his children. Even when he was awake a feeding tube in his throat meant that he was unable to speak. As Diana recalled: 'He wasn't able to ask where his children were. Goodness knows what he was thinking because no one was telling him.'

Understandably Diana found it hard to concentrate on the cookery course she had enrolled in a few days before her father suffered his stroke. For three months she went by Underground to the Wimbledon home of Elizabeth Russell where for many years she schooled the daughters of knights, dukes and earls in the delights of sauces, sponges and soufflés. As far as Diana was concerned it was another set of 'velvet hairbands'. She had joined the course at her parents' insistence and while it wasn't her idea of fun at the time it seemed a better alternative than being behind a typewriter. Often the glutton in Diana got the better of her and she was frequently told off for dipping her fingers into pans filled with gooey sauces. She completed the course a few pounds heavier and clutching a diploma for her efforts.

As her father began his fight back to health, Diana's mother took a hand in guiding her career. She wrote to Miss Betty Vacani, the legendary dance teacher who taught three generations of royal children, and asked if there was a vacancy for a student ballet teacher at grade two level. There was. Diana passed her interview and, in the spring term, began at the Vacani dance studio on the Brompton Road. It neatly combined her love of children with her enjoyment of dance. Again she only lasted three months but for once it wasn't her fault.

In March, her friend Mary-Ann Stewart-Richardson invited her to join her family on their skiing holiday in the French Alps. Diana fell badly on the ski slopes, tearing all the tendons in her left ankle. For three months she was in and out of plaster as the tendons slowly healed. It marked the end of her aspirations as a dance teacher.

In spite of her misadventure, Diana looked back on that trip to Val Claret as one of the most enjoyable and carefree holidays of her life. It was also where she first met many of the people who later became loyal and supportive friends. When Diana joined the Stewart-Richardsons they were just coming to terms with a family tragedy. She naturally felt out of place in their chalet and accepted the invitation of Simon Berry, the son of a wealthy wine merchant, to join his chalet party instead.

Berry and three other old Etonians, James Bolton, Alex Lyle and Christian de Lotbiniere, were the brains behind 'Ski Bob' travel. This was a company, named after their Eton housemaster Bob Baird, which had been formed when they discovered that they were too young legally to book holidays themselves. So these young entrepreneurs started their own company and within the 20-strong group, which mainly comprised old Etonians, the greatest accolade was to be called 'Bob'.

Diana was soon Bob, Bob, Bobbing along. 'You're skating on thin ice,' she yelled in her Miss Piggy voice as she skied dangerously close behind members of the group. She joined in the pillow fights, charades and satirical singsongs. Diana was teased mercilessly about a framed photograph of Prince Charles, taken at his Investiture in 1969, which hung in her school dormitory. 'Not guilty', she said. It was a gift to the school. When she stayed in the Berry chalet she slept on the living-room sofa. Not that she got much sleep. Medical student James Colthurst liked to regale the slumbering throng with unwelcome early-morning renditions of Martin Luther King's famous 'I had a dream' speech or his equally unamusing Mussolini impersonation.

Adam Russell, the great-grandson of Prime Minister Stanley Baldwin and now a deer farmer in Dorset, was not overly impressed by Diana when she first walked in. He recalled: 'When she arrived she made a rude comment followed by a giggle. I thought, "Oh God, a giggler, help." Once you got behind that she was very much more composed. But she was lacking in self-confidence when she should have had lots. Very bubbly and giggly but not in a vacuous way.' When he too was injured, they kept each other company and during their conversations he saw the reflective, rather sad side to her character. He said: 'She seemed a happy person on the surface but underneath she had been deeply affected by her parents' divorce.'

Her sister Sarah, then working for Savills, a leading estate agent, found what was to become, for a time, the most famous address in Britain. A three-bedroomed apartment in a mansion block at 60, Coleherne Court was Diana's coming-of-age present from her parents. In July 1979 she moved into the £50,000 apartment and immediately set to work furnishing the rooms in a warm but simple Habitat style that was popular at the time. The white walls were repainted in pastel shades, the sitting room became pale primrose yellow while the bathroom was bright with red cherries. Diana had always promised her schoolfriend Carolyn Bartholomew a room when she got her own apartment. She was as good as her word. Sophie Kimball and Philippa Coaker stayed for a while but in August Diana and Carolyn were joined by Anne Bolton, who also worked for Savills, and Virginia Pitman, the oldest member of the quartet. It was these three who stayed with her throughout her romance with Prince Charles.

Diana later looked back on those days at Coleherne Court as the happiest time of her life. It was juvenile, innocent, uncomplicated and above all fun. 'I laughed my head off there,' she said and the only black cloud was when the apartment was burgled and she had most of her jewellery stolen. As landlady, she charged the others £18 a week and organized the cleaning rotas. Naturally she had the largest room, complete with double bed. So that no one would forget her status, the words 'Chief Chick' were emblazoned on her bedroom door. 'She always had the rubber gloves on as she clucked about the place,' recalled Carolyn. 'But it was her house and when it is your own you are incredibly proud of it.'

At least she never had to worry about washing piles of dirty dishes and cups. The girls rarely cooked in spite of the fact that Virginia and Diana had completed expensive *cordon bleu* courses. Diana's two specialities were chocolate roulades and Russian borscht soup which friends asked her to make and then deliver to their apartments. Usually the girls devoured the roulade before it left Coleherne Court. Otherwise they lived on Harvest Crunch cereal and chocolate. 'We stayed remarkably plump,' observed Carolyn.

The houseproud teenager was also tidying up her career. Shortly after moving into her apartment she found a job where she was truly in her element. For several afternoons a week she went to work at the Young England kindergarten run by Victoria Wilson and Kay Seth-Smith in St Saviour's church hall in Pimlico. She taught the children painting, drawing and dancing and joined in the games they devised. Victoria and Kay were so impressed with her rapport with the children that they asked her to work in the morning as well. On Tuesdays and Thursdays she looked after Patrick Robinson, the son of an American oil executive, work which she 'adored'.

There were still loose ends in her working week so her sister Sarah took it upon herself to tie them up. She employed her as a cleaner at her house in Elm Park Lane, Chelsea. Sarah's flatmate Lucinda Craig Harvey recalled: 'Diana hero-worshipped her but Sarah treated her like a doormat. She told me not to be embarrassed about asking Diana to do the washing up and so on.' Diana, who did the vacuuming, dusting, ironing and washing, was paid £1 an hour and took a quiet satisfaction in her labours. When she became engaged to Prince Charles Diana referred to her cleaning job in her reply to Lucinda's letter of congratulation. 'Gone are the days of Jif and dusters. Oh dear, will I ever see them again?'

She escaped her sister's gimlet gaze when she returned to the privacy of her own apartment. Perhaps this was just as well since the jolly but rather juvenile japes her sister embarked upon might not have pleased her. Diana and Carolyn would regularly while away a quiet evening ringing people with silly names who appeared in the telephone directory. Another favourite pastime was planning raids on the various apartments and cars owned by their friends. Carolyn recalled: 'We used to do midnight runs, we were always skimming around London on undercover operations in Diana's Metro.'

Those who offended the girls in some way were paid back with interest. Doorbells were rung in the dead of night, early-morning alarm calls were made, friends' cars had their locks covered in sticky tape. On one occasion James Gilbey, then working for a car rental company in Victoria, woke to find his prize Alfa Romeo car covered in eggs and flour which had set like concrete. For some reason he had let down Diana on a date so she and Carolyn had taken their revenge.

It wasn't all one-way traffic. One evening James Colthurst and Adam Russell secretly tied two huge 'L' plates to the front and rear of Diana's Honda Civic car. She managed to pull them off but as she drove down the street she was followed by a cacophony of tin cans tied to the bumper. Once again eggs and flour were used by Diana and Carolyn in high-spirited retaliation.

Indeed this innocent, totally unsophisticated fun continued throughout her romance with Prince Charles. 'We were the giggling lavatorial girls we've always been portrayed as, but somewhere there was a spark of maturity,' said Carolyn. Certainly the constant parade of young men calling round for a chat and tea, if there was any, or to take the girls out for the evening were friends who happened to be boys. For the most part Diana's escorts were old Etonians whom she had met while skiing or elsewhere. Harry Herbert, now the 8th Earl of Carnarvon and son of the Queen's former racing manager, James Boughey, a lieutenant in the Coldstream Guards, farmer's son George Plumptre, who asked her to the ballet the day she got engaged, the artist Marcus May and Rory Scott, a dashing lieutenant in the Royal Scots Guards, often came to call, along with Simon Berry, Adam Russell and James Colthurst. 'We were all just friends together,' Simon Berry remembered.

The men in her life were clean-cut, well-bred, reliable, unpretentious and good company. 'Diana is an Uptown girl who has never gone in for downtown men,' observed Rory Scott. If they wore a uniform or had been cast aside by Sarah, so much the better. She felt rather sorry for Sarah's rejects and often tried, unsuccessfully, to be asked out by them.

So she did washing for William van Straubenzee, one of Sarah's old boyfriends, and ironed the shirts of Rory Scott, who had then starred in a television documentary about Trooping the Colour, and Diana regularly stayed for weekends at his parents' farm near Petworth, West Sussex. She continued caring for his wardrobe during her royal romance, on one occasion delivering a pile of freshly laundered shirts to the back entrance of St James's Palace, where Rory was on duty, in order to avoid the press. James Boughey was another military man who took her out to restaurants and the theatre and Diana visited Simon Berry and Adam Russell at their rented house on the Blenheim estate when they were undergraduates at Oxford.

There were lots of boyfriends but none became lovers. The sense of destiny which Diana had felt from an early age shaped, albeit unconsciously, her relationships with the opposite sex. She said: 'I knew I had to keep myself tidy for what lay ahead.'

As Carolyn observed: 'I'm not a terribly spiritual person but I do believe that she was meant to do what she is doing and she certainly believes that. She was surrounded by this golden aura which stopped men going any further; whether they would have liked to or not, it never happened. She was protected somehow by a perfect light.'

It was a quality noted by her old boyfriends. Rory Scott said roguishly: 'She was very sexually attractive and the relationship was not a platonic one as far as I was concerned but it remained that way. She was always a little aloof, you always felt that there was a lot you would never know about her.'

In the summer of 1979 another boyfriend, Adam Russell, completed his language degree at Oxford and decided to spend a year travelling. He left unspoken the fact that he hoped the friendship between himself and Diana could be renewed and developed upon his return. When he arrived home a year later it was too late. A friend told him: 'You've only got one rival, the Prince of Wales.'

That winter Diana's star began to move into the royal family's orbit. She received an unexpected Christmas bonus in the form of an invitation to join a royal house party at Sandringham for a shooting weekend in February. Lucinda Craig Harvey, known to all her friends as Beryl, remembers Diana's excitement and the irony of the subsequent conversation. They were chatting about the weekend while Diana, ever the Cinderella, was on her knees cleaning the kitchen floor. Diana said: 'Guess what, I'm going on a shooting weekend to Sandringham.' Lucinda replied: 'Gosh, perhaps you are going to be the next Queen of England.' As she wrung out a cloth which she was using to mop the floor Diana joked: 'Beryl, I doubt it. Can you see me swanning around in kid gloves and a ballgown?'

As Diana's life was taking a new direction, her sister Sarah was in crisis. She and Neil McCorquodale, a former Coldstream

Guards officer, had abruptly called off their wedding which had been planned for later in February. In true Spencer style — it is certainly not a family for the faint-hearted — there were angry words and exchanges of letters between the interested parties. While Sarah was trying to sort out the mess — they eventually married in May 1980 at St Mary's church near Althorp — Diana was having fun. For once Diana was in what she called 'a grown up' social setting. This for Diana was the satisfaction of that Sandringham weekend, not her proximity to Prince Charles. She was still in awe of the man, her sense of respect mellowed by a feeling of deep sympathy for the Prince whose 'honorary grandfather', Earl Mountbatten, had been assassinated by the IRA just six months previously. In any case the following Monday as she scrubbed her sister's floors this aristocratic Cinderella had to pinch herself to make sure that her weekend had not been some idle pipe dream.

For whatever that small voice of intuition was telling her about her destiny, common sense decreed that the Prince already had a full hand of potential suitors. She travelled to King's Lynn and then on to Sandringham with Lady Amanda Knatchbull, the granddaughter of the murdered Earl. Lord Mountbatten had strenuously pressed his granddaughter's suit not only on the Prince of Wales but on the royal family. After all it was he, in the face of George VI's reservations, who had been instrumental in clearing the decks for the union of Princess Elizabeth and his nephew Prince Philip.

While commentators have dismissed her as a serious contender, those who worked intimately with the Prince and watched Mountbatten's machinations at first hand were convinced that marriage between Prince Charles and Amanda Knatchbull was a virtual certainty. A glance through his working diary for 1979 shows how frequently Prince Charles stayed at Broadlands, the Mountbatten family seat, ostensibly for fishing and shooting weekends. In the aftermath of Mountbatten's murder in August 1979, Charles's friendship with Lady Amanda developed and he spent several weekends in her company as they tried to come to terms with their loss. If Mountbatten, the unofficial 'queenmaker', had lived, royal history might have been very different.

While Amanda may be considered as the 'official candidate' whose breeding and background made her eminently acceptable at Court, the Prince was also conducting a stormy relationship with Anna Wallace, the daughter of a Scottish landowner, whom he had met while fox hunting in November 1979. She was the latest of a long line of girlfriends, drawn for the most part from the upper reaches of the aristocracy, who had appeared on his romantic horizon. However, Anna, fiery, wilful and impulsive, was temperamentally unsuitable for the regulated routine of royalty. Not for nothing was she known as 'Whiplash Wallace'. Prince Charles, a man who by his own admission fell in love easily, pressed his suit even though his advisers told him that she had other boyfriends.

Their relationship became so serious that, according to at least one account, he asked her to marry him. She is said to have turned him down but that rebuff did little to dampen his ardour. In May they were discovered by journalists lying on a rug by the river Dee on the Queen's estate at Balmoral. The Prince was furious at this intrusion into his private life and authorized his friend Lord Tryon, who was present at the picnic, to shout a four-letter word at the journalists concerned.

The end of their romance in the middle of June was just as tempestuous. She complained bitterly when he virtually ignored her during a ball to celebrate the Queen Mother's 80th birthday at Windsor Castle. Anna was overheard to rage: 'Don't ignore me like that again. I've never been treated so badly in my life. No one treats me like that, not even you.' On their next public appearance he treated her in precisely the same way. She watched with mounting fury as he danced the night away with Camilla Parker Bowles at a polo ball held at Stowell Park, the Gloucestershire estate owned by Lord Vestey. He was so eager for Camilla's company that he did not even ask his hostess, Lady Vestey, to take the floor. In the end, Anna borrowed Lady Vestey's BMW car and drove off into the night, angry and humiliated at her very public snub. Within a month she had married Johnny Hesketh, the younger brother of Lord Hesketh.

With hindsight it is tempting to ask if her outrage was directed at the Prince or at the woman who held him in such thrall, Camilla Parker Bowles. If Prince Charles had been serious about marrying Anna then she, a worldly-wise 25-year-old, would have been aware of his friendship with Camilla. She would have known, as Diana discovered too late, that Camilla's famous vetting of Charles's girlfriends was not so much to assess their potential as a royal bride but to see how much of a threat they posed to her relationship with Prince Charles.

She might also have simply got tired of playing second fiddle to the Prince's pastimes. Throughout his bachelor years — and during his marriage — his partners have simply fitted in to his lifestyle. They were interested spectators while he played polo, went fishing or fox hunting. When he entertained them to dinner, they travelled to his apartment at Buckingham Palace, not the other way around. His staff organized boxes for concerts or the opera and even remembered to send flowers to his escorts. 'A charming male chauvinist' is how one friend describes him. His behaviour, as the Victorian constitutionalist Walter Bagehot had noted a hundred years earlier, was the prerogative of princes. He wrote: 'All the world and the glory of it, whatever is most attractive, whatever is most seductive, has always been offered to the Prince of Wales of the day, and always will be. It is not rational to expect the best virtue where temptation is applied in the most trying form at the frailest time of human life.'

That summer of 1980 Prince Charles was a man of settled habits and inflexible routine. A former member of his Household, reviewing the collapse of the Waleses' marriage, sincerely believed that he would have remained single if he had been given the choice. He recalled: 'It's very sad really. He would never have got married, of course, because he was happy with his bachelor life. If he had his fishing tackle ready, his polo ponies saddled and a £5 note for the church collection he was perfectly content. It was great fun. You would wake him up at six in the morning and say: "Right, Sir, we are going here" and off we would go.' His relationship with Camilla Parker Bowles, who eagerly adapted her life to his diary, dovetailed perfectly with his lifestyle.

Unfortunately for Charles, his title brought obligations as well as privileges. His duty was to marry and produce an heir to the throne. It was a subject Earl Mountbatten discussed endlessly with the Queen during afternoon tea at Buckingham Palace while Prince Philip let it be known that he was growing impatient with his son's irresponsible approach to marriage. The ghost of the Duke of Windsor haunted the minds of the family, patently aware that the older he became the more difficult it would be to find a virginal, Protestant aristocrat to be his bride.

His quest for a wife had developed into a

233

national pastime. The Prince, then nearly 33, had already made himself a hostage to fortune by declaring that 30 was a suitable age to settle down. He publicly acknowledged the problems of finding a suitable bride. 'Marriage is a much more important business than falling in love. I think one must concentrate on marriage being essentially a question of mutual love and respect for each other . . . Essentially you must be good friends, and love, I'm sure, will grow out of that friendship. I have a particular responsibility to ensure that I make the right decision. The last thing I could possibly entertain is getting divorced.'

On another occasion he declared that marriage was a partnership where his wife was not simply marrying the man but a way of life. As he said: 'If I'm deciding on whom I want to live with for fifty years — well, that's the last decision I want my head to be ruled by my heart.' Thus marriage in his eyes was primarily the discharge of an obligation to his family and the nation, a task made all the more difficult by the immutable nature of the contract. In his pragmatic search for a partner to fulfil a role, love and happiness were secondary considerations.

The meeting which was to set Prince

Charles and Lady Diana Spencer irrevocably on the road to St Paul's Cathedral took place in July 1980 on a hay bale at the home of Commander Robert de Pass, a friend of Prince Philip, and his wife Philippa, a lady-in-waiting to the Queen. Diana was invited to stay at their house in Petworth, West Sussex, by their son Philip. 'You're a young blood,' he told her, 'you might amuse him.'

During the weekend she drove to nearby Cowdray Park to watch the Prince play polo for his team, Les Diables Bleus. At the end of the game the small house party trooped back to Petworth for a barbecue in the grounds of the de Pass' country home. Diana was seated next to Charles on a bale of hay and, after the usual pleasantries, the conversation moved on to Earl Mountbatten's death and his funeral in Westminster Abbey. In a conversation which she later recalled to friends Diana told him: 'You looked so sad when you walked up the aisle at Lord Mountbatten's funeral. It was the most tragic thing I've ever seen. My heart bled for you when I watched. I thought: "It's wrong, you're lonely, you should be with somebody to look after you." '

Her words touched a deep chord. Charles saw Diana with new eyes. Suddenly, as she later told her friends, she found herself overwhelmed by his enthusiastic attentions. Diana was flattered, flustered and bewildered by the passion she had aroused in a man 12 years her senior. They resumed their conversation, chatting away late into the evening. The Prince, who had important paperwork to attend to at Buckingham Palace, asked her to drive back with him the following day. She refused on the grounds that it would be rude to her hosts.

However, from then on their relationship began to develop. Her flatmate, Carolyn Bartholomew, recalled: 'Prince Charles was coming quietly on to the scene. She certainly had a special place for him in her heart.' He invited her to a performance of Verdi's *Requiem* — one of her favourite works — at the Royal Albert Hall. Her grandmother, Ruth, Lady Fermoy, went along as their chaperone and accompanied them when they returned to Buckingham Palace for a cold buffet supper in his apartments. His memo to his valet, Stephen Barry, relating to the meeting is typical of the elaborate planning undertaken for the simplest royal date. It read: 'Please ring Captain Anthony Asquith [a former equerry] before going out shooting and tell him that I have asked Lady Diana Spencer (Lady Fermoy's granddaughter) to come to the Albert Hall and dinner afterwards at BP on Sunday evening. Please ask him if this can be arranged and she will arrive with her grandmother at the Albert Hall. If it is all right, please ask him to ring back at lunchtime when we will be in the House. C.' [The House is Buckingham Palace.]

The problem is that the invitation must have come rather late, as Carolyn recalled: 'I walked in about six o'clock and Diana went: "Quick, quick I've got to meet Charles in 20 minutes." Well, we had the funniest time ever, getting the hair washed, getting it dried, getting the dress, where's the dress. We did it in 20 minutes flat. But I mean, how dare he ask her so late.'

She had scarcely recovered her composure from that frantic evening before he invited her to join him on the royal yacht *Britannia* during Cowes Week. For many years the royal yacht, the oldest ship in the Royal Navy until it was decommissioned in 1997, was a familiar sight in the waters of the Solent during the August regatta and Prince Philip played host to a party which usually included his German relatives along with Princess Alexandra, her husband, the late Honourable Sir Angus Ogilvy, and numerous yachting friends.

On that weekend Diana had Lady Sarah

Armstrong-Jones, Princess Margaret's daughter, and Susan Deptford, who later became Major Ronald Ferguson's second wife, to keep her company. She went water skiing while Prince Charles went windsurfing. Stories that she lightheartedly tipped him off his board do not ring true of Diana, who was totally in awe of him. Indeed she felt 'fairly intimidated' by the atmosphere on board the royal yacht. Not only were his friends so much older than herself, but they seemed aware of Prince Charles's strategy towards her. She found them too friendly and too knowing. 'They were all over me like a bad rash,' she told her friends. For a girl who likes to be in control it was profoundly disconcerting.

There was little time to reflect on the implications as Prince Charles had already asked her to Balmoral for the weekend of the Braemar Games early in September. The Queen's Highland castle retreat, set in 40,000 acres of heather and grouse moor, is effectively the Windsors' family seat. Ever since Queen Victoria bought the estate in 1848 it has had a special place in the affections of the royal family. However, the very quirks and obscure family traditions which have accrued over the years can intimidate newcomers. 'Don't sit there,' they chorus at an unfortunate guest foolish enough to try and sit in a chair in the drawing room which was last used by Queen Victoria. Those who successfully navigate this social minefield, popularly known as 'the Balmoral test', are accepted by the royal family. The ones who fail vanish from royal favour as quickly as the Highland mists come and go.

So the prospect of her stay at Balmoral loomed large in Diana's mind. She was 'terrified' and desperately wanted to behave in the appropriate manner. Fortunately rather than staying in the main house, she was able to stay with her sister Jane and husband Robert Fellowes who, as he was a member of the royal Household, enjoyed a grace and favour cottage on the estate. Prince Charles rang her every day, suggesting she join him for a walk or a barbecue.

It was a 'wonderful' few days until the glint of a pair of binoculars across the river Dee spoiled their idyll. They were carried by royal journalist James Whitaker who had spotted Prince Charles fishing by the banks of the river. The hunters had become the hunted. Diana immediately told Charles that she would make herself scarce so while he continued fishing she hid behind a tree for half an hour hoping vainly that the journalists would go away. Cleverly she used the mirror from her powder compact to watch the unholy trinity of James Whitaker and rival photographers Ken Lennox and Arthur Edwards as they tried to capture her on film. She foiled their efforts by calmly walking straight up through the pine trees, her head muffled with a headscarf and flat cap, leaving Fleet Street's finest clueless as to her identity.

They soon picked up her trail and from then on her private life was effectively over. Reporters waited outside her apartment day and night, while photographers badgered her at the Young England kindergarten where she worked. On one occasion she agreed to pose for photographs on the condition that she would then be left alone. Unfortunately during the photo session the light was behind her and made her cotton skirt seem see-through, revealing her legs to the world. 'I knew your legs were good but I didn't realize they were that spectacular,' Prince Charles is reported to have commented. 'And did you really have to show them to everybody?'

While Prince Charles could afford to be amused, Diana was quickly discovering the exacting price of royal romance. She was telephoned in the early hours of the morning about stories in newspapers and yet dared not take the communal telephone off the hook in case any of their families became ill during the night. Each time she went out in her distinctive red Metro she was followed by a press posse. However, she never lost control, giving polite but non-committal answers to endless questions about her feelings for the Prince. Her engaging smile, her winsome manner and her impeccable behaviour soon endeared her to the public. Her flatmate Carolyn Bartholomew said: 'She played it just right. She didn't in any way splash it across the newspapers because that ruined her sister's chances. Diana was very aware that if anything special had to be cultivated it should take place without any pressure from the press.'

None the less, there was constant stress which tested her reserves to the limit. In the privacy of her apartment she could afford to show her feelings. 'I cried like a baby to the four walls, I just couldn't cope with it,' she recalled. Prince Charles never offered to help and when, in desperation, she contacted the press office at Buckingham Palace, they told her that she was on her own. While they washed their hands of any involvement, Diana dipped deep into her inner resources, drawing upon her instinctive determination to survive.

What made it worse was that Prince Charles seemed less concerned about her predicament than that of Camilla Parker Bowles. When he called Diana on the phone he often spoke in sympathetic tones about the rough time Camilla was getting because there were three or four journalists outside her home. Diana bit her lip and said nothing, never mentioning the virtual siege she was living under. She didn't think that it was her place to do so nor did she want to appear to be a burden to the man she loved.

As the romance gathered momentum, Diana began to harbour doubts about her new friend Camilla Parker Bowles. She seemed to know everything that Diana and Charles had discussed in their rare moments of privacy and was full of advice on how best to handle Prince Charles. It was all very strange. Even Diana, an absolute beginner in the rules of love, was starting to suspect that this was not the way most men conducted their romances. For a start she and Charles were never on their own. At her first visit to Balmoral when she stayed with her sister Jane, the Parker Bowleses were prominent among the house guests. When Charles invited her to dine at Buckingham Palace the Parker Bowleses or his skiing companions, Charles and Patti Palmer-

Tomkinson, were always present.

On 24 October 1980 when Diana drove from London to Ludlow to watch Prince Charles race his horse Alibar in the Clun Handicap for amateur riders, they spent the weekend with the Parker Bowleses at Bolehyde Manor in Wiltshire. The following day Charles and Andrew Parker Bowles went out with the Beaufort Hunt while Camilla and Diana spent the morning together. They made a return visit to Bolehyde Manor the following weekend.

During that first weekend Prince Charles showed Diana around Highgrove, the 353-acre Gloucestershire home he had bought in July — the same month he had started to woo her. As he took her on a guided tour of the eight-bedroomed mansion, the Prince asked her to organize the interior decoration. He liked her taste though she felt that it was a 'most improper' suggestion as they were not even engaged.

So Diana was deeply distressed when the *Sunday Mirror* newspaper ran a front-page story claiming that, on 5 November, Diana drove from London for a secret meeting with Prince Charles aboard the royal train in a siding at Holt in Wiltshire. For once Buckingham Palace came to her assistance. The Queen authorized her press secretary to demand a retraction. There was an exchange of letters which the editor, Bob Edwards, published coincidentally on the same day that Prince Charles flew to India and Nepal for an official tour. Diana insisted that she had been in her apartment, exhausted after a late night at the Ritz hotel where she and Prince Charles had attended Princess Margaret's 50th birthday party. 'The whole thing has got out of control, I'm not so much bored as miserable,' confided Diana to a sympathetic neighbour who just happened to be a journalist.

Her mother, Frances Shand Kydd, also took the opportunity to enter the fray on behalf of her youngest daughter. In early December she wrote a letter to *The Times* complaining about the lies and harassment Diana had endured since the romance became public.

'May I ask the editors of Fleet Street, whether, in the execution of their jobs, they consider it necessary or fair to harass my daughter daily, from dawn until well after dusk? Is it fair to ask any human being, regardless of circumstances, to be treated in this way?' While her letter galvanized 60 Members of Parliament to draft a motion 'deploring the manner in which Lady Diana Spencer is being treated by the media' and led to a meeting between editors and the Press Council, the siege of Coleherne Court continued.

Sandringham, the royal family's winter fortress, was also surrounded by the media. The House of Windsor, protected by police, press secretaries and endless private acres, showed less composure than the House of Spencer. The Queen shouted: 'Why don't you go away?' at the crowd of hacks, while Prince Charles heckled: 'A very happy New Year, and to your editors a particularly nasty one!' Prince Edward was even said to have fired a shotgun over the head of a *Daily Mirror* photographer.

Back at Coleherne Court, the beleaguered garrison managed to outwit the enemy when it mattered. On one occasion, when Diana was due to stay with Prince Charles at Broadlands, she stripped the sheets from her bed and used them to lower her suitcase from the kitchen window to the street below, out of sight of the waiting news-hounds. On another occasion she climbed over dustbins and went through the fire exit of a Knightsbridge store, and on another occasion she and Carolyn abandoned her car and jumped on a red double-decker bus to evade photographers. When the bus got caught in traffic they dashed off it and ran through a nearby Russell and Bromley shoe store. 'That was brilliant fun,' said Carolyn, 'like being on a drag hunt in the middle of London.'

They had organized a decoy system whereby Carolyn drove Diana's car to entice her press pursuers away and then Diana would emerge from Coleherne Court and walk off in the other direction. Even her grandmother, Ruth, Lady Fermoy, joined in the subterfuge.

Diana, having spent Christmas 1980 at Althorp, returned to London to spend New Year's Eve with her flatmates. The next day she drove to Sandringham but first left her distinctive Metro at Kensington Palace where her grandmother's silver VW Golf was waiting. Away she went in the VW, leaving the gentlemen of the press behind.

As the hysterical media juggernaut pushed Charles and Diana along to the altar, she had to try and come to terms with her own feelings and thoughts about the Prince of Wales. It was not easy. She had never had a real boyfriend before and so had no yardstick by which to compare Charles's behaviour. During their bizarre courtship she was his willing puppy who came to heel when he whistled. It was no more than he expected. As the Prince of Wales, he was used to being the centre of attention and the focus of flattery and praise. He called her Diana, she addressed him as 'Sir'.

He aroused her mothering instincts. When she came back from a date with the Prince she would be full of sympathy for him, uttering phrases like 'they work him too hard' or 'it's appalling the way they push him around'. In her eyes he was a sad, lonely man who needed looking after. And she was hopelessly, utterly besotted with him. He was the man she wanted to be with for the rest of her life and she was willing to jump through any hoop and over any hurdle to win him. Diana regularly asked her flatmates for advice on how she should conduct her romance. As Carolyn recalled: 'It was pretty normal procedure that goes on between girls. Some of it I can't disclose, some of it would have been on the lines of: "Make sure you do this or that." It was a bit of a game.'

As she bathed in the warm glow of first love, she was occasionally unsettled by shards of doubt. Surprisingly, it was her grandmother, Ruth, Lady Fermoy, a lady-in-waiting to the Queen Mother, who sounded one of the first notes of caution. Far from engineering the union, as has been widely suspected, her grandmother advised her about the difficulties of marrying into the royal family. 'You must understand that their sense of humour and lifestyle are very different,' she warned her. 'I don't think it will suit you.'

Diana was also troubled by other worries. There was Prince Charles's clique of syco-phantic friends, many of them middle-aged, who were too fawning and deferential. She instinctively felt that that kind of attention wasn't good for him. Then there was the ever-present Mrs Parker Bowles who seemed to know everything they were doing almost before they had done it. During their courtship Diana had asked Charles about his previous girlfriends. He had told her candidly that they were married women because, in his words, 'they were safe'; they had their husbands to think about. Yet Diana truly believed he was in love with her because of the devoted way he behaved in her presence. At the same time she couldn't help but wonder about the fact that in the space of 12 months he had been involved in three relationships, Anna Wallace, Amanda Knatchbull and herself, any one of which could have ended in marriage.

Those doubts disappeared following a telephone call she received while Prince Charles was on a skiing holiday in Klosters,

Switzerland. During his call, made from the chalet of his friends Charles and Patti Palmer-Tomkinson, he said that he had something important to ask her when he returned. Instinct told her what that 'something' was and that night she talked until the small hours with her flatmates discussing what she should do. She was in love, she thought he was in love with her and yet she was concerned that there might be another woman hovering in the background.

Charles returned to England on 3 February 1981, looking fit and tanned. That Thursday he joined HMS *Invincible,* the Royal Navy's latest aircraft carrier, for manoeuvres, and returned to London where he spent the night at Buckingham Palace. He had arranged to see Diana the following day, Friday 6 February, at Windsor Castle. It was here that the Prince of Wales formally asked Lady Diana Spencer to be his bride.

The actual proposal took place late that evening in the Windsor nursery. He told her how much he had missed her while he was away skiing and then asked her simply to marry him. At first she treated his request in a lighthearted way and broke into a fit of giggles. The Prince was deadly serious, emphasizing the earnestness of his proposal by reminding her that one day she would be Queen. While a small voice inside her head told her that she would never become Queen but would have a tough life, she found herself accepting his offer and telling him repeatedly how much she loved him. 'Whatever love means,' he replied, a phrase he was to use again during their formal engagement interviews with the media.

He left her and went upstairs to telephone the Queen, who was at Sandringham, and inform her of the happy outcome of his proposal. In the meantime Diana pondered her fate. Despite her nervous laughter, Diana had given the prospect much thought. Besides her undoubted love for Prince Charles, her sense of duty and her deep desire to carry out a useful role in life were factors in her fateful decision.

When she returned to her apartment later that night her friends were eager for news. She flopped down on her bed and announced: 'Guess what?' They cried out in unison: 'He asked you.' Diana replied: 'He did and I said: "Yes please." ' After the congratulatory hugs and tears and kisses, they opened a bottle of champagne before they went for a drive round London nursing their secret.

She told her parents the next day. They

were naturally thrilled but when she told her brother Charles of her marriage plans at their mother's London apartment he wise-cracked: 'Who to?' He recalled: 'When I got there she looked absolutely blissful and was beaming away. I just remember her as really ecstatic.' Did he feel then that she was in love with the role or the person? 'From the baptism of fire she had got from the press she knew that she could handle the role too. She looked as happy as I have ever seen her look. It was genuine because nobody with insincere motives could look that happy. It wasn't the look of somebody who had won the jackpot but of somebody who looked spiritually fulfilled as well.'

Her sister Sarah, for so long the Spencer girl in the spotlight, now had to make way for Diana. While she was happy for her younger sister, she admitted to being rather envious of Diana's new-found fame. It took her some time to adjust to her new billing as sister to the future Princess of Wales. Jane took a more practical approach. While she shared in the bride-to-be's euphoria, as the wife of the Queen's assistant private secre-tary, she couldn't help but be concerned about how Diana would cope with royal life.

This was for the future. Two days later Diana took a well-earned break, her last as a private citizen. She joined her mother and stepfather on a flight for Australia where they travelled to his sheep station at Yass in New South Wales. They stayed at a friend's beach house and enjoyed ten days of peace and seclusion.

While Diana and her mother started planning guest lists, wardrobe requirements and the other details for the wedding of the year, the media vainly attempted to discover her hiding place. The one man who did know was the Prince of Wales. As the days passed, Diana pined for her Prince and yet he never telephoned. She excused his silence as due to the pressure of his royal duties. Finally she called him, only to find that he was not in his apartment at Buckingham Palace. It was only after she called him that he telephoned her. Soothed by that solitary telephone call, Diana's ruffled pride was momentarily mollified when she returned to Coleherne Court. There was a knock on the door and a member of the Prince's staff appeared with a large bouquet of flowers. However, there was no note from her future husband and she concluded sadly that it was simply a tactful gesture by his office.

These concerns were forgotten a few days later when Diana rose at dawn and travelled to the Lambourn home of Nick Gaselee,

Charles's trainer, to watch him ride his horse, Alibar. As she and his detective observed the Prince put the horse through its paces on the gallops Diana was seized by another premonition of disaster. She said that Alibar was going to have a heart attack and die. Within seconds of her uttering those words, 11-year-old Alibar reared its head back and collapsed to the ground with a massive coronary. Diana leapt out of the Land Rover and raced to Charles's side. There was nothing anyone could do. The couple stayed with the horse until a vet officially certified its death and then, to avoid waiting photographers, Diana left the Gaselees in the back of the Land Rover with a coat over her head.

It was a miserable moment but there was little time to reflect on the tragedy. The inexorable demands of royal duty took Prince Charles on to Wales, leaving Diana to sympathize with his loss by telephone. Soon they would be together forever, the subterfuge and deceit ended. It was nearly time to let the world into their secret.

The night before the engagement announcement, which took place on 24 February 1981, she packed a bag, hugged her loyal friends and left Coleherne Court forever. She had an armed Scotland Yard bodyguard for company, Chief Inspector Paul Officer, a philosophical policeman who was fascinated by runes, mysticism and the after-world. As she prepared to say goodbye to her private life, he told her: 'I just want you to know that this is the last night of freedom ever in the rest of your life, so make the most of it.'

Those words stopped her in her tracks. 'It was like a sword went in my heart.'

3
'SUCH HOPE IN MY HEART'

The quest of the handsome prince was complete. He had found his fair maiden and the world had its fairytale. In her ivory tower, Cinderella was unhappy, locked away from her friends, her family and the outside world. As the public celebrated the Prince's fortune, the shades of the prison house closed inexorably around Diana.

For all her aristocratic breeding, this innocent young kindergarten teacher felt totally at sea in the deferential hierarchy of Buckingham Palace. There were many tears in those three months and many more to come after that. Weight simply dropped off, her waist shrinking from 29 inches when the engagement was announced down to 23 1/2 inches on her wedding day. It was during this turbulent time that her bulimia, which would take nearly a decade to overcome, began. The note Diana left her friends at Coleherne Court saying: 'For God's sake, ring me up — I'm going to need you', proved painfully accurate.

As her friend Carolyn Bartholomew, who watched her waste away during her engagement, recalled: 'She went to live at Buckingham Palace and then the tears started. This little thing got so thin. I was so worried about her. She wasn't happy, she was suddenly plunged into all this pressure and it was a nightmare for her. She was dizzy with it, bombarded from all sides. It was a whirlwind and she was ashen, she was grey.'

Her first night at Clarence House, then the Queen Mother's London residence, was the calm before the coming storm. She was left to her own devices when she arrived, no one from the royal family, least of all her future husband, thinking it necessary to welcome her to her new world. The popular myth paints a homely picture of the Queen Mother clucking around Diana as she schooled her in the subtle arts of royal protocol while the Queen's senior lady-in-waiting, Lady Susan Hussey, took the young woman aside for tuition in regal history. In reality, Diana was given less training in her new job than the average supermarket checkout operator.

Diana was shown to her first-floor bedroom by a servant. There was a letter lying on her bed. It was from Camilla Parker Bowles and had been written several days before the engagement was officially announced. The friendly note invited her to lunch. It was during that meeting, arranged to coincide with Prince Charles's trip to Australia and New Zealand, that Diana became suspicious. Camilla kept asking if Diana was going to hunt when she moved to Highgrove. Nonplussed by such an odd question, Diana replied in the negative. The relief on Camilla's face was clear. Diana later realized that Camilla saw Charles's love of hunting as a conduit to maintaining her own relationship with him.

It wasn't clear at the time. Then again, nothing was. Diana soon moved into rooms at Buckingham Palace where she, her mother and a small team had to organize her wedding and her wardrobe. She quickly appreciated that the only thing the royal family like to change is their clothes. With the year divided into three official seasons and often involving four formal changes of clothes a day, her wardrobe of one long dress, one silk shirt and a smart pair of shoes was wholly inadequate. During her romance she had regularly raided her friends' wardrobes so that she would have a presentable outfit to go out in. While her mother helped her choose the famous blue engagement suit which she bought from Harrods, she asked her sisters' friend Anna Harvey, then the fashion editor of *Vogue* magazine, for advice on building up her formal wardrobe.

She began to understand that her working clothes had not just to be fashionable but also to cope with the vagaries of walkabouts, the intrusion of photographers and her ever-present enemy, the wind. Slowly she discovered tricks of the trade such as weighting her hems so that they didn't blow up in a breeze and she gradually acquired a coterie of designers, including Catherine Walker, David Sassoon and Victor Edelstein.

At first there was no grand plan, it was simply a case of choosing who was around or who had been recommended by her new friends from *Vogue.* She picked two young designers, David and Elizabeth Emanuel, to make the wedding dress because she had been impressed by their work when she attended a photo shoot at Lord Snowdon's Kensington studio. They also made the evening gown for her first official engagement, a charity gala in the City of London, which created almost as big a sensation as the dress which graced St Paul's Cathedral a few months later.

The black taffeta silk ballgown was strapless and backless with a plunging, gravity-defying décolletage. Prince Charles was not impressed with the outfit. While she thought black was the smartest colour a girl her age could wear, he had different ideas. When she appeared in her finery at the door of his study he commented unfavourably saying that only people in mourning wore black. Diana replied that she was not yet a member of his family and, what's more, she had no other dress suitable for the occasion.

That spat did little for her confidence as she faced a battery of cameras waiting outside Goldsmiths Hall. She was un-schooled in the niceties of royal behaviour and felt absolutely terrified that she would embarrass her fiancé in some way. 'It was a horrendous occasion,' she told her friends. During the course of the evening she met Princess Grace of Monaco, a woman she had always admired from afar.

She noticed Diana's uncertainty and, ignoring the other guests who were still buzzing over Diana's choice of dress, whisked her off to the powder room. Diana poured her heart out about the publicity, her sense of isolation and fears about what the future held in store. 'Don't worry,'

Princess Grace joked. 'It will get a lot worse.'

At the end of that momentous month of March, Prince Charles flew to Australia for a five-week visit. Before he climbed the gangway of the RAF VC10 he grasped her arm and kissed her on each cheek. As she watched his aeroplane taxi away, she broke down and wept. This vulnerability further endeared her to the public. However, her tears were not what they seemed. Before he had left for the airport, he had attended to a few last-minute details in his study at Buckingham Palace. Diana was chatting to him when the telephone rang. It was Camilla. Diana wondered whether to sit there or leave and let them make their farewells in private. She left her fiancé alone but told friends afterwards that the episode broke her heart.

She was now alone in the ivory tower. For a girl used to the noise and chaos of an all-girls apartment, Buckingham Palace felt like anywhere but home. Diana found it a place of 'dead energy' and grew to despise the smooth evasions and subtle equivocations employed by courtiers, particularly when she asked them directly about her fiancé's relationship with Camilla Parker Bowles. Lonely and feeling sorry for herself, she regularly wandered from her second-floor apartment to the kitchens to chat to the staff. On one famous occasion Diana, barefoot and casually dressed in jeans, buttered toast for an astonished footman.

She found some solace in her love of dancing, inviting the West Heath School pianist, Lily Snipp, and Wendy Mitchell, her dance teacher, to Buckingham Palace to give her private lessons. For 40 minutes Diana, dressed in a black leotard, went through a routine that combined ballet with tap dancing.

During those momentous days Miss Snipp kept a diary which gives a first-hand feeling of the misgivings felt by Lady Diana Spencer as the wedding day approached. The first entry in Miss Snipp's diary, on Friday 5 June 1981, recorded details of Diana's first lesson. She wrote: 'To Buckingham Palace to play for Lady Diana. We all worked hard at the lesson, no time wasted. When the lesson was over Lady Diana, with her tongue in her cheek, said: "I suppose Miss Snipp will now go direct to Fleet Street." She has a good sense of humour — she will need it in the years to come.'

The most poignant lesson, which proved to be the last, was held a few days before the wedding. Diana's thoughts were on the profound changes ahead. Miss Snipp noted: 'Lady Diana rather tired — too many late nights. I delivered silver salt-cellars — present from West Heath School — very beautiful and much admired. Lady Diana counting how many days of freedom are left to her. Rather sad. Masses of people outside of Palace. We hope to resume lessons in October. Lady Diana said: "In 12 days' time I shall no longer be me." '

Even as she spoke those words Diana must have known that she had left behind her bachelor persona as soon as she had entered the Palace portals. In the weeks following the engagement she had grown in confidence and self-assurance, her sense of humour frequently bubbling to the surface. Lucinda Craig Harvey saw her former cleaning lady on several occasions during her engagement, once at the 30th birthday party of her brother-in-law, Neil Mc-Corquodale. 'She had a distance to her and everyone was in awe of her,' she recalled. It was a quality also noticed by James Gilbey. 'She has always been seen as a typical Sloane Ranger. That's not true. She was always removed, always had a determination about her and was very matter-of-fact, almost dogmatic. That quality has now developed into a tremendous presence.'

While she was in awe of Prince Charles, deferring to his every decision, she didn't appear to be overcome by her surroundings. Inwardly she may have been nervous, outwardly she appeared calm, relaxed and ready to have fun. At Prince Andrew's 21st-birthday party, which was held at Windsor Castle, she was at her ease among friends. When her future brother-in-law asked where he could find the Duchess of Westminster, the wife of Britain's richest aristocrat, she joked: 'Oh Andrew, do stop name dropping.' Her ready repartee, cutting but not vicious, was reminiscent of her eldest sister Sarah when she was the queen bee of the Society circuit.

'Don't look so serious, it's not working,' joked Diana as she introduced Adam Russell to the Queen, Prince Charles and other members of the royal family in the receiving line at the ball held at Buckingham Palace two days before her wedding. Once again she seemed good humoured and relaxed in her grand surroundings. There wasn't the slightest sign that a few hours earlier she had collapsed in paroxysms of tears and seriously considered calling the whole thing off.

The cause of the tears was the arrival, a few days earlier, of a parcel at the busy

Buckingham Palace office which she shared with Michael Colbourne, who was then in charge of the Prince's finances, and several others. Diana insisted on opening it, despite firm remonstrations from the Prince's right-hand man. Inside was a gold chain bracelet with a blue enamel disc and the initials 'F' and 'G' entwined. The initials stand for 'Fred' and 'Gladys', the nicknames used by Camilla and Charles which Diana had been made aware of by friends. It had come home to her earlier when she discovered that the Prince had sent a bouquet of flowers to Camilla when she had been ill. Once again he had used that nickname.

Work in the Prince's office at Buckingham Palace came to a halt when Diana confronted her husband-to-be about his proposed gift. In spite of her angry and tearful protests Charles insisted on giving the token to the woman who had haunted their courtship and who subsequently cast a long shadow across their married life. The full enormity of the charade hit her two days before the wedding when she attended a rehearsal at St Paul's Cathedral. As soon as the camera lights were switched on, it triggered the churning emotions in her heart and she broke down and wept inconsolably.

The public glimpsed her frustration and

desperation the weekend before the wedding when she left a polo field at Tidworth in floods of tears. By then, though, the television cameras were in place for the wedding, the cake had been baked, the crowds were already gathering on the pavement and the sense of happy anticipation was almost palpable. On the Monday before her wedding day, Diana gave serious consideration to calling a halt to the whole affair. At lunchtime she knew that Prince Charles had gone to present Camilla with her gift, even leaving behind his senior bodyguard, Chief Inspector John McLean.

At the time he was seeing Camilla, Diana had lunch with her sisters at Buckingham Palace and discussed her predicament with them. She was confused, upset and bewildered by the train of events. At that moment, as she seriously considered calling off the wedding, they made light of her fears and premonitions of the disaster which lay ahead. 'Bad luck, Duch,' they said, using the family nickname for their younger sister, 'your face is on the tea-towels so you're too late to chicken out.'

Her head and heart were in turmoil but no one would have guessed it when later that evening she and Charles entertained 800 of their friends and family at a ball inside Buckingham Palace. It was a memorable night of riotous jollity. Princess Margaret attached a balloon to her tiara, Prince Andrew tied another to the tails of his dinner jacket while royal bar staff dispensed a cocktail called 'A Long Slow Comfortable Screw up against the Throne'. Rory Scott recalled dancing with Diana in front of the then Prime Minister, Margaret Thatcher, and embarrassing himself by continually standing on Diana's toes.

The comedian Spike Milligan held forth about God, Diana gave a priceless diamond and pearl necklace to a friend to look after while she danced; while the Queen was observed looking through the programme and saying in bemused tones: 'It says here they have live music', as though it had just been invented. Diana's brother, Charles, just down from Eton, vividly remembered bowing to one of the waiters. 'He was absolutely weighed down with medals,' he recalled, 'and by that stage, with so many royal people there, I was in automatic bowing mode. I bowed and he looked surprised. Then he asked me if I wanted a drink.'

For most of the guests the evening passed in a haze of euphoria. 'It was an intoxicatingly happy atmosphere,' recalled Adam Russell. 'Everyone horribly drunk and then catching taxis in the early hours, it was a blur, a glorious, happy blur.'

On the eve of the wedding, which Diana spent at Clarence House, her mood was much improved when Charles sent her a signet ring engraved with the Prince of Wales's feathers and an affectionate card which said: 'I'm so proud of you and when you come up I'll be there at the altar for you tomorrow. Just look 'em in the eye and knock 'em dead.'

While his loving note helped to soothe her misgivings, it was difficult to control the inner turmoil which had been building up over the months. During dinner that evening with her sister Jane, she ate everything she could and then was promptly sick. The stress and tension of the occasion were partly to blame but the incident was also an early symptom of bulimia nervosa, the condition which took pernicious hold later that year. She later said: 'The night before the wedding I was very, very calm, deathly calm. I felt I was a lamb to the slaughter. I knew it and I couldn't do anything about it.'

She woke early on the morning of 29 July 1981, which was not surprising as her room overlooked the Mall where the singing, chattering crowds had been gathering for days.

It was the start of what she later described as 'the most emotionally confusing day of my life'. Listening to the crowds outside, she felt a deathly composure combined with great anticipation at the event which lay ahead.

Her hairdresser Kevin Shanley, make-up artist Barbara Daly and David and Elizabeth Emanuel were on hand to ensure that the bride looked her best. They succeeded. Her brother, Charles, remembers his sister's transformation. 'She was never one for make-up but she did look fantastic. It was the first time in my life I ever thought of Diana as beautiful. She really did look stunning that day and very composed, not showing any nerves although she was slightly pale. She was happy and calm.'

Her father, who gave her away, was thrilled. 'Darling, I'm so proud of you,' he said as she walked down the staircase at Clarence House. As she climbed into the Glass Coach with her father, Diana had several practical considerations to overcome. Her dressmakers realized too late that they had not taken the size of the coach into consideration when they had designed the ivory silk wedding gown with its 25-foot-long train. In spite of all Diana's efforts it was badly crushed in the short journey to

St Paul's.

She also knew that it was her priority to get her father, physically impaired since his stroke, down the long aisle. 'It was a deeply moving moment for us when he made it,' observed Charles Spencer. Earl Spencer loved the carriage ride, waving enthusiastically to the crowds. As they reached St Martin-in-the-Fields church the cheering was so loud he thought that they had arrived at St Paul's and prepared to get out of the carriage.

When they finally arrived at the cathedral, the world held its collective breath and Diana, with her father leaning heavily on her arm, walked with painful slowness down the aisle. Diana had plenty of time to spot the guests, who included Camilla Parker Bowles. As she walked down the aisle her heart brimmed over with love and adoration for Charles. When she looked at him through her veil her fears vanished and she thought that she was the luckiest girl in the world. She had such hope for the future, such belief that he would love, nurture and protect her from the difficulties that lay ahead. That moment was watched by 750 million people gathered around television sets in more than 70 countries. It was, in the words of the Archbishop of Canterbury, 'the stuff of which fairytales are made'.

But for the moment she had to concentrate on dipping a formal curtsy to the Queen, a consideration which had greatly exercised her mind in the previous few days. When the newly created Princess of Wales emerged from St Paul's Cathedral to the cheers of the crowd, hope and happiness brimmed in her heart. She convinced herself that the bulimia, which had scarred her engagement, was simply an attack of pre-wedding nerves and that Mrs Parker Bowles was consigned to history. She later spoke of those hours of heady emotion in a voice of wry amusement: 'I had tremendous hopes in my heart.'

She was proved bitterly wrong. In Diana's mind this unworkable triangle engendered a decade of angst, anguish and anger. There were no winners. As Diana pithily observed in a memorable line: 'There were three of us in this marriage so it was a bit crowded.' A friend of both of them, who watched this unhappy saga unfold over the following decade, conceded: 'I am sorry for the tragedy of it all. My heart bleeds for the whole misunderstanding but it bleeds most for Diana.'

But on that July day, Diana basked in the warm affection of the crowds who lined the route back to Buckingham Palace where the royal family and their guests enjoyed the traditional royal wedding breakfast. By then she was simply too weary to think clearly, feeling totally overwhelmed by the spontaneous display of affection from the patriotic crowd.

She was longing for some peace and privacy, believing that now the wedding was over she would slip back into relative obscurity. The royal couple found that seclusion at Broadlands, Earl Mountbatten's home in Hampshire, where they spent the first three days of their honeymoon, followed by a leisurely Mediterranean cruise on board the royal yacht *Britannia* which they joined at Gibraltar. Prince Charles had his own ideas about married life. He brought along his fishing tackle which he used at their Hampshire retreat, together with half a dozen books by his friend and mentor, the South African philosopher and adventurer Sir Laurens van der Post. It was his idea that they should read his books together and then discuss van der Post's mystical ideas at mealtimes.

Diana, on the other hand, wanted to spend time really getting to know her husband. For much of their engagement his royal duties had taken him away from her side. On board the royal yacht, with its 21 officers and 256 men, they were never left alone. Evening meals were black-tie affairs attended by selected officers. While they discussed the day's events, a Royal Marine band played in an adjoining room. The nervous tension of the build-up to the wedding had left the royal couple absolutely drained. For much of the time they slept and when she wasn't sleeping Diana frequently visited the kitchens, the domain of 'Swampie' Marsh and fellow chefs. They were amused by the way she consumed endless bowls of ice cream or asked them to make her special snacks in between the normal meals.

Over the years royal staff and her friends were puzzled by Diana's appetite, particularly as she always appeared to be so slim. She was frequently found raiding the refrigerator at Highgrove late in the evening, and once startled a footman by eating an entire steak and kidney pie when she was staying at Windsor Castle. Her friend Rory Scott remembers her eating a 1lb bag of sweets in short order during a bridge evening while her admission that she ate a bowl of custard before she went to bed added to the perplexity concerning her diet.

In fact, virtually from the moment she

became the Princess of Wales, Diana suffered from bulimia, a fact which helped to explain her erratic dietary behaviour. As Carolyn Bartholomew, who was instrumental in convincing Diana to seek medical help, observed: 'It's been there through her royal career, without a doubt. I hate to say it but I feel that it may erupt when she feels under pressure.' For Diana, the last few months had been an emotional rollercoaster as she had tried to come to terms with her new life as a public figure and the suffocating publicity as well as her husband's ambiguous behaviour towards her. It was an explosive cocktail and it took just one spark to bring on her condition. The week after they became engaged, according to Diana, Charles put his arm around her waist and commented on what he considered to be her chubby figure. It was an innocent enough remark but it triggered something inside her. Shortly afterwards she made herself sick. It was a profound release of tension and in some hazy way gave her a sense of control over herself and a means of releasing the anger she felt.

Their honeymoon gave no respite. In fact it became much worse as Diana would make herself sick four, sometimes five times a day. The ever-present shadow cast by

Camilla merely served to throw fuel on the flames. Reminders were everywhere. On one occasion they were comparing engagements in their respective diaries when two photographs of Camilla fell out from the pages of Charles's diary. Amid the tears and the angry words, she pleaded with him to be honest about how he felt about her and Camilla. Those words fell on deaf ears. Several days later they entertained the Egyptian President, Anwar Sadat, and his wife Jihan on board the royal yacht. When Charles appeared for dinner, Diana noticed that he was sporting a new pair of cufflinks in the shape of two 'C's entwined. He admitted that they were from Camilla but passed them off as a simple gesture of friendship. Diana didn't see it that way. As she commented angrily to friends later, she could not see why Charles needed these constant reminders of Camilla.

In public, however, Diana appeared buoyant and happy. She joined in a singsong in the sailors' mess, playing 'What shall we do with a drunken sailor?' after drinking from a can of beer. 'We were all tickled pink,' recalls one sailor. One moonlit night they enjoyed a barbecue in a bay on the coast of Ithaca. It was organized by the yacht's officers, who did all the cooking. After they had eaten, a Royal Marine accordionist came ashore, song sheets were handed out, and the night air rang to the sound of Boy Scout songs and sea shanties.

In its own way, the honeymoon finale was the high point of the trip. For days the officers and men had rehearsed a farewell concert. There were more than 14 acts, from stand-up comics to bawdy singalongs. The royal couple returned to Britain looking fit, tanned and very much in love and flew to join the Queen and the rest of the royal family on the Balmoral estate.

But the Highland mists did little to soothe Diana's troubled spirit. Indeed when they arrived at Balmoral, where they stayed from August to late October, the full impact of life as Princess of Wales began to hit home. She had believed, like many others in the royal family, that her fame would be transitory, her star soon fading following the wedding. Everyone, even newspaper editors, was caught unawares by the Princess Diana phenomenon. Their readers could not get enough of Diana; her face was on every magazine cover, every aspect of her life attracted comment and anyone who had ever known her was tracked down to be interviewed by the voracious media.

In a little under a year this insecure High

School dropout had undergone a process of deification by press and public. Her very ordinariness was celebrated; everyday gestures such as opening a car door herself or buying a bag of sweets were acclaimed as evidence of a very human princess. Everyone was infected, even the royal family's guests at Balmoral that autumn. Diana was profoundly confused. She had not altered overmuch in the 12 months since she was covering cars with eggs and flour and ringing doorbells with her giggling friends.

As she mingled with the guests at the Queen's Scottish home she realized that she was no longer treated as a person but as a position, no longer a flesh and blood human being with thoughts and feelings but a symbol where the very title 'Her Royal Highness, the Princess of Wales' distanced her not only from the wider public but from those within the intimate royal circle. Protocol decreed that she should be addressed as 'Your Royal Highness' on first reference and 'Ma'am' thereafter. Of course everyone curtsied too. Diana was disconcerted. 'Don't call me ma'am, call me Duch,' she told a friend shortly after her marriage. But no matter how much she tried she could not prevent the shift in perceptions towards her.

She realized that everyone looked at her with new eyes, handling her like a precious piece of porcelain to be admired but not touched. Diana was treated with kid gloves when all she needed was some sensible advice, a cuddle and a consoling word. Yet the confused young woman who was the real Diana was in grave danger of drowning in the tidal wave of change which had turned her world upside-down. For the watching world, she smiled and laughed, seeming perfectly delighted with her husband and new-found status. At a famous photocall by the Bridge of Dee on the Balmoral estate, Diana told the assembled media that she could 'highly recommend' married life. However, away from the cameras and microphones, the couple argued continually. Diana was always on edge, suspecting Camilla's presence in Charles's every action. At times she believed that he was seeking Camilla's advice about his marriage or making arrangements to see her. As a close friend commented: 'They had shocking rows about her, real stinkers, and I don't blame Diana one bit.'

She lived on an emotional see-saw, her jealousy matched by a sublime devotion to Charles. Diana was still totally besotted with him and Charles, in his own way, in love with her. They went for long rambles around the hills which overlook Balmoral and as they lay in the heather he read out passages from books by the Swiss psychiatrist Carl Jung or Laurens van der Post. Charles was happy and if he was content, so was Diana. The touching love letters they exchanged were testimony to that growing bond of affection.

But these romantic interludes were mere pauses in Diana's worries about public life, anxieties which did little to subdue her bulimic condition. She was continually sick, her weight falling drastically until she had literally shrunk to 'skin and bone'. At this critical juncture in her life she felt that there was no one in whom she could confide. She assumed, correctly, that the Queen and other members of the royal family would take her husband's side. In any event the royal family, both by training and inclination, shy away from emotional breast beating. They live in a world of contained feelings and regimented activity. It was assumed by them that Diana would somehow be able to assume their rigid code of behaviour overnight.

Nor did she feel she could approach her own family for assistance. Her parents and sisters were sympathetic but expected her to conform to the existing status quo. Her girlfriends, particularly her former flatmates, would have rallied round but she did not feel that she could inflict upon them such a burden of responsibility. She sensed that, like the rest of the world, they wanted the royal fairytale to work. They believed in the myth and Diana could not bring herself to tell them the awful truth. She was terribly alone and dreadfully exposed. Inexorably her thoughts turned to suicide, not because she wanted to die but because she desperately wanted help.

Her husband took matters into his own hands by asking Laurens van der Post to come to Scotland to see what he could do. His ministrations had little effect so in early October she flew to London for professional counselling. She saw several doctors and psychologists at Buckingham Palace. They prescribed various tranquillizers to calm her down and recover her equilibrium. However, Diana vigorously fought against their advice. She knew in her heart that she did not need drugs, she needed rest, patience and understanding from those around her. Just as she was bombarded by voices telling her to accept the doctors' recommendations she discovered that she was pregnant. 'Thank Heavens for William,' she later said as it meant she could now quite properly forsake the pills she was proffered by arguing that she did not want to risk harming the baby she was carrying.

Her pregnancy was a reprieve. It was a reprieve that would not last long.

4
'MY CRIES FOR HELP'

The sound of voices raised in anger and hysterical sobbing could be plainly heard coming from the suite of rooms occupied by the Prince and Princess of Wales at Sandringham House. It was shortly after Christmas but there was little festive feeling between the royal couple. Diana was then three months pregnant with Prince William and felt absolutely wretched. Her relationship with Prince Charles was rapidly unravelling. The Prince seemed incapable of understanding or wishing to comprehend the turmoil in Diana's life. She was suffering dreadfully from morning sickness, she was haunted by Camilla Parker Bowles and she was desperately trying to accommodate herself to her new position and new family.

As she later told friends: 'One minute I was a nobody, the next minute I was Princess of Wales, mother, media toy, member of this family, and it was just too much for one person to handle.' She had pleaded, cajoled and quarrelled violently as she tried to win the Prince's assistance. In vain. On that January day in 1982, her first New Year within the royal family, she now threatened to take her own life. He accused her of crying wolf and prepared to go riding on the Sandringham estate. She was as good as her word. Standing on top of the wooden staircase she hurled herself to the ground, landing in a heap at the bottom.

The Queen was one of the first to arrive on the scene. She was horrified, physically shaking with the shock of what she had witnessed. A local doctor was summoned while George Pinker, Diana's gynaecologist, travelled from London to visit his royal patient. Her husband simply dismissed her plight and carried on with his plan to go riding. Fortunately Diana was not seriously hurt by the fall although she did suffer severe bruising around her stomach. A full check-up revealed that the foetus had not been injured.

The incident was one of many domestic crises which crowded in upon the royal couple in those tumultuous early days. At every turning point they put a greater distance between each other. As James Gilbey observed of her suicide attempts: 'They were messages of complete desperation. Please, please help.' In the first years of their married life, Diana made several suicide bids and numerous threats. It should be emphasized that they were not serious attempts to take her life but cries for help.

On one occasion she threw herself against a glass display cabinet at Kensington Palace while on another she slashed at her wrists with a razor blade. Another time she cut herself with the serrated edge of a lemon slicer; on yet another occasion, during a heated argument with Prince Charles, she picked up a penknife lying on his dressing table and cut her chest and her thighs. Although she was bleeding her husband studiously scorned her. As ever he thought that she was faking her problems. Later on, her sister Jane, who saw her shortly afterwards, remarked on the score marks on her body. Jane was horrified when she learned the truth.

As Diana later told friends: 'They were desperate cries for help. I just needed time to adjust to my new position.' One friend who watched their relationship deteriorate points to Prince Charles's disinterest and total lack of respect for her at a time when Diana badly needed help. 'His indifference pushed her to the edge whereas he could have romanced her to the end of the world. They could have set the world alight. Through no fault of his own, because of his own ignorance, upbringing and lack of a whole relationship with anyone in his life, he instilled this hatred of herself.'

This is a partisan appraisal. In the early days of their marriage Prince Charles did, for a time, try to ease his wife into the royal routine. Her first big test was a three-day visit to Wales in October 1981. The crowds made it painfully obvious who was the new star of the show — the Princess of Wales. Charles was left apologizing for not having enough wives to go round. If he took one side of the street during a walkabout the crowd collectively groaned, it was his wife they had come to see. 'I seem to do nothing but collect flowers these days,' he said. 'I know my role.' Behind the smiles there were other muttered concerns. The first sight of the Princess on a rainswept quayside in Wales came as a shock to royal watchers. It was the first chance to see Diana close up since the long honeymoon and it was like looking at a different woman. She wasn't just slim, she was painfully thin.

She had lost weight before the wedding; that was only to be expected — but the girl moving through the crowds, shaking hands and accepting flowers, looked positively transparent. Diana was two months pregnant — and feeling worse than she looked. She chose the wrong clothes for the torrential rain which followed their every move, she was wracked by severe morning sickness and absolutely overwhelmed by the crowds who turned out to see her.

Diana admitted that she wasn't easy to handle during that baptism of fire. She was often in tears as they travelled to the various venues, telling her husband that she simply could not face the crowds. She didn't have the energy or the resources to cope with the prospect of meeting so many people. There were times, many times, when she longed to be back in her safe bachelor apartment with her jolly, uncomplicated friends.

While Prince Charles sympathized with his tearful wife he insisted that the royal roadshow had to go on. He was understandably apprehensive when Diana made her first speech, partly in Welsh, at Cardiff City Hall when she was presented with the Freedom of the City. While Diana passed that test with aplomb, she discovered another truism about royal life. However well she did, however hard she tried, she never earned a word of praise from her husband, the royal family or their courtiers. In her vulnerable, lonely position a little applause would have worked wonders. 'I remember her saying that she was trying so damn hard and all she needed was a pat on the back,' recalled a friend. 'But it wasn't forthcoming.' Every day she fought back the waves of nausea in order to fulfil her public engagements. She had such a morbid fear of letting down her husband and the royal family 'firm' that she performed her official duties when she was quite clearly unwell. On two occasions she had to cancel engagements, on others she looked pale and sickly, acutely aware that she was not helping her husband. At least after her pregnancy was officially announced on 5 November 1981 Diana could publicly discuss her condition. The weary Princess said: 'Some days I felt terrible. No one told me I would feel like I did.' She confessed to a passion for bacon and tomato sandwiches and took to telephoning her friend, Sarah Ferguson, the daughter of Charles's polo manager, Major Ronald Ferguson. The irrepressible redhead regularly left her job at a London art dealer and drove round to Buckingham Palace to cheer up the royal mother-to-be.

In private it was no better. She stalwartly refused to take any drugs, once again arguing that she could not hold herself responsible if the baby were born deformed, perhaps thinking back to her elder brother who died soon after birth. At the same time she acknowledged that she was now seen by the rest of the royal family as 'a problem'. At formal dinners at Sandringham or Windsor Castle she frequently had to leave the table to be ill. Instead of simply going to bed, she insisted on returning, believing that it was her duty to try and fulfil her obligations.

If daily life was difficult, public duties were a nightmare. The visit to Wales had been a triumph but Diana had felt overwhelmed by her popularity, the size of the crowds and the proximity of the media. She was riding a tiger and there was no way of escape. For the first few months she trembled at the thought of performing an official engagement on her own. Where possible she would join Charles and remain by his side, silent, attentive but still terrified. When she accepted her first solo public duty, to switch on the Christmas lights at Regent Street in London's West End, she was paralysed with nerves. She felt sick as she made a brief speech which was delivered in a rapid monotone. At the end of that engagement she was glad to return home to Buckingham Palace.

It didn't get any easier. The girl who would only appear in school plays if she had a non-speaking part was now centre stage. It took, by her own admission, six years before she felt comfortable appearing in her starring role. Fortunately for her the camera had already fallen in love with the new royal cover girl. However nervous she may have felt inside, her warm smile and unaffected manner were a photographer's delight. For once the camera did lie, not about the beauty she was becoming but in camouflaging the vulnerable personality behind her effortless capacity to dazzle.

She believed that she was able to smile through the pain thanks to qualities she inherited from her mother. When friends asked how she was able to display such a sunny public countenance she said: 'I've got what my mother has got. However bloody you are feeling you can put on the most amazing show of happiness. My mother is an expert at that and I've picked it up. It kept the wolves from the door.'

The ability to become this smiling persona in public was helped by the nature of Diana's bulimia, her binging and purging allowing her to maintain a relatively steady weight. At the same time Diana's healthy lifestyle of regular exercise, little alcohol and early nights gave her the energy to carry on with her royal duties.

At the same time her deep sense of duty and obligation impelled her to keep up appearances for the sake of the public. As she later recalled: 'The public side of her was very different from the private side. They wanted a fairy princess to come and touch them and turn everything into gold. All their worries would be forgotten. Little did they realize that the individual was crucifying herself inside.' Diana, an unwilling international media celebrity, was having to learn on the hoof. There was no training, backup or advice from within the royal system. Everything was piecemeal and haphazard. Charles's courtiers were used to dealing with a bachelor of fixed habits and a set routine. Marriage changed all that. During the preparations for the wedding there was consternation that Prince Charles would not be able to afford his share of the expense. 'Sums were worked out on the backs of envelopes, it was chaos,' recalled one former member of his Household. The momentum which continued long after the wedding took everyone by surprise. Even though extra staff were drafted in, Diana herself sat down to answer many of the 47,000 letters of congratulation and 10,000 gifts which the wedding generated.

She frequently had to pinch herself with the absurdity of it all. One moment she was cleaning floors for a living, the next receiving a pair of brass candlesticks from the King and Queen of Sweden or making small talk with the President of Somewhere or Other. Fortunately her upbringing had given her the social training to cope with these situations. This was just as well because the federal structure of the royal family means that everyone keeps to their own province.

As well as coming to terms with her public role, the fledgling princess had two houses to furnish and decorate. Prince Charles admired her sense of style and colour and left the burden of decoration to her. However, she did need professional help. She welcomed her mother's suggestion of Dudley Poplak, a discreet South African-born interior designer who had furnished her own homes. He set to work on Apartments Eight and Nine at Kensington Palace and Highgrove.

His main task was tastefully to accommodate as many wedding presents into their new homes as was practicable. An 18th-century travelling commode from the Duke and Duchess of Wellington, a pair of Georgian chairs from the people of Bermuda and wrought-iron gates from the neighbouring village of Tetbury were just a sample of the cornucopia of presents which had descended on the royal couple.

For much of her pregnancy Diana stayed at Buckingham Palace while painters and carpenters worked at their new London home. It wasn't until five weeks before Prince William was born that the royal couple moved into Kensington Palace, the home also of Princess Margaret, the Duke and Duchess of Gloucester and their immediate neighbours, Prince and Princess Michael of Kent. By then Diana was truly at the end of her tether. She was constantly watched by photographers and reporters while newspapers commented on her every action. Unknown to the Princess, the Queen had already summoned Fleet Street newspaper editors to Buckingham Palace where her press secretary requested that Diana be given a little peace and privacy. The request was ignored.

In February, when Charles and Diana flew to Windermere Island in the Bahamas, they were followed by representatives from two tabloid newspapers. The Princess, then five months pregnant, was photographed running through the surf in a bikini. She and

Charles were furious at the publication of the pictures while the Palace, reflecting their outrage, remarked that it was one of 'the blackest days in British journalism'. The honeymoon between the press, the Princess and the Palace was effectively over.

This daily media obsession with Diana further burdened her already overstretched mental and physical resources. The bulimia, the morning sickness, her collapsing marriage and her jealousy of Camilla conspired to make her life intolerable. Media interest in the forthcoming birth was just too much to bear. She decided to have the labour induced even though her gynaecologist, George Pinker, has been quoted as saying: 'Birth is a natural process and should be treated as such.' While she was well aware of her mother's trauma following the birth of her brother John, her instincts told her that the baby was well. 'It's well cooked,' she told a friend before she and Prince Charles travelled to the private Lindo wing of St Mary's Hospital in Paddington, west London.

Her labour was, like her pregnancy, seemingly interminable and difficult. Diana was continually sick and at one point Mr Pinker and his fellow doctors considered performing an emergency Caesarean operation.

During her labour Diana's temperature soared dramatically, which in turn gave rise to concern for the baby's health. In the end Diana, who had an epidural injection in the base of her spine, was able to give birth thanks to her own efforts, without resorting to forceps or an operation.

Joy was unconfined. At 9.03 p.m. on 21 June 1982 Diana produced the son and heir which was cause for national rejoicing. When the Queen came to visit her grandchild the following day her comment was typical. As she looked at the tiny bundle she said drily: 'Thank goodness he hasn't got ears like his father.' The second in line to the throne was still known officially as 'Baby Wales' and it took the couple several days of discussion before they arrived at a name. Prince Charles admitted as much: 'We've thought of one or two. There's a bit of an argument about it, but we'll find one eventually.' Charles wanted to call his first son 'Arthur' and his second 'Albert', after Queen Victoria's consort. William and Harry were Diana's choices while her husband's preferences were used in their children's middle names.

When the time came, she was similarly firm about the boys' schooling. Prince Charles argued that they should be brought up initially by Mabel Anderson, his childhood nanny, and then a governess employed to educate the boys for the first few years in the privacy of Kensington Palace. This was the way Prince Charles had been reared and he wanted his boys to follow suit. Diana suggested that her children should go to school with other youngsters. To her it was essential that her children grew up in the outside world and not be hidden away in the artificial environment of a royal palace.

Within the confines of the royal schedule Diana attempted to bring up her children as normally as possible. Her own childhood was evidence enough of the emotional harm which can be wrought when a child is passed from one parental figure to another. She was determined that her children would never be deprived of the cuddles and kisses that she and her brother Charles craved when they were young. While Barbara Barnes, the nanny to Lord and Lady Glenconner's children, was employed it was made clear that Diana would be intimately involved in her children's upbringing. Initially she breastfed the boys, a subject she discussed endlessly with her sister Sarah.

For a time the joy of motherhood overcame her eating disorder. Carolyn Bartholomew who visited her at Kensington Palace three days after William was born recalled: 'She was thrilled with both herself and the baby. There was a contentment about her.' The mood was infectious. For a time Charles surprised his friends by his enthusiasm for the nursery routine. 'I was hoping to do some digging,' he told Harold Haywood, secretary of the Prince's Trust one Friday evening. 'But the ground's so hard that I can't get the spade in. So I expect I'll be nappy changing instead.' As William grew, stories filtered out about the Prince joining his son in the bath, of William flushing his shoes down the lavatory or of Charles cutting short engagements to be with his family.

There were darker tales too: that Diana was suffering from anorexia; that Prince Charles was concerned about her health; that she was beginning to exert too much influence on his friends and their staff. In reality, the Princess was suffering both from bulimia and a severe case of postnatal depression. The events of the previous year had left her mentally drained while she was physically exhausted because of her chronic illness.

The birth of William and the consequent psychological reaction triggered off the black feelings she harboured about her husband's relationship with Camilla Parker Bowles. There were tears and panicked telephone calls when he didn't arrive home on time, nights without sleep when he was away. A friend clearly recalls the Princess telephoning him in tears. Diana had accidentally overheard her husband talking on a mobile telephone while having a bath. She was deeply upset when she heard him say: 'Whatever happens, I will always love you.'

She was weepy and nervy, anxious about her baby — 'Is he all right Barbara?' she would ask her new nanny — while neglecting herself. It was a desperately lonely time. Her family and friends were now at the margins of her new life. At the same time she knew that the royal family perceived her not only as a problem but also as a threat. They were deeply concerned about Prince Charles's decision to give up shooting as well as his inclination towards vegetarianism. As the royal family have large estates in Scotland and Norfolk where hunting, shooting and fishing are an integral part of land management, they were very worried about the future. Diana was blamed for her husband's change of heart. It was a woeful misreading of her position.

Diana felt that she was in no position to

influence her husband's behaviour. Changes in his wardrobe were one thing, radical alterations in the traditional country code were quite another. In fact, Charles's highly publicized conversion to vegetarianism can more properly be laid at the door of his former bodyguard, Paul Officer, who frequently argued with him during long car journeys about the virtues of a non-meat diet.

She was also beginning to see the lie of the land with her in-laws. During a ferocious argument with Diana, Charles made clear the royal family's position. He told her in no uncertain terms that his father, the Duke of Edinburgh, had agreed that if, after five years, his marriage was not working he could go back to his bachelor habits. Whether those sentiments, uttered in the heat of the moment, were true or not was beside the point. They had the effect of placing Diana on her guard in her every dealing with her in-laws.

At Balmoral her mood grew even more depressed. The weather hardly lifted her spirits. It rained continually and when the Princess was photographed leaving the castle *en route* to London the media jumped to the conclusion that she was bored with the Queen's Highland retreat and wanted to go shopping. In fact, she returned to Kensington Palace for professional treatment for her chronic depression. Over a period of time she was seen by a number of psychotherapists and psychologists who adopted differing approaches to her varied problems. Some suggested drugs, as they had when she was pregnant with William, others tried to explore her psyche.

One of the first to treat her was the noted Jungian psychotherapist the late Dr Alan McGlashan, a friend of Laurens van der Post, who had consulting rooms conveniently near to Kensington Palace. He was intrigued to analyse her dreams and encouraged her to write them down before he discussed the hidden messages they may have contained. She later said that she was not convinced by this form of treatment. As a result he discontinued his visits. However, his involvement with the royal family did not end there and he regularly discussed many confidential matters with Prince Charles who would often visit his practice near Sloane Street.

Another doctor, David Mitchell, was more concerned to discuss and analyse Diana's conversations with her husband. He came to see her every evening and asked her to recount the events of that day. She admitted frankly that their dialogues consisted more of tears than words. There were other professional counsellors who saw the Princess. While they had their own ideas and theories, Diana did not feel that any of them came close to understanding the true nature of the turmoil in her heart and mind.

On 11 November, Diana's doctor, Michael Linnett, mentioned his concern about her health to her former West Heath pianist, Lily Snipp. She recorded in her diaries: 'Diana looked very beautiful and very thin. (Her doctor wants her to increase her weight — she has no appetite.) I enquired after Prince William — he slept 13 hours last night! She said that she and Charles are besotted parents and their son is wonderful.'

With savage irony, when Diana was in the depths of despair, the tide of publicity turned against her. She was no longer the fairytale Princess but the royal shopaholic who lavished a fortune on an endless array of new outfits. It was Diana who was held responsible for the steady stream of royal staff who had left their service during the previous 18 months and it was the Princess who was accused of forcing Charles to abandon his friends, change his eating habits and his wardrobe. Even the Queen's press secretary had described their relationship as 'rumbustious'. At a time when dark thoughts of suicide continually crossed her mind, gossip columnist Nigel Dempster described her as 'a fiend and a monster'. While it was an appalling parody of the truth, Diana took the criticism very much to heart.

Later her brother unwittingly reinforced the impression that she hired and fired staff when he said: 'In a quiet way she has weeded out a lot of the hangers-on who surrounded Charles.' While he was referring to the Prince's fawning friends, it was interpreted as a comment on the high staff turnover at Kensington Palace and Highgrove.

In reality, Diana was struggling to keep her head above water, let alone undertake a radical management restructuring programme. Yet she shouldered the blame for what the media gleefully called: 'Malice at the Palace', describing the Princess as 'the mouse that roared'. In a moment of exasperation she told James Whitaker: 'I want you to understand that I am not responsible for any sackings. I don't just sack people.' Her outburst came following the resignation of Edward Adeane, the Prince's private secretary and a member of the family who had helped to guide the monarchy since the days of George V.

In truth, Diana got on rather well with Adeane, who introduced her to many of the women she accepted as her ladies-in-waiting while she was an enthusiastic matchmaker, continually trying to pair off the difficult bachelor with unattached ladies. When the Prince's devoted valet, Stephen Barry, who later died of Aids, resigned, the blame was laid at Diana's door. She had anticipated as much when he talked to her about leaving as they watched the sun go down over the Mediterranean during the honeymoon cruise. He, like the Prince's detective John McLean and several other staff who served the Prince during his bachelorhood, knew that it was time to leave once he was safely married. So it proved.

As she endeavoured to come to terms with the realities of her marriage and royal life, there were moments in those early years when Diana sensed that she actually could cope and could make a positive contribution to the royal family and the wider nation. Those first glimmerings occurred in tragic circumstances. When Princess Grace of Monaco died in a motor car accident in September 1982, Diana was determined to attend her funeral. She felt a debt of gratitude to the woman who had been so kind to her during that first traumatic public engagement 18 months before as well as an empathy with someone who, like her, had come into the royal world from the outside. Initially she discussed her desire to go to the funeral with her husband. He was doubtful and told her that she would have to ask the Queen's private secretary for approval. She sent him a memo — the usual form of royal communication — but he replied negatively, arguing that it wasn't possible as she had only been doing the job for a short time. Diana felt so strongly about the issue that, for once, she would not take no for an answer. This time she wrote directly to the Queen, who raised no objections to the request. It was her first solo foreign trip representing the royal family and she returned home to praise from the public for her dignified manner at the highly charged and at times mawkish funeral service.

Other challenges were on the horizon. Prince William was still at the crawling stage when they were invited to visit Australia by the government. There was much controversy in the media about how Diana had defied the Queen to take Prince William on her first major overseas visit. In fact it was the Australian Prime Minister, Malcolm

Fraser, who was instrumental in this decision. He wrote to the royal couple saying that he appreciated the problems facing a young family and invited them to bring the Prince along as well. Until that moment they were reconciled to leaving him behind for the proposed four-week tour. Fraser's considerate gesture enabled them to lengthen the visit to include a two-week trip to New Zealand. The Queen's permission was never requested.

During the visit William stayed at Woomargama, a 4,000-acre sheep station in New South Wales, with nanny Barbara Barnes and assorted security personnel. While his parents could only be with him during the occasional break in a hectic schedule, at least Diana knew that he was under the same skies. His presence in the country was a useful talking point during their endless walkabouts and Diana in particular delighted in chatting about his progress.

That visit was a test of endurance for Diana. There have been few other occasions since then of such remorseless enthusiasm. In a country of 17 million people, around one million actually travelled to see the Prince and Princess of Wales as they journeyed from city to city. At times the welcome bordered on frenzy. In Brisbane where 300,000 people packed together in the city centre, hysteria ran as high as the baking 95-degree temperature. There were many moments when an unexpected surge in the crowd could have resulted in catastrophe. No one in the royal entourage, including the Prince of Wales, had ever experienced this kind of adulation.

Those first few days were traumatic. Diana was jet-lagged, anxious and sick with bulimia. After her first engagement at the Alice Springs School of the Air, she and her lady-in-waiting, Anne Beckwith-Smith, consoled each other. Behind closed doors Diana cried her eyes out with nervous exhaustion. She wanted William; she wanted to go home; she wanted to be anywhere but Alice Springs. Even Anne, a mature, practical 29-year-old, was devastated. That first week was an ordeal. She had been thrown in at the deep end and it was a question of sink or swim. Diana drew deeply on her inner resolve and managed to keep going.

While Diana looked to her husband for a lead and guidance, the way the press and public reacted to the royal couple merely served to drive a wedge between them. As in Wales, the crowds complained when Prince Charles went over to their side of the street during a walkabout. Press coverage focused on the Princess; Charles was confined to a walk-on role. It was the same later that year when they visited Canada for three weeks. As a former member of his Household explained: 'He never expected this kind of reaction. After all, he was the Prince of Wales. When he got out of the car people would groan. It hurt his pride and inevitably he became jealous. In the end it was rather like working for two pop stars. It was all very sad and is one reason why now they do everything separately.'

In public Charles accepted the revised status quo with good grace; in private he blamed Diana. Naturally she pointed out that she never sought this adulation, quite the opposite, and was frankly horrified by media attention. Indeed, for a woman suffering from a condition directly related to self-image, her smiling face on the front cover of every newspaper and magazine did little to help.

Ultimately, the success of that gruelling tour marked a turning point in her royal life. She went out a girl, she returned home a woman. It was nothing like the transformation she would undergo a few years later but it signalled the slow resurrection of her inner spirit. For a long time she had been out of control, unable to cope with the everyday demands of her new royal role. Now she had developed a self-assurance and experience which allowed her to perform on the public stage. There were still tears and traumas but the worst was over. She gradually started to pick up the threads of her life. For a long time she had not been able to face many of her friends. Confined to a prison, she knew that she would find it unbearable to hear the news from her former circle. In their terms, talk about their holidays, dinner parties and new jobs seemed mundane compared to her new status as an international superstar. But for Diana this chatter signified freedom, a freedom she could no longer enjoy.

At the same time Diana did not want her friends to see her in such a wretched, unhappy state. She was rather like an injured animal, wanting to lick her wounds in peace and privacy. Following her tours of Australia and Canada she felt enough confidence to renew her friendships and wrote a number of letters asking how everyone was and what they were doing. One was to Adam Russell, whom she arranged to meet at an Italian restaurant in Pimlico.

The woman he saw was very different from the happy, mischievous girl he knew from the ski slopes. More confident certainly but beneath the banter Diana was a very lonely and unhappy young woman. 'She was really feeling the bars of the cage chafing. At that time she hadn't come to terms with them,' he recalled.

Her greatest luxury in life was to sit down with baked beans on toast and watch television. 'That's my idea of paradise,' she told him. The most obvious sign of Diana's new life was the sight of her Scotland Yard bodyguard who was seated at a nearby table. It took her a long time to come to terms with that presence; the proximity of an armed police officer was the most potent reminder of the gilded cage she had now entered. It was the little things she missed such as those blissful moments of privacy when she could listen to her favourite music on the car stereo at full blast. Now she had to consider another person's wishes at all times.

In the early days she would go for an evening 'burn up' in her car around Central London, leaving her armed Scotland Yard bodyguard behind. On one occasion she was chased through the streets by a car full of excited young Arabs. Later on she used to drive to a favourite beach on the south coast so that she could enjoy the wind in her hair and the tang of the sea breeze on her face. She loved being by water, be it the river Dee or the sea. It was where she liked to think, to commune with herself.

The presence of a bodyguard was a constant reminder of the invisible veil which separated her from her family and friends. It was the awareness that she was now a possible target for an anonymous terrorist or an unknown madman. The bloody attempt to kidnap Princess Anne on the Mall, just yards from Buckingham Palace, and the successful break-in to the Queen's bedroom by an unemployed labourer, Michael Fagan, were ample proof of the constant danger the royal family faced. Diana was typically matter-of-fact in response to this ever-present threat. She went to the headquarters of the Special Air Services in Hereford to take a 'terrifying' driving course where she learned the basic techniques in handling a possible terrorist attack or kidnap attempt. Thunderflashes and smoke bombs were thrown at her car by her 'enemies' to make sure that the training was as realistic as possible. On another occasion she went to Lippitts Hill in Loughton, Essex, where officers from the Metropolitan Police receive weapons training. There she learned how to handle a .38 calibre Smith and Wesson revolver and a Hechler and Koch machine pistol, which were standard issue to members of the Royal Protection squad.

She had become reconciled to the idea of an eternal shadow; she discovered that, far from being a threat, her bodyguards were much wiser sounding boards than many of the gentleman courtiers who fluttered around her. Police officers like Sergeant Allan Peters and Inspector Graham Smith became avuncular father figures, defusing tricky situations and deflating overweening subjects alike with a joke or a crisp command. They also brought her mothering instincts to the fore. She remembered their birthdays, sent notes of apology to their wives when they had to accompany her on an overseas tour and ensured that they were 'fed and watered' when she went out with them from Kensington Palace. When Graham Smith contracted cancer, she invited him and his wife on holiday to Necker in the Caribbean and also on a Mediterranean cruise on board the yacht owned by Greek tycoon John Latsis.

When she was dining with friends at San Lorenzo, a favourite restaurant in Knightsbridge, one of her detectives, Inspector Ken Wharfe, would join the Princess's table at the end of the meal and regale the assembled throng with his jokes. Perhaps she reserved her fondest memories for Sergeant Barry Mannakee who became her bodyguard at a time when she felt lost and alone in the royal world. He sensed her bewilderment and became a shoulder for her to lean on and sometimes to cry on during this painful period. The affectionate bond that built up between them did not go unnoticed either by Prince Charles or by Mannakee's colleagues. Shortly before the wedding of the Duke and Duchess of York in July 1986 he was transferred to other duties, much to Diana's dismay. In the following spring he was tragically killed in a motorcycle accident.

For much of this unhappy early chapter in Diana's royal life, she had excluded those who had been near and dear to her, although Prince Charles still saw his former friends, particularly the Parker Bowleses and the Palmer-Tomkinsons. The Prince and Princess attended the Parker Bowleses' house-warming party when they moved from Bolehyde Manor to Middlewick House, 12 miles from Highgrove, and Charles regularly saw Camilla when he went fox hunting. At Kensington Palace and Highgrove the couple entertained little, so rarely in fact that their butler Allan Fisher described working for the Waleses as 'boring'. It was a meagre diet: an annual dinner for Charles's polo-playing friends, a 'boys only' evening or the occasional lunch with friends like Catherine Soames, Lady Sarah Armstrong-Jones and Sarah Ferguson.

The tours, new homes, new baby and Diana's illnesses took a heavy toll. In her desperation she consulted Penny Thornton, an astrologer introduced to her by Sarah Ferguson. Diana admitted to Penny that she couldn't bear the pressure of her position any longer and that she had to leave the system. 'One day you will be allowed out but you will be allowed out as opposed to divorcing,' Penny told her, confirming Diana's existing opinion that she would never become Queen.

The mood in 1984 was not helped by the fact that she was pregnant with Prince Harry. Once again she suffered badly from morning sickness although it wasn't as bad as the first time. When she returned from a solo engagement in Norway, Diana was still in the early stages of pregnancy. She and the late Victor Chapman, the Queen's former assistant press secretary, took turns to use the lavatory on the flight home.

Characteristically he was suffering from a hangover, she from morning sickness. It was during those months of waiting that she felt in her heart that her husband was once again seeing Camilla. She felt the signs were there. Late-night telephone calls, unexplained absences and other minor but significant changes in his usual routine. Ironically during that time, Charles and Diana enjoyed the happiest period of their married life. The balmy summer months before Harry's birth were a time of contentment and mutual devotion. But a storm cloud hovered on the horizon. Diana knew that Charles was desperate for their second child to be a girl. A scan had already shown that her baby was a boy. It was a secret she nursed until the moment he was born at 4.20 p.m. on Saturday, 15 September in the Lindo wing at St Mary's Hospital. Charles's reaction finally closed the door on any love Diana may have felt for him. 'Oh God, it's a boy,' he said, 'and he's even got red hair' [a common Spencer trait which eventually sparked inaccurate speculation that Harry was the son of Diana's lover, ginger-haired army officer James Hewitt]. With these dismissive remarks he left for Kensington Palace. The following day he played polo. From that moment, as Diana told friends:

'Something inside me died.' It was a reaction which marked the beginning of the end of their marriage.

5
'DARLING, I'M ABOUT
TO DISAPPEAR'

It was a routine request from the Queen to her daughter-in-law, the Princess of Wales. Royal Ascot race week loomed and she was in the process of drawing up a guest list for the traditional house party at Windsor Castle. Would the Princess like to recommend two single girls of good breeding who would be acceptable guests? She duly put forward the names of two friends, Susie Fenwick and Sarah Ferguson, the daughter of Prince Charles's polo manager Major Ronald Ferguson.

Sarah, a vivacious redhead known by one and all as 'Fergie', first met Diana during the early days of her romance with Prince Charles when she watched him play polo at Cowdray Park near the Sussex home of Sarah's mother, Susie Barrantes. Fourth cousins by marriage, the girls had been aware of each other for much longer and had a number of friends in common. They soon became good friends. Sarah was invited to Diana's wedding and entertained her royal friend in her apartment near Clapham Junction in South London.

At one of Sarah's cocktail parties at her home in Lavender Gardens, Diana met Paddy McNally, a motor racing entrepreneur who enjoyed an uneven and ultimately unhappy romance with Fergie. It was Paddy who, on a June day in 1985, dropped Sarah at Windsor Castle's private entrance where she was met by a footman and taken to her room by one of the Queen's ladies-in-waiting. By the side of her bed there was a card, embossed with the Queen's cipher, giving the times of meals and table placements as well as a note saying how the various guests would be conveyed to the racecourse, either in open carriages or in black Daimler saloons. Even though her family had rubbed shoulders with the royal family for years, Sarah was understandably nervous. She arrived promptly in the Green Drawing Room for pre-lunch drinks and then found herself seated next to Prince Andrew, who was on leave from his Royal Navy flying duties.

They discovered an instant rapport. He teased her by trying to feed her chocolate profiteroles. She refused, playfully punching

his shoulder and claiming one of her interminable diets as an excuse. 'There are
always humble beginnings; it's got to start
somewhere,' said Andrew at their engagement interview eight months later. While
Diana was billed as the matchmaker in this
royal romance, the truth was that she never
noticed the romantic spark between her
brother-in-law and one of her best friends.
After all, Sarah was involved in a long-term
relationship with Paddy McNally while
Andrew still had a soft spot for Kathleen
'Koo' Stark, an American actress who had
excited considerable media interest because
of her appearance in soft-porn films.

Diana had been favourably impressed
when she met Koo during her romance with
Andrew. The Princess had known Andrew
since childhood and had always been aware
that beneath the brash, noisy mask was a
much shrewder and lonelier character than
he or his family would admit. Charles was
only ever jealous of him when he served
with some distinction as a helicopter pilot
during the Falklands War. While he returned
from that campaign with greater maturity,
even his best friends would never describe
him as a man of great ambition. In his free
time he was happy to watch cartoons and
videos on TV or wander around the various

royal apartments, chatting to kitchen staff or watching Diana perform her ballet exercises at Kensington Palace. Diana had seen how Koo Stark, gentle, quiet and utterly devoted, had given this rather lonely man the affection and friendship he was seeking. So when Andrew started seeing Sarah, the Princess took a back seat. She told her friend: 'I'm there if you need me.' As their romance developed, Diana was happy to agree to Andrew's requests that he and Sarah stay at Highgrove for the weekend. As Sarah's stepmother, Susan Ferguson, said: 'Things got better and better between them as the weeks passed by. There was never any "Is it on or is it off?" It wasn't as complicated because they got on so well. That was the nice thing about it, a straightforward love story. Of course, if Sarah hadn't been a friend of the Princess of Wales the situation would have been far more difficult in the early stages. She made it easier for Sarah to see him. You have to remember that in his position it is very difficult to meet women.'

As with Diana's romance, events began to take on a momentum of their own. The Queen invited Sarah to stay at Sandringham in January 1986; soon after, Charles and Diana took her skiing to Klosters in

Switzerland. Diana loaned Sarah a black-and-white check coat when they visited Prince Andrew on board his ship, HMS *Brazen*, which was docked in the Port of London. Diana deftly guided Sarah through her first public appearance with members of the royal family. Compared with the aspiring newcomer, Diana seemed the accomplished performer in front of the cameras. She had blossomed into a sophisticated beauty whose innate sense of style was celebrated the world over.

The traumas of child-bearing, home-making and marriage-building behind her, it seemed to the outsider that Diana had at last come to terms with her royal role. After all, she was still basking in the plaudits following her first television appearance since her engagement. A few weeks earlier she and Prince Charles had been interviewed at Kensington Palace by the veteran newsreader Sir Alastair Burnet. She was pleased that she had answered his questions clearly and calmly, a fact which did not go unnoticed by other members of the royal family. At the same time High Society was still buzzing about her impromptu performance on the stage of the Royal Opera House, Covent Garden, with the ballet star Wayne Sleep. They had secretly choreographed a routine to Billy Joel's song 'Uptown Girl', using her drawing room at Kensington Palace as their rehearsal studio. Prince Charles watched the Gala performance from the royal box completely oblivious to his wife's plan.

Two numbers before the end she left his side and changed into a silver silk dress before Wayne beckoned her on stage. The audience let out a collective gasp of astonishment as they went through their routine. They took eight curtain calls, Diana even dropping a curtsy to the royal box. In public Prince Charles confessed himself 'absolutely amazed' by Diana's display; in private he expressed his strong disapproval of her behaviour. She was undignified, too thin, too showy.

This totally negative attitude was what she had now come to expect. No matter how hard she tried or what she did, every time she struggled to express something of herself, he crushed her spirit. It wore her down. During the wedding preparations for Sarah and Andrew, there was further evidence of his indifference towards her when they flew to Vancouver to open the mammoth Expo exhibition. Before they went, there were further rumblings about her health and what the tabloids liked to call her 'pencil slim' physique. It was rumoured that Diana had used the summer break at Balmoral to have an operation on her nose. Her physical appearance had changed so much during the last four years that plastic surgery seemed to be the only credible explanation. But chronic eating disorders such as bulimia and anorexia do produce physiological changes and this was the case with the Princess. Diana was fortunate that she did not suffer from hair loss, skin complaints or dental problems as a result of starving her body of essential vitamins and minerals.

Discussion about her diet resurfaced when she fainted during a visit to the California stand during the opening of Expo. Throughout her chronic bulimia, Diana had always managed to eat her breakfast. Before this visit she hadn't eaten for days, only nibbling at a Kit Kat chocolate bar during the flight to Canada's Pacific coast. She felt ghastly as they looked round the various stands. Finally, she put her arm on her husband's shoulder, whispered: 'Darling, I think I'm about to disappear', and promptly slid down his side. Her lady-in-waiting, Anne Beckwith-Smith, and their deputy private secretary, David Roycroft, helped her to a private room where she recovered her composure.

When she finally rejoined her husband she found little sympathy. In a mood of irritated exasperation he told her bluntly that if she was going to faint she should have done so in private. When she returned to the penthouse suite they occupied in the Pan Pacific hotel overlooking Vancouver Bay, Diana flopped down and sobbed her eyes out. She was exhausted, hadn't eaten and was distressed by her husband's uncaring attitude. It was what she had come to expect but his disapproving tone still hurt.

While the rest of the party advised that it would sensible if the Princess missed that night's official dinner and got some sleep, Charles insisted that she must take her place at the top table, arguing that her absence would create an unnecessary sense of drama. By now Diana realized that she needed help for her condition but knew that this was neither the time nor the place to voice those fears. Instead, she allowed the doctor accompanying the tour to prescribe medication to help her through the evening. She managed to finish that leg of the visit but when they arrived in Japan Diana seemed pale, distracted and clearly unwell. Her mood was not helped on their return to Kensington Palace when, shortly before the royal wedding, Barry Mannakee was transferred to other duties. He had been the only one within her immediate circle in whom she could confide her worries about being isolated, about her condition and her position as an outsider within the royal family. With his departure, she felt very lonely indeed.

In some ways the arrival of the Duchess of York made her life less bearable. The newly created Duchess bounded into her new role like an over-excited labrador. At her first Balmoral, a holiday experience which used to leave Diana drained and dispirited, the Duchess seemed to take it in her stride. She went riding with the Queen, carriage driving with the Duke of Edinburgh and made a point of spending time with the Queen Mother. The Duchess has always had a chameleon personality, readily conforming to the desires of others. She did it when she mixed with the Verbier set, the well-heeled, sophisticated but savagely sarcastic friends of her former lover, Paddy McNally, and she did it now as she adapted to life within the royal family.

Slightly older than Diana but infinitely more experienced in the ways of the world, the Duchess displayed enthusiasm where

Diana showed dismay, hearty jollity compared with Diana's droopy silences, and boundless energy against the Princess's constant illness. Fergie was an immediate hit inside the family; Diana was still seen as an enigmatic stranger who held herself aloof. When Fergie arrived like a breath of fresh air, Prince Charles was not slow to make the comparison. 'Why can't you be more like Fergie?' he asked. It made a change from his usual refrain, which was to compare her to his much beloved grandmother, the Queen Mother, but the message was the same.

Diana was deeply confused. Her face graced the cover of a million magazines and the public sang her praises, yet her husband and his family rarely gave her a word of encouragement, congratulation or advice. Little wonder then that Diana, who at the time had no sense of self-worth or self-esteem, accepted the royal family's view that she should strive to be more like her sister-in-law. This point was reinforced when the Prince and Princess of Wales went to Majorca as guests of King Juan Carlos of Spain at the Marivent Palace. While the public thought Diana had engineered this 'bucket and spade holiday' to escape the rigours of Balmoral, the holiday was Prince Charles's idea. There was even ridiculous gossip romantically connecting Diana with Juan Carlos. Actually the King was much closer to Charles than the Princess who found him far too much of a playboy for her tastes. On that first holiday Diana had a miserable time. She was sick for much of the week whereas Charles was fêted by their hosts. Word soon reached the rest of the royal family. Once again Diana was the problem; once again her husband asked: 'Why can't you be more like Fergie?'

While the complete absence of support and the atmosphere of disapproval and criticism undermined Diana's self-confidence, the problem was reinforced by society's expectations of the royal family. Essentially, royal men are judged by what they say, royal women by how they look. As she blossomed into a natural beauty, Diana was defined by her appearance not by her achievements. For a long time Diana accepted the role of the docile helpmate to her crusading, articulate husband. Her astrologer Felix Lyle observed: 'One of the worst things that happened to her was that she was put on a pedestal which didn't allow her to develop in the direction that she wanted but one which has forced her to be concerned about image and perfection.'

Diana was praised for simply existing. For being, not for doing. As one of her informal advisers said: 'She was only expected by the royal system to be a clothes horse and an obedient wife. If that is the way you are defined, there is little to praise other than the choice of clothes. If the clothes were partially picked by others then there is nothing to praise. They set her nothing praiseworthy to do.' The Duchess of York, this boisterous, independent and energetic young woman, was viewed by Prince Charles, his family and the media as a welcome arrival and a suitable role model for the Princess of Wales. The whole world seemed to encourage Diana to follow her lead.

The first signal of the change in her behaviour was Prince Andrew's stag night when the Princess of Wales and Sarah Ferguson dressed as policewomen in a vain attempt to gatecrash his party. Instead they drank champagne and orange juice at Annabel's nightclub before returning to Buckingham Palace where they stopped Andrew's car at the entrance as he returned home. Technically the impersonation of police officers is a criminal offence, a point not neglected by several censorious Members of Parliament. For a time this boisterous mood reigned supreme within the royal family. When the Duke and Duchess hosted a party at Windsor Castle as a thank-you for everyone who had helped organize their wedding, it was Fergie who encouraged everyone to jump, fully clothed, into the swimming pool. There were numerous noisy dinner parties and a disco in the Waterloo Room at Windsor Castle at Christmas. Fergie even encouraged Diana to join her in an impromptu version of the can-can.

This was but a rehearsal for their first public performance when the women, accompanied by their husbands, flew to Klosters for a week-long skiing holiday. On the first day they lined up in front of the cameras for the traditional photocall. For sheer absurdity this annual spectacle takes some beating as 90 assorted photographers laden with ladders and equipment scramble through the snow for positions. Diana and Sarah took this silliness at face value, staging a cabaret on ice as they indulged in a mock conflict, pushing and shoving each other until Prince Charles announced censoriously: 'Come on, come on!' Until then Diana's skittish sense of humour had only been seen in flashes, invariably clouded by a mask of blushes and wan silences. So it was a surprised group of photographers who chanced across the Princess in a Klosters café that same afternoon. She pointed to the outsize medal on her jacket, joking: 'I have awarded it to myself for services to my country because no one else will.' It was an aside which spoke volumes about her underlying self-doubt. The mood of frivolity continued with pillow fights in their chalet at Wolfgang, although it would be wrong to characterize the mood on that holiday as a glorified schoolgirls' outing. As one royal guest commented: 'It was good fun but within reason. You have to mind your p's and q's when royalty, particularly Prince Charles, is present. It is quite formal and can be rather a strain.'

On one occasion Charles, Andrew and Sarah watched a video in the chalet while Diana went out to a local disco where she danced with Peter Greenall, a member of the brewing family, and chatted to old Etonian Philip Dunne, one of Sarah's childhood friends. Indeed it was the Duchess, who always had a bulging address book even before she entered the royal world, who was asked by Prince Charles to invite two single men along on their holiday. He wanted to make sure that his wife and other female guests, who did not ski as well as he did, had suitable company. The Duchess chose

Dunne, a merchant banker who was later described as a 'Superman lookalike', and David Waterhouse, then a captain in the Household Cavalry. While the majority of the ski party went on taxing off-piste runs, the two men accompanied Catherine Soames, the former wife of Conservative Member of Parliament Nicholas Soames, and Diana on less exacting slopes. They got along famously. Diana found Waterhouse to be a man of great good humour with a magnetic personality. Philip was 'very sweet' but no more. Indeed, she was much more friendly with his sister Millie who then worked at Capital Radio running the 'Help a London Child' appeal.

Ironically, it was Dunne who became the focus of attention when that summer the unsettled marriage of the Prince and Princess of Wales was examined in some detail. It began with another innocent invitation, this time from Philip's mother, Henrietta, who lived with her husband, Thomas Dunne, then the Lord Lieutenant of Hereford and Worcester, at Gatley Park. The Dunnes were away for a shooting weekend and so were delighted to offer their home for a house party. The skiing companions were present as well as a dozen other friends. The dozen friends were conveniently forgotten when a gossip columnist mischievously reported that she had stayed alone with Dunne at his parents' home. Actually Diana was much closer to Waterhouse, enjoying his lively sense of humour.

The public concern about the marriage of the Prince and Princess of Wales was matched by a growing sense of irritation with the behaviour of younger members of the royal family. The breezy mood of hedonism which everyone enjoyed in the early years of Fergie's royal life was now beginning to grate. Diana was forewarned by her astrologer Penny Thornton. When she visited her in the spring of 1987 she told the Princess that everything she did during the next few months she would pay for. The skittish behaviour on the ski slopes was followed in April by criticism when Diana was seen giggling as she reviewed the passing-out parade of young army officers at Sandhurst. She subsequently explained that it was the commanding officer's weak jokes as well as her anxiety before making a short speech which caused the nervous laughter. Unfortunately the damage was done and at Royal Ascot two months later she once again came in for critical scrutiny. Photographers captured the moment when Diana and Sarah poked their friend Lulu Blacker in the backside with their rolled umbrellas.

The watching world chorused its disapproval. 'Far too much frivolity', sniffed the *Daily Express* while other commentators accused the women of behaving like actresses in a soap opera. Much was made of Diana's behaviour at the wedding of the Duke of Beaufort's son, the Marquis of Worcester, to the actress Tracy Ward. It was noted that while Prince Charles left early, she danced until the early hours with a number of partners including the gallery owner David Ker, art dealer Gerry Farrell and Philip Dunne. Her dancing style, which was angrily energetic, aroused much comment although little was made of the fact that Charles spent much of the evening locked in conversation with Camilla Parker Bowles.

The name of Philip Dunne appeared once more when he was wrongly described as her partner at a David Bowie concert at Wembley Stadium. In fact, it was David Waterhouse who was photographed talking to her while the man sitting next to her, Viscount Linley, was conveniently cut out of the picture. Diana was in tears when she saw the picture in Monday's papers. She was aware of the media interest in her male friends and so was annoyed with herself for allowing David Waterhouse to sit so near. It was a salutary lesson, compounded by the fact that she got, in her words, 'slapped wrists' for wearing a pair of leather trousers at the concert. Once again she was trying to behave like Fergie but courtiers at Buckingham Palace did not feel her apparel was suitable for a future queen.

Worse was to come. On 22 September, Prince Charles flew to Balmoral while Diana and the children remained at Kensington Palace. They were not to see each other for well over a month. The strain told. Each time she left Kensington Palace she was conscious that she was being followed by photographers who hoped to capture her at an unguarded moment. The Princess, Julia Samuel and David Waterhouse were snapped as they emerged from a West End cinema. Waterhouse didn't help matters by leaping over a pedestrian barrier and racing off into the night. On another occasion a freelance cameraman claimed he photographed the Princess indulging in some horseplay with David Waterhouse and other friends when she emerged from the mews home of Kate Menzies. At the same time other cameramen were busy in Scotland. Lady Tryon, known as 'Kanga' and one of Charles's trusted confidantes from his bachelor days, was photographed by his side. However, no one in the press mentioned the name of Camilla Parker Bowles, who was also among the house guests.

While the public were unaware of Camilla's presence, the Princess knew full well that Mrs Parker Bowles was spending much time with Prince Charles. A sense of injustice burned deeply inside her. Every time she was spotted with an unattached man it made banner headlines while her husband's 'friendship' with Camilla barely raised an eyebrow. As Philip Dunne, David Waterhouse and later James Gilbey and Captain James Hewitt realized to their cost, meetings with the Princess of Wales produced a high price in publicity and unwelcome personal attention. With hindsight, there was a large dollop of hypocrisy in her protests.

The crisis in the relationship of the Prince and Princess of Wales became a matter of comment not merely for tabloid newspapers but also for serious journals, radio, television and the foreign media. For once the Palace took notice of the media storm. TV personality Jimmy Savile, who was exposed after his death in 2011 as a notorious sexual predator, and who often acted as a high-powered go-between in royal circles at the time, offered his services. In October, as speculation about the Waleses' marriage reached fever-pitch, he suggested to the estranged royal couple that it would be an effective public relations exercise if they visited Dyfed in south Wales, which had been devastated by flooding. It would, he argued, help to blunt the damaging gossip.

That short trip was not a success. The mood was set when Diana joined her husband at RAF Northolt for the short flight to Swansea. In a scene witnessed by numerous members of staff, the estrangement between the couple was made plain. Diana was already agitated before she saw her husband but she was unprepared for his hostility as she boarded the BAe 146 jet of the Queen's Flight. When she tried to explain that she had had a terrible time from the media, who had followed her every move, the Prince was completely unsympathetic. 'Oh God, what is the matter?' he said in resigned tones as she talked about the difficulty of performing her public duties in such an atmosphere. He refused to listen and for much of the flight ignored her presence. 'It was terrible,' she told friends later. 'I was crying out for help.' The distance in their personal relations was underlined when, at the end of the visit, they returned once more to opposite ends of the country.

It was time for the Princess to take stock. She remembered the occasion well, driving out of the claustrophobia of Kensington Palace with its spy cameras, watchful courtiers and prison walls to her favourite stretch of beach on the Dorset coast. As she walked the lonely sands, Diana realized that any hopes she may have harboured of a reconciliation with her husband were over. His hostile indifference made thoughts of starting afresh completely unrealistic. She had tried to conform to everything he wanted but her efforts at aping the behaviour of the Duchess of York, whom Prince Charles so admired, had been an unmitigated disaster. It brought Charles no closer to her and only served to make a mockery of her public image. The Princess for her own part felt deeply uncomfortable with the world of shallow frivolity epitomized by the Duchess of York. She knew in her heart that in order to survive she had to rediscover the real Diana Spencer, the girl whose character had for seven years been forsaken and submerged. It was time to face the facts of her life. For a long time she had been out of control, meekly agreeing to the wishes of her husband, the royal family and the media. On that long lonely walk she began to accept the challenges of her position and her destiny. Now was the moment to start believing in herself.

6

'MY LIFE HAS
CHANGED ITS COURSE'

The Princess of Wales was feeling sorry for herself. Her skiing holiday had been spoiled by a nasty dose of influenza which confined her to bed for days. Early in the afternoon of 10 March 1988, the bedraggled figure of the Duchess of York appeared at her bedside in their secluded rented chalet at Wolfgang near the town of Klosters. Fergie, who was then pregnant with Princess Beatrice, was skiing down the black Christobel run when she took an uncharacteristic tumble and landed ignominiously on her back in a mountain stream.

She was examined by a local doctor and, pale and shaken, driven back to the chalet. As the women were chatting, they heard a helicopter fly over. They were both filled with foreboding that there had been an avalanche which had somehow affected their skiing party. They were all on tenter-hooks when shortly afterwards Prince

Charles's press secretary, Philip Mackie, came into the chalet. He didn't know there was anyone upstairs and the women could hear him saying: 'There's been an accident.' When he had completed his telephone call they shouted down and asked him what was wrong. Mackie, a former deputy editor of the *Edinburgh Evening News,* tried to shrug off the questions. 'We'll tell you soon,' he said. For once Diana would not be put off by a Palace courtier and was insistent he told them what was going on. He told them that there had been an accident on the slopes and one of the party was dead.

For what seemed like an eternity the Princess and her sister-in-law sat at the top of the stairs, hardly daring to breathe let alone move, as they waited anxiously for more news. Minutes later a call came through to say the victim was a man. Shortly afterwards Prince Charles, sounding shocked and distressed, rang and told Philip Mackie that he was all right but Major Hugh Lindsay, a former equerry to the Queen, had been killed. Everyone started shaking in the first paroxysms of grief. As the Duchess burst into tears, Diana, her stomach churning with emotion, thought it best to deal with practicalities before the full impact of the tragedy overtook them.

She packed Hugh's suitcase while Fergie was given his passport to hand to Inspector Tony Parker, Charles's bodyguard. The Princess carefully placed Hugh's signet ring, his watch and his black curly wig, which, the night before, he had used for his hilarious Al Jolson impersonation, in the suitcase.

When the suitcase was ready Diana took it downstairs and slid it under Tony Parker's bed so that it would be readily available when they left. The chalet was in uproar that evening with an endless stream of visitors. A Swiss coroner arrived to ask about the circumstances of the accident, which occurred when an avalanche overcame the party as they skied down the Wang, a notorious, virtually perpendicular slope which regularly claims lives during the season. Another arrival was Charles Palmer-Tomkinson whose wife, Patti, was undergoing a seven-hour operation on her legs following injuries she had sustained during the avalanche. Diana was most concerned about Prince Charles's inclination to return to the slopes the following day. The Prince was not immediately convinced that they should abandon their holiday but Diana prevailed. She appreciated that he was suffering from shock and could not at that awful time comprehend the enormity of the tragedy.

For once Diana felt absolutely in command of a very trying situation. In fact she was quite bossy, telling her husband that it was their responsibility to return to Britain with Hugh's body. It was, she argued, the least they could do for his wife, Sarah, a popular member of the Buckingham Palace press office who had only been married for a few months and was expecting their first child.

The next day the party flew back to RAF Northolt outside London where Sarah, then six months pregnant with Alice, watched as her husband's coffin was unloaded, with due military ceremony, from the aircraft. As the royal party stood with Sarah, Diana remembered thinking: 'You just don't know what you are going to go through in the next few days.' Her instincts proved too painfully true. Sarah stayed with Diana and her sister Jane for a few days at Highgrove as she tried to come to terms with Hugh's death. There were tears from dawn till dusk as she and Diana talked about Hugh and what he had meant to her. His loss was all the harder to bear because he had been killed overseas.

The tragedy had a profound effect on Diana. It taught her that not only could she cope with a crisis but she could also take control and make significant decisions in the face of opposition from her husband.

Klosters was the beginning of the slow process of awakening to the qualities and possibilities which lay within herself.

A terse telephone call from her friend Carolyn Bartholomew opened another window into herself. For some time Carolyn had been concerned about Diana's bulimia and had discovered to her horror that chronic deprivation of vital minerals such as chromium, zinc and potassium could lead to depression and tiredness. She telephoned Diana and urged her to see a doctor. Diana didn't have the will to discuss her problems with a specialist. Carolyn issued a sharp ultimatum. Either the Princess saw a doctor or she would tell the world about Diana's condition, which she had so far managed to keep secret. Diana spoke to the Spencer family's local doctor who recommended her to Dr Maurice Lipsedge, a specialist in eating disorders who worked at Guy's Hospital in central London. From the moment he walked into her drawing room at Kensington Palace, she sensed that he was an understanding man in whom she could place her trust. He wasted no time with social niceties, asking her immediately how many times she had tried to commit suicide. While she was taken aback by this abrupt question, her reply was equally forthright: 'Four or five times.'

He fired questions at her for two hours before telling her that he could help her to recover in no time at all. In fact he was confident enough to state categorically that if she managed to keep her food down, in six months' time she would be a new person. Dr Lipsedge concluded that the problem did not lie with the Princess but with her husband. For the next few months he visited her every week. He encouraged her to read books about her condition. Even though she had to read them secretly in case they were seen by her husband or members of staff, she found herself inwardly rejoicing as she turned over the pages. 'This is me, this is me, I'm not the only one,' she told Carolyn.

The doctor's diagnosis bolstered her budding sense of self-esteem. She needed every scrap of help. Even as she started the long haul to recovery, her husband derided her efforts. At mealtimes he would watch her eat and say: 'Is that going to reappear later? What a waste.' Dr Lipsedge's prediction proved correct. After six months the improvement was noticeable. It felt, she said, as if she had been born again. Before she had begun her treatment she had been regularly sick four times a day. Now this was reduced to once every three weeks. However, whenever staying with the royal family at Balmoral, Sandringham or Windsor, the tensions and pressures triggered a more serious recurrence. The same was true of Highgrove, the couple's country house which the Princess perceived as Charles's territory where he entertained friends, such as the Parker Bowleses and members of his set. From the beginning she had disliked the Georgian manor house, and the passage of time merely exacerbated those feelings. Each weekend she spent there with her husband brought on anxiety followed shortly by an attack of bulimia.

At the same time that she determined finally to conquer her bulimia she decided to confront the woman about whom she had felt such anxiety and anger. This confrontation happened when she and Prince Charles attended the 40th birthday party of Camilla Parker Bowles's sister, Annabel Elliot, which was held at Ham Common near Richmond Park. There was an unspoken assumption among the 40 guests that Diana would not attend and so there was a frisson of surprise among the assembled company when she walked in. After dinner, Diana, who was chatting to guests in an upstairs room, noted the absence of her husband and

Camilla Parker Bowles. She went downstairs and found her husband, Camilla and another guest chatting. The Princess asked the others to leave because she had something important to say to Camilla.

They duly departed and an expectant hush fell over the company. There followed a brisk conversation in which Diana gave voice to her feelings about what she believed to be the nature of the relationship between Camilla and her husband. Diana had long been concerned about the influence of 'the Highgrove Set' on her husband. When they were at their Gloucestershire retreat she routinely pressed the 'last number redial' button on his mobile telephone and invariably found herself connected to Middlewick House, the Parker Bowleses' Wiltshire home. She was also aware of the regular correspondence between her husband and Mrs Parker Bowles. The meetings between members of the Highgrove Set and Prince Charles while out fox hunting or as guests at Balmoral and Sandringham merely fuelled her suspicions.

During that conversation, seven years of pent-up anger, jealousy and frustration came flooding out. She told her: 'I'm sorry I'm in the way, I obviously am in the way and it must be hell for both of you but I do know what's going on. Don't treat me like an idiot.' The experience resulted in a profound change in Diana's attitude. Although she still felt tremendous resentment towards her husband and Camilla and the Highgrove Set, it was no longer the consuming passion in her life.

It was during this time that she became good friends with Mara and Lorenzo Berni, who, at the time, ran the San Lorenzo restaurant in fashionable Beauchamp Place in Knightsbridge. Mara, who died in 2012, had the reputation of an Italian earth mother, regularly asking guests about their star signs, the meaning of their names and the importance of the planets. While Diana had been visiting the restaurant for some years, Mara and Lorenzo first came properly into her life in the early 1990s. She was waiting for her lunchtime guest when Mara, who tended to be protective and attentive to favoured guests, wandered over to her table and sat down. Putting her hand on Diana's wrist she told her that she understood what she was going through. Diana was sceptical and asked her to justify her statement. In a few sentences Mara painted a portrait of Diana's solitary, sorrowful life, the changes she was undergoing and the path she would take. Diana was transfixed, astonished by her acute observations on the nature of her life which she thought she had managed to disguise from the outside world.

She peppered Mara with questions about her future, if she would find happiness and if she would ever escape from the royal system. From then on, San Lorenzo became not just a restaurant but a safe haven from her turbulent life at Kensington Palace. Mara and Lorenzo became comforting counsellors who listened as the Princess discussed her many woes. As their friend James Gilbey observed: 'Mara and Lorenzo are highly attuned, very perceptive and have seen a lot of unhappiness and frustration in Diana. They have been able to help her come to terms with her situation.' The couple encouraged Diana's interest in astrology, tarot cards and other realms of alternative metaphysics such as clairvoyance and hypnotism. Such things were something of a tradition in the royal family. Author John Dale has traced what he calls the 'psychic bloodline of the royal family' back to the days of Queen Victoria. Over the years, claims Dale, numerous members of the royal family, including the late Queen Mother, the Queen and Prince Philip have attended seances and other investigations into the paranormal. Around this time Diana was first introduced to the astrologer Debbie Frank, whom she continued to consult over the years. Hers is a gentle technique which combines general counselling and analysis concerning the present and the future as they relate to the conjunction of planets appropriate to Diana's birth time and date. Born under the sign of Cancer, Diana has many qualities typical of that sign: protective, tenacious, emotionally attuned and nurturing.

When she first began investigating the possibilities of the spiritual world, Diana was very open, almost too open, to belief. She was so much at sea in her world that she clutched at any prediction, in the way that a drowning man clutches at flotsam. As her confidence in herself grew, she started to see these methods of self-analysis and forecast as tools and guides rather than as a lifeline to grab on to. She found astrology interesting, occasionally relevant and reassuring, but in no way at all the dominant motivation of her life. As her friend Angela Serota observed: 'Learning about the inner growth in ourselves is the most important part of life. This is her next journey.'

This interest was a vital stepping stone on her road to self-knowledge. Her open-minded approach to philosophies outside mainstream Western thought echoed that expressed by Prince Charles. Just as the Prince and other members of the royal family have allied themselves to alternative medicine and holistic beliefs, so Diana independently explored alternative methods of approaching the world. Astrology was one such field of inquiry. For most of her adult life Diana had allowed herself to be governed by others, particularly her husband. Consequently her true nature was submerged for so long that it took time for it to resurface. Her voyage of self-discovery was by no means a smooth passage. For every day she felt at peace with herself there were weeks of depression, anxiety and self-doubt. During these black periods the counselling of therapist Stephen Twigg was crucial and the Princess readily acknowledged the debt she owed him. After training in Swedish and deep tissue massage, he evolved a coherent philosophy towards health which, as with Chinese medicine, links the mind and body in the pursuit of well-being. He started visiting Kensington Palace ostensibly to perform relaxing massage in December 1988.

Her appreciation of Stephen Twigg did not surprise Baroness Falkender, former political secretary to the Labour Prime Minister Harold Wilson, who had been one of his patients for some time following her illness with breast cancer. She stated: 'He must have helped her an awful lot as he has helped me. He is a remarkable character. While he is extremely good at therapeutic massage, he has a complete philosophy of life which is challenging and helps you find your own path in life. He makes you feel confident and relaxed and that in turn gives you a new lease of life.'

During his consultations with Diana, which lasted around an hour, he discussed everything from vitamin supplements to the meaning of the universe as he endeavoured to enable his patient to understand herself and bring into harmony her physical, mental and spiritual components. It was at his suggestion that Diana tried vitamin supplements, used detoxifying processes and started to follow the Hay diet, which is a system of eating based on keeping carbohydrates and proteins apart in a defined eating pattern. As with all his patients, he discussed processes whereby individuals affirm their positive characteristics and examine threatening situations in their lives — for instance, Diana's visits to Balmoral, which made her feel so vulnerable and excluded. 'Remember,' he told her, 'it's not so much that you are stuck with the royal family, rather they are stuck with you.'

As Twigg said: 'People like Diana show us all that it doesn't matter how much you have or what benefits you are born with, your world can still be restricted by unhappiness and ill health. It still takes courage to recognize these limitations, to confront them and change your life.'

She experimented with other techniques, including hypnotherapy with Roderick Lane and aromatherapy, an ancient art which involves the use of aromatic oils to reduce stress, promote physical health and a serenity of mind. 'It has a deep relaxing effect,' says Sue Beechey, a Yorkshirewoman who has been practising the art for 20 years. She would make up the oils in her Chelsea practice before taking them to Kensington Palace. Diana often combined aromatherapy with a session of acupuncture, a Chinese healing art in which needles are used to puncture the skin at certain defined points in order to restore the balance of 'chi energy' which is essential to good health. The needles stimulate invisible lines of energy called meridians which run beneath the skin. The acupuncture was performed by Oonagh Toffolo, a trained nurse from County Sligo in Ireland who also treated Prince William from time to time as well as the Princess. Like Jane Fonda and Shirley MacLaine, the Princess of Wales also had faith in the healing power of crystals.

During this period she would keep physically fit with a daily swim at Buckingham Palace as well as exercise classes and the occasional workout with the London City Ballet of which she was patron. She also had a personal instructor who trained her in the subtle skills of tai chi chuan, a slow-moving form of meditation popular in the Far East. The movements are graceful and flowing and follow a set pattern, enabling an individual to harmonize mind, body and spirit. Her appreciation was all the more discerning because of her lifelong love of ballet. This gentle physical activity was matched by the inner peace she found through quiet meditation and prayer, often with Oonagh Toffolo whose Catholic faith had been tempered by her work in India and the Far East.

While she still read romantic fiction by authors such as Danielle Steele, who would send her signed copies of her latest books, she was drawn to works dealing with holistic philosophy, healing and mental health. Often in the morning she would explore the thinking of the Bulgarian philosopher Mikhail Ivanov. It was a quiet meditation in a crowded day. She cherished a blue leather-bound copy of *The Prophet* by the Lebanese philosopher Kahlil Gibran which was given to her by Adrian Ward-Jackson whom she helped to nurse as he was dying of Aids.

Her preoccupations at that time owed little to her husband, whose interest in holistic medicine, architecture and philosophy is widely recognized. When he saw her reading a book called *Facing Death* while she was on holiday he asked her bluntly what she was doing wasting her time reading about those issues. However, she was no longer afraid of coming to terms with her own feelings nor of confronting the uncomfortable and disturbing emotions of others as they approached death or for that matter seeing humour and joy in situations of intense sorrow. Her love of choral music, 'because it touches the depths', was eloquent testimony to her serious reflective spirit. If cast away on a desert island her first three choices of music to have with her would have been Mozart's *Mass in C* and the requiems by Fauré and Verdi.

The counselling, the friendships and the holistic therapies she embraced during this period enabled her to win back her personality, a character which had been smothered by her husband, the royal system, and the public's expectations towards their fairytale princess. The woman behind the mask was not a flighty, skittish young thing nor a vision of saintly perfection. She was, however, a much quieter, introverted and private person than many would like to have believed. As Carolyn Bartholomew said: 'She has never liked the media although they've been friends to her. Actually she has always been shy of them.'

As she matured the physical changes in her became noticeable. When she asked Sam McKnight to cut her hair in a shorter, sportier style it was a public statement of the way she felt she had altered. Her voice, too, was a barometer of the way she had matured. When she spoke of the 'dark ages', her tone was flat and soft, almost fading to nothing, as though dredging thoughts from a dim recess of her heart which she only visited with trepidation. When she was feeling 'centred', and in charge of herself, her voice was lively, colourful and brimming with wry amusement. When Oonagh Toffolo first visited Diana at Kensington Palace in September 1989 she observed that the Princess was timid and would never look her straight in the eye. She said: 'Over the last two years she has got in touch with her own nature and has found a new confidence and sense of liberation which she had never known before.' Her observation was borne out by others. As one friend who first met Diana in 1989 recalled: 'My initial impression was of a very shy and retiring person. She bowed her head low and hardly looked at me when she spoke. Diana emanated such sadness and vulnerability that I just wanted to give her a hug. She has matured enormously since that time. She now has a purpose in life and is no longer the lost soul of that first meeting.'

Her willingness to take on challenging and difficult causes such as Aids was a reflection of her new-found confidence. As her interests moved into the world of health she found that she had less time to devote to her portfolio of patronages and sometimes this had awkward results. For example, she endured a sticky meeting with executives from a ballet company who made it clear that they would like her to devote more time to their cause. As she said afterwards: 'There are more important things in life than ballet, there are people dying in the streets.' During the winter of 1991 and 1992 she made seven private visits to hostels for the homeless, often accompanied by the late Cardinal Basil Hume, then the head of the Roman Catholic church in England and

Wales who was patron of a trust for the homeless. On one trip in January 1992 she and Cardinal Hume spent nearly two hours with homeless youngsters at a hostel on the South Bank of the Thames. Some teenagers, many with drink and drug problems, greeted her presence with aggressively hostile questions, others were simply surprised that she had bothered to see them on a cold Saturday night.

As she was talking, a drunken Scotsman lurched into the room. 'Hey, you're gorgeous,' he slurred, totally oblivious of to whom he was talking. When he was told about the identity of the Princess, he was unconcerned. 'I don't care who she is, she's gorgeous.' While Cardinal Hume was deeply embarrassed, Diana, perfectly at ease among these young people, found the incident amusing. In spite of these lapses in manners, she felt very comfortable on these occasions, far more so than when she mixed with the royal family and their courtiers. At Royal Ascot in 1991 she attended the race meeting for just two days out of five before undertaking other engagements. In the past she used to enjoy Ascot's annual parade of fashion and horseflesh, but she later found it frivolous. As she said to friends: 'I don't like the glamorous occasions any more. I feel uncomfortable with them. I would much rather be doing something useful.'

Ironically, it was Prince Charles's love of polo which gave Diana a greater understanding of her own worth. The Prince broke his right arm during a game at Cirencester in June 1990. He was taken to a local hospital but, after weeks of rest and recuperation, his arm failed to respond to treatment and a second operation was advised. His friends Charles and Patti Palmer-Tomkinson recommended the University Hospital in Nottingham.

Even though it was a National Health Service hospital, the Prince was duly ensconced in his own ward, which had been newly decorated. He brought along with him, from Kensington Palace, his butler Michael Fawcett and his personal chef. During Diana's visits to see her husband, she spent much time with other patients, particularly in the intensive care unit. She sat with Dean Woodward who was in a coma following a car accident and when he recovered she paid a private visit to his family home. It was a spontaneous gesture but Diana was horrified when news of these secret visits reached a wider audience after the family sold their story to national newspapers.

An incident which meant a great deal to

Diana took place in that same hospital away from the cameras, smiling dignitaries and the watchful public. The drama began uneventfully three days earlier in a backyard in Balderton, a village near Newark, when a housewife, Freda Hickling, collapsed with a brain haemorrhage. When Diana first saw her behind the screens in the intensive care unit she was on a life-support system. Her husband Peter sat with his wife, holding her hand. Diana, who was visiting patients in the hospital, had been told by the consultant that there was little hope of recovery. She quietly asked Peter if she should join him. For the next two hours she sat holding the hands of Peter and Freda Hickling before the specialist informed Peter that his wife was dead. Diana then joined Peter, his stepson, Neil, and Neil's girlfriend, Sue, in a private room. Sue, who was so shocked at seeing Freda Hickling on a life-support machine, did not recognize Diana at first, vaguely thinking she was someone from television. 'Just call me Diana,' said the Princess. She chatted about everyday matters; the size of the hospital, Prince Charles's arm; and asked about Neil's forestry business. Eventually Diana decided that Peter could do with a large gin and asked her detective to find one. When he failed to reappear, the Princess successfully found one herself.

Peter, a 53-year-old former council worker, recalled: 'She was trying to keep our spirits up. For somebody who didn't know anything about us she was a real professional at handling people and making quick decisions about them. Diana did a great job to keep Neil calm. By the time we left he was chatting to Diana as though he had known her all his life and gave her a kiss on the cheek as we walked down the steps.'

His sentiments were endorsed by his stepson, Neil, who said: 'She was a very caring, understanding person, somebody you can rely on. She understood about death and grief.'

As Neil and Peter were making the funeral arrangements they were surprised and touched to receive a letter, sent on 4 September 1990, from the Princess on Kensington Palace writing paper. (shown on page 359).

It was another watershed event for a woman who had for so long believed herself worthless, with little to offer the world other than her sense of style. Her life in the royal family had been directly responsible for creating this confusion. As James Gilbey said: 'When she went to Pakistan last year she was amazed that five million people turned out just to see her. Diana has this extraordinary battle going on in her mind. "How can all these people want to see me?" and then I get home in the evening and lead this mouselike existence. Nobody says: "Well done." She has this incredible dichotomy in her mind. She has this adulation out there and this extraordinary vacant life at home. There is nobody and nothing there in the sense that nobody is saying nice things to her — apart of course from the children. She feels she is in an alien world.'

Little things meant so much to Diana. She didn't seek praise, but at public engagements if people thanked her for helping, it turned a routine duty into a very special moment. In the early years she never believed the plaudits she received but later she became much more comfortable accepting a kind word and a friendly gesture. It made her day if she felt that her presence made a difference. She discussed with church leaders, including the Archbishop of Canterbury and several leading bishops, the blossoming of this deep-seated need within herself to help the sick and dying. 'Anywhere I see suffering, that is where I want to be, doing what I can,' she said. Visits to specialist hospitals such as Stoke Mandeville or

September 4th
1990.

Dear Peter,

I have been thinking
of you & Neil so much during
the last few days — I can't
imagine what you must be
going through, the pain & total
devastation.

You were extraordinarily brave
on Saturday, but I worried
continually about how you would
cope returning to your home.

I wanted you to know how
much you're in my thoughts &
prayers & I hope you'll forgive me
for enclosing something which may
bring some comfort —

This comes with my love &
heartfelt sympathy to a very
special person,

from,

Diana.

the Great Ormond Street Hospital for Sick Children were not a chore but deeply satisfying. As America's then First Lady, Barbara Bush, discovered when she joined the Princess on a visit to an Aids ward of the Middlesex Hospital in July 1991 there was nothing maudlin about Diana's attitude towards the sick. When a bed-bound patient burst into tears as the Princess was chatting to him, Diana spontaneously put her arms around him and gave him an enormous hug. It was a touching moment which affected the First Lady and others who were present. While she spoke later of the need to give Aids sufferers a cuddle, for Diana this moment was a personal achievement. As she held him to her, she was her own self rather than conforming to her role as a princess.

While her involvement with Aids counselling initially met with some hostility, which was regularly translated into anonymous hate mail, it was part of her desire to help the forgotten victims in society. Her work with leprosy, drug addiction, the homeless and sexually abused children brought her in contact with problems and issues to which there are no easy solutions. As her friend Angela Serota said: 'She took on Aids because she saw this group of people for whom nothing was being done to help. It is a mistake to think that she is only interested in Aids and the Aids question. She cares about sickness and illness.'

Diana embraced the personal and social issues generated by Aids with candour and compassion. As her brother, Charles, said: 'It's been good for her to champion a really difficult cause. Anybody can do your run-of-the-mill charity work but you have to be genuinely caring and able to give a lot of yourself to take on something that other people wouldn't dream of touching.' He saw those qualities at first hand when he asked an American friend, who was dying of Aids, to be one of the godfathers at the christening of his daughter Kitty. The flight from New York left him fatigued and he was understandably nervous to be in the royal presence. 'Diana realized straightaway what was wrong,' recalled Charles, 'and went to him and started talking in a really Christian way. She wanted to know that he was all right and getting through the day. Her concern meant an enormous amount to him.'

It was her concern and commitment to a friend which in 1991 involved her in what was perhaps the most emotional period of her life up to that point. For five months she secretly helped to care for Adrian Ward-

Jackson who had discovered that he was suffering from Aids. It was a time of laughter, joy and much sorrow as Adrian, a prominent figure in the world of art, ballet and opera, gradually succumbed to his illness. A man of great charisma and energy, Adrian initially found it difficult to come to terms with his fate when in the mid-1980s he was diagnosed as HIV positive. His work as deputy chairman of the Aids Crisis Trust, where he first met the Princess, had made him fully aware of the reality of the condition. Finally he broke the news in 1987 to his great friend Angela Serota, a dancer with the Royal Ballet until a leg injury cut short her career and now prominent in promoting dance and ballet. For much of the time, Angela, a woman of serenity and calm practicality, nursed Adrian, always with the support of her two teenage daughters.

He was well enough to receive a CBE at Buckingham Palace in March 1991 for his work in the arts — he was a governor of the Royal Ballet, chairman of the Contemporary Arts Society and a director of the Theatre Museum Association — and it was at a celebratory lunch held at the Tate Gallery that Angela first met the Princess. In April 1991 Adrian's condition deteriorated and he was confined to his Mayfair apartment where Angela was in almost constant attendance. It was from that time that Diana made regular visits, once even bringing her children, Princes William and Harry. From that time Angela and the Princess began to forge a supportive bond as they cared for their friend. Angela recalled: 'I thought she was utterly beautiful in a very profound way. She has an inner spirit which shines forth though there was also a sense of pervasive unhappiness about her. I remember loving the way she never wanted me to be formal.'

When Diana brought the boys to see her friends, a reflection of her firmly held belief that her role as mother was to bring them up in a way that equipped them for every aspect of life and death, Angela saw in William a boy much older and more sensitive than his years. She recalled: 'He had a mature view of illness, a perspective which showed awareness of love and commitment.'

At first Angela kept in the background, leaving Diana alone in Adrian's room where they chatted about mutual friends and other aspects of life. Often Diana brought Angela, whom she called 'Dame A', a gift of flowers or similar token. Angela recalled: 'Adrian loved to hear about her day-to-day work and he loved, too, the social side of life. She made him laugh but there was always the perfect degree of understanding, care and solicitude. This is the point about her, she is not just a decorative figurehead who floats around on a cloud of perfume.' The mood in Mount Street was invariably joyous, that sense of happiness that understands about pain. As Angela said: 'I don't see death as sad or depressing. It was a great journey he was going on. The Princess was very much in tune with that spirit. She also loved coming for herself, it was an intense experience. At the same time Adrian was revitalized by the healing quality of her presence.' Angela read from a number of works by St Francis of Assisi, Kahlil Gibran and the Bible as well as giving Adrian frequent aromatherapy treatments. A telephone call from Mother Teresa of Calcutta, who also sent a medallion via Indian friends, gave great pleasure. At his funeral Diana was passed a letter from Mother Teresa saying how much she was looking forward to meeting her when she visited India. Unfortunately Mother Teresa was ill at that time so the Princess made a special journey to Rome where she was recuperating. None the less that affectionate note meant a great deal to the Princess at the time.

When Diana was unable to visit, she telephoned the apartment to check on her friend's condition. On her 30th birthday she wore a gold bracelet which Adrian had given to her as a sign of their affection and solidarity. Nevertheless, Diana's quiet and long-standing commitment to be with Adrian when he died almost foundered. In August his condition worsened and doctors advised that he should be transferred to a private room at St Mary's Hospital, Paddington, where he could be treated more effectively. However, Diana had to leave London for a holiday cruise in the Mediterranean with her family on board a yacht owned by the Greek millionaire John Latsis. Provisional plans were made to fly her from the boat by helicopter to a private plane so that she could be with her friend at the end. Before she left London, Diana visited Adrian in his home. 'I'll hang on for you,' he told her. With those words emblazoned on her heart, she flew to Italy, ticking off the hours until she could return.

At the end of the holiday she went straight from the airport to St Mary's Hospital. Angela recalled: 'Suddenly there was a knock on the door. It was Diana. I flung my arms around her and took her into the room to see Adrian. She was still dressed in a T-shirt and sporting a sun tan. It was wonderful for Adrian to see her like that.'

She eventually went home to Kensington Palace but returned the following day with all kinds of goodies. Her chef Mervyn Wycherley had packed a large picnic hamper for Angela while Prince William walked into the room almost dwarfed by his present of a large jasmine plant from the Highgrove greenhouses. Diana's decision to bring William was carefully calculated. By then Adrian was off all medication and very much at peace with himself. 'Diana would not have brought her son if Adrian's appearance had been upsetting,' said Angela. On his way home, William asked his mother: 'If Adrian starts to die when I'm at school will you tell me so that I can be there?'

Once more royal duty called and this time Diana had to join the Queen and the rest of the family during their annual retreat at Balmoral. She left on the strict understanding that she was to be called the moment Adrian's condition deteriorated, having previously worked out that it would take her seven hours to drive to London from Scotland.

On Monday, 19 August he started to fade. Canon Roger Greenacre had already administered last communion but, in the evening, nurses were so alarmed by Adrian's condition that they woke Angela from a catnap and told her that she had better telephone Diana. The last scheduled evening flight to London had departed so Diana tried to hire a private plane. There were none available. Instead she decided to drive the 600 miles from Balmoral to London with her detective. After driving through the night, the Princess arrived at the hospital at 4 a.m. She maintained a vigil for hours, holding Adrian's hand and stroking his brow.

A similar watch was maintained throughout Tuesday and Wednesday. 'We shared everything,' recalled Angela. 'In the end it was a very long march.' Little wonder then that by Wednesday morning Diana felt drained. She was in the corridor snatching a catnap when in a room four doors away the alarm bells sounded. A mother who had just had a cardiac operation had a further, fatal seizure. Unfortunately the woman's children and family were in the room at the time. As doctors and nurses dashed around with electronic equipment Diana spent her time comforting the distraught relatives. For them it was the grief of disbelief. One moment their mother was talking, the next she was dead. Diana spent much time with them before they left the hospital. As they said goodbye the eldest son told her: 'God has taken our mother but has put an angel in her place.'

By Thursday the news had leaked out and a group of photographers waited for her outside the hospital. 'People thought Diana only came in at the end,' said Angela. 'Of course it wasn't like that at all, we shared it all.' In the early hours of Thursday, 23 August the end came. When Adrian died, Angela went next door to telephone Diana. Before she could speak Diana said: 'I'm on my way.' Shortly after she arrived they said the Lord's Prayer together and then Diana left her friends to be alone for one last time. 'I don't know of anybody else who would have thought of me first,' said Angela. Then the protective side of Diana took over. She made up a bed for her friend, tucked her in and kissed her goodnight.

As her friend slept, Diana realised that it would be best for Angela to be with her family on holiday in France. She packed her suitcase for her and telephoned her husband in Montpellier to tell him that Angela was flying out as soon as she awoke. Then Diana walked upstairs to see the baby ward, the same unit where her own sons were born. She felt that it was important to see life as well as death, to try and balance her profound sense of loss with a feeling of rebirth. In those few months Diana had learned much about herself, reflecting the new start she had made in life.

It was all the more satisfying because for once she had not bowed to the royal family's pressure. She knew that she had left Balmoral without first seeking permission from the Queen and during the following days it was insisted that she return promptly. The family felt that a token visit would have sufficed and seemed uneasy about her display of loyalty and devotion which clearly went far beyond the traditional call of duty. Her husband had never shown much regard for her interests and he was less than sympathetic concerning the amount of time she spent caring for her friend. They failed to appreciate that she had made a commitment to Adrian Ward-Jackson, a commitment she was determined to keep. It mattered not whether he was dying of Aids, cancer or some other disease; she had given her word to be with him at the end. She was not about to breach his trust. At that critical time she felt that her loyalty to her friends mattered as much as her duty towards the royal family. As she recalled to Angela: 'You both need me. It's a strange feeling being wanted for myself. Why me?'

While the Princess was Angela's guardian angel at Adrian's funeral, holding her hand throughout the service, it was at his memorial service that her friend really needed Diana's shoulder to cry on. It didn't happen. They tried hard to sit together for the service but Buckingham Palace courtiers would not allow it. As the service at St Paul's Church in Knightsbridge was a formal occasion, the royal family had to sit in pews on the right, the family and friends of the deceased on the left. In grief, as with so much in Diana's life, the heavy hand of royal protocol prevented the Princess from fulfilling this very private moment in the way she would have wished. During the service Diana's grief was apparent as she mourned the man whose road to death had given her such faith in herself.

The Princess no longer felt that she had to disguise her true feelings from the world. She could be herself rather than hide behind a mask. Those months nurturing Adrian had reordered her priorities in life. As she wrote to Angela shortly afterwards: 'I reached a depth inside which I never imagined was possible. My outlook on life has changed its course and become more positive and balanced.'

7

'I Don't Rattle
Their Cages'

In June 1991 the Princess of Wales was enjoying lunch with a friend at San Lorenzo when her conversation was interrupted by her bodyguard. He broke the news that her eldest son, Prince William, had been involved in an accident at his private boarding school. Details were sketchy but it was clear that the Prince had suffered a severe blow to his head while he and a fellow pupil were playing with a golf club in the grounds of Ludgrove School in Berkshire. As she hurried from the restaurant, Prince Charles was driving from Highgrove to the Royal Berkshire Hospital in Reading where William was taken for tests.

While Prince William had a CT scan to assess the damage to his head, doctors at the Royal Berkshire advised his parents that it would be sensible to transfer him to the Great Ormond Street Hospital for Sick Children in central London. As the convoy sped along the M4 motorway, Diana travelled with her son in the ambulance while Prince Charles followed behind in his Aston Martin sports car. While William, who was 'chirpy and chatty' during the journey, was prepared for surgery, neurosurgeon Richard Hayward, the Queen's physician Dr Anthony Dawson, and several other doctors surrounded his parents to explain the position. In numerous conversations they were told that he had suffered a depressed fracture of the skull and required an immediate operation under general anaesthetic. They made it clear that there were potentially serious risks, albeit relatively small, both in the operation itself and in the possibility that the Prince could have suffered damage to the brain during the initial accident.

Satisfied in his mind that his son was in safe hands, Prince Charles left the hospital to go to a performance of Puccini's *Tosca* at Covent Garden where he was host to a party of a dozen European Union officials including the Environmental Commissioner who had flown in from Brussels. Meanwhile Prince William, holding his mother's hand, was wheeled into surgery for the 75-minute operation. Diana waited anxiously in a nearby room until Richard Hayward walked in to tell her that her son was fine. It was, she said later, one of the longest hours of her life. As she sat with William in his private room, his father boarded the royal train for an overnight journey to North Yorkshire where he was due to attend an environmental study.

Diana held her son's hand and watched as nurses, who came in every 20 minutes, tested his blood pressure and reflexes and shone a light in his eyes. As had been explained to William's parents, a rapid rise in blood pressure, which can prove fatal, is the most feared side-effect of an operation on a head injury. Hence the regular checks. These were suspended at about 3 a.m. when the fire alarm shattered the night-time silence.

The following morning Diana, tired and overwrought, was deeply concerned about newspaper reports which discussed the chances of William suffering from epilepsy. That was just one of a number of worries. As she discussed the issue with a friend, she observed: 'You have to support your children in the bad as well as the good times.' She was not alone in that conclusion. As Prince Charles wandered over the Yorkshire Dales on his green mission, a phalanx of psychologists, royal watchers and indignant mothers condemned the Prince for his behaviour. 'What kind of dad are you?' asked the headline in the *Sun* newspaper.

His decision to put duty before family may have come as a shock to the general public but it was no surprise to his wife. Indeed she accepted his decision to go to the opera as nothing out of the ordinary. For her it was another example in a continuing pattern rather than an aberration. One friend who spoke to her minutes after William came out of the operating theatre commented: 'Had this been an isolated incident it would have been unbelievable. She wasn't surprised. It merely confirmed everything she thought about him and reinforced the feeling that he found it difficult to relate to the children. She got no support at all, no cuddles, no affection, nothing.'

James Gilbey reinforced this view: 'Her reaction to William's accident was horror and disbelief. By all accounts it was a narrow escape. She can't understand her husband's behaviour so, as a result, she just blocks it out. Diana thinks: "I know where my loyalties lie: with my son." '

When the Prince was made aware of the public's wrath, once again his reaction came as no surprise to his wife: he blamed her. Charles accused her of making an 'awful nonsense' about the severity of the injury and affected innocence about the possibility that the future heir to the throne could have suffered brain damage. The Queen, who had been briefed by Prince Charles, was surprised and rather shocked when Diana informed her that while her grandson was on the mend it had not been a cut and dried operation.

Several days after the accident, William was recovering sufficiently well to allow the Princess to fulfil a commitment to visit Marlow Community Hospital. As she was leaving, an old man in the crowd collapsed with an attack of angina. Diana rushed over to help rather than leaving it to others. When the Prince saw the media coverage of her sympathetic actions, he accused Diana of behaving like a martyr. His sour response typified the yawning gulf between them and gave substance to Diana's observations on the media interest in their 10th wedding anniversary the following month. She asked in her matter-of-fact way: 'What is there to celebrate?'

The dramatically different manner in which the couple responded to William's injury publicly underlined what those within their immediate circle had known for some time: the fairytale marriage between the Prince of Wales and Lady Diana Spencer was over in all but name. The breakdown of their marriage and the virtual collapse of their professional relationship was a source of sadness to many of their friends. This much-discussed union which began with such high hopes had now reached an impasse of mutual recrimination and chilling indifference. The Princess had told friends that spiritually their marriage ended the day Prince Harry was born in 1984. The couple, who had had separate bedrooms at their homes for years, stopped sharing the same sleeping quarters during an official visit to Portugal in 1987. Little wonder then that she found an article in the *Tatler* magazine which posed the question: 'Is Prince Charles too sexy for his own good?' absolutely hilarious because of its unintentional irony.

Such was their mutual antipathy at this time that friends observed that Diana found her husband's very presence upsetting and disturbing. He in turn viewed his wife with indifference tinged with dislike. When a Sunday newspaper reported how the Prince had pointedly ignored her at a concert at Buckingham Palace to celebrate the Queen Mother's 90th birthday, she remarked to friends that she found their surprise rather odd. 'He ignores me everywhere and has done for a long time. He just dismisses me.'

She would, for example, never contemplate making any input into any of his special interests such as architecture, the environment or agriculture. Painful experience told her that any suggestions would be treated with ill-disguised contempt. 'He makes her feel intellectually insecure and inferior and constantly reinforces that message,' noted a close friend. When Charles took his wife to see the Oscar Wilde play *A Woman of No Importance,* to celebrate his 43rd birthday, the irony was not lost on her friends.

A man of considerable charm and humour, Prince Charles also has the unerring ability to freeze out those who disagree with him. That ability was extended to a trio of private secretaries who contradicted him once too often and numerous other courtiers and staff as well as his wife. Diana's mother experienced his ruthless streak as well as his obdurate nature at Prince Harry's christening. When he complained to her that her daughter had delivered a boy with red hair, Mrs Shand Kydd, a woman of fierce integrity, told him firmly that he should be thankful that his second son was born healthy. From that moment the Prince of Wales effectively excluded his mother-in-law from his life. The experience made her much more sympathetic to her daughter's plight.

This divide between the royal couple became too wide to paper over for the sake of their public image. Before Christmas 1991 the Princess of Wales was due to travel to Plymouth to fulfil a rare joint public engagement. She had been with Prince Edward until midnight at a Mozart concert but the following morning she cancelled the visit saying that she had influenza. Although she did feel ill following the concert the thought of spending the day with her husband made her even more inclined to spend the day in bed.

The constant tightrope that courtiers had to walk between the royal couple's public and private life was illustrated when the Princess of Wales was told about her father's death on 29 March 1992 while she was on a skiing holiday in Lech, Austria. She was prepared to fly home on her own, leaving Prince Charles to stay with their children. When he insisted on returning with her, she made the point that it was a bit late for him to start acting the caring husband. In her grief she did not wish to be part of a palace public relations scheme. For once she dug her heels in. She sat in their hotel room with her husband, his private secretary and press secretary ranged against her. They insisted he return with her for the sake of his public image. She refused. Finally, a telephone call was made to the Queen who was staying at Windsor Castle to arbitrate on this increasingly bitter matter. The Princess bowed to her ruling that they should fly home together. At the airport, they were duly met by the assembled media who reported the fact that the Prince was lending his support at Diana's hour of need. The reality was that as soon as the royal couple arrived at Kensington Palace, Prince Charles immediately went to Highgrove, leaving Diana to grieve alone. Two days later Diana drove to the funeral while Charles flew in by helicopter. The friend to whom Diana related this story commented: 'He only flew home with her for the sake of his public image. She felt that at a time when she was grieving the death of her father she could at least be given the opportunity to behave in the way she wanted rather than go through this masquerade.'

As a close friend commented: 'She seems to dread Charles's appearance. The days when she is happiest is when he is in Scotland. When he is at Kensington Palace she feels absolutely at a loss and like a child again. She loses all the ground she has built up when she is on her own.'

The changes in her at such times were physical ones. Her speech, normally rapid, energetic, coloured and strong, degenerated instantly when he was with her. Diana's voice became monosyllabic and flat, suffused with an ineffable weariness. It was the same tone that infected her speech when she talked about her parents' divorce and what she calls 'the dark ages', the period in her royal life until the late 1980s during which time she was emotionally crushed by the royal system.

In his presence she reverted to the girl she had been a decade before. She giggled over nothing, started biting her nails — a habit she had given up some time ago — and took on the hunted look of a nervous fawn. The strain in their home when they were together was palpable. As Oonagh Toffolo observed: 'It is a different atmosphere at Kensington Palace when he is there. It is tense and she is tense. She doesn't have the freedom she would like when he's around. It is quite sad to see the stagnation there.' Another frequent guest simply called it 'The Mad House'.

When Prince Charles arrived home from a private visit to France she found his presence so oppressive that she literally ran out of Kensington Palace. Diana telephoned a friend who was grieving over the death of a loved one. She could sense that her chum was crying and said: 'Right, I'm coming over now.' As her friend recalled: 'She came instantly for me but when she arrived she was visibly unsettled. Diana told me: "I'm here for you but I'm also here for me. My husband appeared and I just had to fly out and escape." She was all of a dither.'

As far as was practicable they led separate lives, joining forces only to maintain a façade of unity. These reunions merely gave the public a glimpse into their isolated existences. At the soccer Cup Final at Wembley in 1991 they sat next to each other but never exchanged a word or glance during the 90-minute game. Not long afterwards, Prince Charles missed his wife's cheek and ended up kissing her neck at the end of a polo match during their tour of India. Even their writing paper which used to have a distinctive entwined 'C' and 'D' had been discarded in favour of individual letterheadings.

When she was at Kensington Palace he would be at Highgrove or Birkhall on the Balmoral estate. At Highgrove she had the large four-poster in the master bedroom; he slept in a brass bed which he borrowed from his son Prince William, because he found its extra width more comfortable after breaking his right arm during a polo match. Even these distant sleeping arrangements led to marital discord. When Prince William asked for his bed back, his father refused. 'Sometimes I don't know who the baby is in this family,' commented Diana caustically. The days when she affectionately called him 'Hubcap' had long gone. As James Gilbey noted: 'Their lives are spent in total isolation. It's not as though they ring each other and have sweet chats each evening and say: "Darling, what have you been doing?" It simply doesn't happen.'

During lunch with a close friend who was also the mother of three young children, Diana told of an incident which underlined not only the state of her relationship with her husband at that time but also the protective nature of her son William. She told her friend that the week that Buckingham Palace decided to announce the separation of the Duke and Duchess of York was understandably a trying time for her. She had lost an amicable companion and was acutely aware that the public spotlight would once again fall on her marriage. Yet her husband seemed unmoved by the furore surrounding the separation.

He had spent a week touring various stately homes, gathering material for a book he was writing on gardening. When he returned to Kensington Palace he failed to see why his wife should feel strained and rather depressed. He airily dismissed the departure of the Duchess of York and launched, as usual, into a disapproving appraisal of Diana's public works, especially her visit to see Mother Teresa in Rome. Even their staff, by now used to these altercations, were dismayed by this attitude and felt some sympathy when Diana told her husband that unless he changed his attitude towards her and the job she was doing she would have to reconsider her position. In tears, she went upstairs for a bath. While she was regaining her composure, Prince William pushed a handful of paper tissues underneath the bathroom door. 'I hate to see you sad,' he said.

She was tormented every day and in every way by the dilemma of her position, continually torn between her sense of duty to the Queen and nation and her desire to find the happiness she craved. Yet in order to find happiness she felt she had to divorce; if she divorced she worried she would inevitably lose the children she lived for and who gave her such joy. At the same time she faced rejection by the public who were unaware of the lonely reality of her life and accepted her smiling image at face value. It was a cruelly circular argument with endless variations and permutations which she discussed regularly with her friends and counsellors.

Her friends saw their marriage deteriorate to a point where it was a war in which no quarter was expected or given. At home the battlegrounds were their children and Charles's relationship with Camilla Parker Bowles. Officially this skirmishing spilt over into their public roles as the Prince and Princess of Wales. She gave him nothing, he offered less. Diana reserved one phrase for their most acerbic confrontations. 'Remember I am the mother of your children,' she said. That particular shell exploded during their set-piece confrontations about Camilla Parker Bowles.

Courtiers were regularly caught in the crossfire. When Prince Charles was licking his wounds following the public condemnation of his behaviour when Prince William cracked his skull, his private secretary, Commander Richard Aylard, attempted to make amends. In a handwritten memo he implored his royal principal to be seen in public with his children more frequently so that he could at least be seen to be behaving as a responsible father. At the conclusion of his missive he heavily underlined in red ink and printed in bold capitals a single word: 'TRY'.

The ploy worked for a while. Prince Charles was seen taking Prince Harry to Wetherby School and was photographed riding and cycling with his sons on the Sandringham estate. But Richard Aylard's modest public relations success was seen as cynical hypocrisy by the Princess of Wales who knew the daily reality of his involvement with his children.

James Gilbey explained: 'She thinks he is a bad father, a selfish father, the children have to tie in with what he's doing. He will never delay, cancel or change anything which he has sorted out for their benefit. It's a reflection of the way he was brought up and it is history repeating itself. That's why she gets so sad when he is photographed riding with the children at Sandringham. When I spoke to her about it she was literally having to contain her anger because she thought the picture would represent the fact that he was a good father whereas she has the real story.'

Over-protective in the way that single-parent families are, she lavished William and Harry with love, cuddles and affection. They were a point of stability and sanity in her topsy-turvy world. She loved them unconditionally and absolutely, working with a singleness of purpose to ensure that they did not suffer the same kind of childhood that she did.

It was Diana who chose their schools, their clothes and planned their outings. She negotiated her public duties around their timetables. A glance through the pages of her official diary signified as much: the dates of their school plays, term times and outings were all highlighted in green ink. They came first and foremost in her life. So while Charles would send a servant to Ludgrove School to give William a tray of plums from the Highgrove estate, Diana would make time to cheer him from the touchline when he played left back for his school soccer team. While Charles's absences were accepted by the boys, there were times naturally when they were keen to see their father. During his convalescence after he had broken his right arm, Charles spent a great deal of time in Scotland, much to the dismay of Prince William. Diana communicated his hurt to her husband which resulted in the Prince sending his son handwritten faxes about his activities.

Diana's friendship with Captain James

Hewitt, which caused some comment in the gossip columns at the time, blossomed precisely because he was a popular 'uncle' figure to her boys. Hewitt, a keen polo player with the laconic sense of humour and reserve reminiscent of a 1930s matinée idol, taught William and Harry the finer points of horsemanship during his visits to Highgrove and helped Diana overcome her reluctance to renew her equine skills. He is a man of great charm who provided Diana with amusing and sympathetic companionship at a time when she needed a shoulder to lean on because of her husband's neglect. During their friendship which, as she later admitted, developed into a full-blown love affair, she helped choose some of his clothes and bought him tasteful presents. She visited his family home in Devon on several occasions where she was entertained by his parents while her boys went riding with Captain Hewitt. The Princess found these weekend breaks a relaxing interlude in a hectic life.

For some time Hewitt was an important figure in Diana's life. The distance which then separated the royal couple was demonstrated by the fact that they marshalled rival battalions of friends in their support. Thus Diana aired her grievances about her husband to a tightly knit phalanx of friends who included her former flatmate Carolyn Bartholomew, Angela Serota, Catherine Soames, the Duke and Duchess of Devonshire, Lucia Flecha de Lima, wife of the then Brazilian ambassador, her sister Jane, who lived at the time a few yards from Diana's apartment, and Lorenzo and Mara Berni. There were other friends such as Julia Samuel, Julia Dodd-Noble, David Waterhouse and the well-known actor Terence Stamp, whom she would see for lunch at his London apartment, who were social friends as opposed to the confidantes she sounded out for advice on her eternal dilemma.

On his side Prince Charles counted on Andrew and Camilla Parker Bowles, Camilla's sister, Annabel, and her husband, Simon Elliot, skiing friends Charles and Patti Palmer-Tomkinson, Conservative MP Nicholas Soames, author Laurens van der Post, Lady Susan Hussey, a long-serving lady-in-waiting to the Queen, Lord and Lady Tryon as well as the Dutch couple Emilie and Hugh van Cutsem.

Diana referred to them dismissively as 'the Highgrove Set'. They paid court to her husband and lip-service to her, allying themselves completely with his perspective on his marriage, his children and his royal life. As a result, friendships foundered as relations between the Prince and Princess degenerated. Diana once described Emilie van Cutsem, a former champion golfer, as her best friend. Inevitably suspicion was rife. When the van Cutsems hosted a dinner for Prince Charles and his circle at a Covent Garden restaurant just before Christmas 1991 the Princess strongly suspected that the date had been chosen because she had a long-standing previous engagement and would be unable to attend.

The week of the Princess of Wales's 30th birthday in 1991 provided graphic evidence of the way their friends had become involved in the rivalry between the royal couple. On the day that a national opinion poll revealed that Diana was the most popular member of the royal family, she received a public slap in the face when a front-page story in the *Daily Mail* revealed that the Princess had turned down her husband's offer of a birthday party at Highgrove. The clear implication, illustrated by quotes from the Prince's friends, was that Diana was behaving in an unreasonable manner. When Prince Charles first suggested the idea of a party, the Gulf War was raging. Diana believed strongly that planning such a party would be frivolous at a time when British troops were involved in the fighting. Also, as her friends were aware, a party at Highgrove comprising many of Charles's cronies was hardly her idea of fun.

The clear implication of the newspaper article was that Prince Charles had complained about his wife to friends who had decided to take action on his behalf. While her husband protested his innocence, it cast a shadow over her birthday, which she celebrated quietly with her sister Jane and their children. It marked a significant private corrosion of the relations between the royal couple.

The resulting adverse publicity forced a temporary public *rapprochement* upon the couple. Prince Charles altered his diary so that he could appear with his wife at various public engagements, including a concert at the Royal Albert Hall, as well as deciding to spend at least part of their 10th wedding anniversary together to placate the media. It was highly contrived and lasted only a matter of weeks before the truce was breached. Their total separation, epitomized by the presence of the hostile 'Highgrove Set', was virtually formalized. But Charles's friends were not the only reason why she loathed her country home. She referred to her trips to their Gloucestershire home as 'a return to prison' and rarely invited her family or friends. As James Gilbey said: 'She dislikes Highgrove. She feels that Camilla lives just down the road and regardless of any effort she puts into the house, she never feels it is her home.'

Diana took some small satisfaction when a Sunday newspaper accurately detailed Camilla's comings and goings, even reporting on the unmarked Ford estate car the Prince used to drive the 12 miles to Middlewick House. This was further authenticated by a former policeman at Highgrove, Andrew Jacques, who sold his story to a national newspaper. 'Mrs Parker Bowles certainly figures larger in the Prince's life at Highgrove than Princess Di,' he claimed, a view endorsed by many of Diana's friends.

So who was the woman who excited Diana's feelings? From the moment photographs of Camilla fluttered from Prince Charles's diary during their honeymoon, the Princess of Wales harboured every kind of suspicion, resentment and jealousy about the woman Charles loved and lost during his bachelor days. Camilla is from sturdy county stock with numerous roots in the aristocracy. She is the daughter of the late Major Bruce Shand, a well-to-do wine merchant, Master of Foxhounds and Vice Lord Lieutenant of East Sussex. Her brother, who died in 2014, was the adventurer and author Mark Shand, who was once an escort of Bianca Jagger and model Marie Helvin, before he married Clio Goldsmith, the niece of the grocery millionaire, the late James Goldsmith. Camilla is related to Lady Elspeth Howe, wife of the late Lord Howe, one-time Chancellor of the Exchequer, and the millionaire builder, the late Lord Ashcombe. Her great-grandmother was Alice Keppel who for many years was the mistress of Edward VII. She was married to a serving Army officer and once said that her job was to 'curtsy first and then leap into bed'.

In his bachelor days Andrew Parker Bowles, who is related to the Earls of Derby and Cadogan and the Duke of Marlborough, was a dashing and popular escort among society debutantes. Before his marriage at the Guards Chapel in July 1973, the charming cavalry officer was a companion for Princess Anne and Sir Winston Churchill's granddaughter Charlotte. A former brigadier, he was holder of the improbable title 'Silver Stick in Waiting to the Queen' and it was in this capacity that he organized the celebration parade along the Mall to mark the Queen Mother's 90th birthday.

Charles first met Camilla in 1972 while he was serving in the Navy and she was dating his polo friend Andrew Parker Bowles, then a captain in the Household Cavalry. He was immediately smitten by this vivacious, attractive young woman who shared his passion for hunting and polo. According to the Prince's biographer, Penny Junor, he fell deeply in love with Camilla. 'She was in love with him and would have married him at the drop of a hat. Alas, he never asked her. He dithered and hedged his bets, and could not resist the charms of other women, until Camilla gave up on him. It was only when she was irretrievably gone that the Prince realized what he had lost.'

Diana frequently discussed her concerns about Camilla with James Gilbey. He provided a sympathetic ear as Diana poured out her feelings of anger and anguish about Camilla. He said that she was unable to put out of her mind the one-time relationship Camilla enjoyed with Prince Charles. 'As a result their marriage is a charade. The whole prospect of Camilla drives her spare. I can understand it. I mean what the hell is that woman doing in her house? This is what she sees as the gross injustice of the thing.'

Gilbey, a motor-trade executive, knew Diana from the age of 17 but became much closer to her when they met at a party hosted by Julia Samuel. They talked long into the night about their respective love lives — he about a failed romance, she about her fading marriage. One of their loving late-night telephone conversations from this time was later to be made embarrassingly public. The so-called Squidgygate tapes revealed that Gilbey and the Princess were more than friends. However, in the summer of 1989 she was concerned about winning her husband back and forcing him to make a break with 'the Highgrove Set'. He recalled: 'There was enormous pride at stake. Her sense of rejection, by her husband and the royal system, was apparent.'

At that time she was under pressure from her own family and the royal family to try and make a new start. Diana even agreed that another baby might provide a solution to the problem. However, her olive branch was met with the negative indifference which then characterized their relations. At times the waves of anger, frustration, wounded pride and sense of rejection threatened to overwhelm her. When Prince Charles was convalescing from his broken right arm in 1990, he spent his days at

Highgrove or Balmoral where Camilla Parker Bowles was a regular visitor. Diana stayed at Kensington Palace, unwanted, unloved and humiliated. She unburdened her feelings to Gilbey: 'James, I'm just so fed up with it. If I let it get to me I will just upset myself more. So the thing to do is to involve myself in my work; get out and about. If I stop to think I'll go mad.'

As a mutual friend, who watched the royal couple's gradual estrangement, noted: 'You can't blame Diana for the anger she must feel given the fact that her husband appears to have this long-standing friendship with another woman. The marriage has deteriorated too much to want to win him back. It's just too late.'

In the early 1990s, Diana's renewed self-confidence and her changed priorities, combined with skilful counselling, blunted the anger she felt towards Camilla. As her marriage crumbled, she began to see Camilla as a less threatening figure and more of a useful means of keeping her husband out of her life. None the less, there were times when she still found her husband's indifference deeply wounding. When Camilla and her husband joined Prince Charles on a holiday in Turkey shortly before his polo accident, she didn't complain, just as she bore, through gritted teeth, Camilla's regular invitations to Balmoral and Sandringham. When Charles flew to Italy in 1991 on a sketching holiday, Diana's friends noted that Camilla was staying at another villa a short drive away. On her return Mrs Parker Bowles made it quite clear that any suggestion of impropriety was absurd. During a rare, family summer holiday when the Prince and Princess and their children joined other guests on a Greek millionaire's yacht Diana noted that her husband kept in touch with Camilla by telephone.

They would meet socially on occasion but there was no love lost between these two women locked into an eternal triangle of rivalry. At social engagements they were at pains to avoid each other. Diana developed a technique in public of locating Camilla as quickly as possible and then, depending on her mood, she watched Charles when he looked in her direction or simply evaded her gaze. 'It was a morbid game,' said a friend. Days before the Salisbury Cathedral spire appeal concert Diana knew that Camilla was going. She vented her frustration in conversations with friends so that on the day of the event the Princess was able to watch the eye contact between her husband and Camilla with quiet amusement.

In December 1991 all those years of pent-up emotion came flooding out at a memorial service for Leonora Knatchbull, the six-year-old daughter of Lord and Lady Romsey, who had died of cancer. As Diana left the service, held at St James's Palace, she was photographed in tears. She was weeping in sorrow but also in anger. Diana was upset that Camilla Parker Bowles, who had only known the Romseys for a short time, was also present at such an intimate family service. It was a point she made vigorously to her husband as they travelled back to Kensington Palace in their chauffeur-driven limousine. When they arrived at Kensington Palace the Princess felt so distressed that she ignored the staff Christmas party, which was then in full swing, and went to her sitting room to recover her composure. Diplomatically, Peter Westmacott, the Waleses' deputy private secretary, sent her avuncular detective, Ken Wharfe, to help calm her.

The incident at the memorial service brought to the surface her resentment at her treatment by the royal system and the charade of life at Kensington Palace. Shortly afterwards she vented that anger and frustration when she spoke to a close friend. She made clear that her sense of duty impelled her to fulfil her obligations as the Princess of Wales yet her difficult private life led her seriously to consider leaving the royal family.

Amid the wreckage of their relationship there were still friends who felt that the rage and jealousy Diana felt towards her husband was a reflection of her innermost desire to win him back. Those observers were in a minority. Most were deeply pessimistic about the future. Oonagh Toffolo noted: 'I had great hopes until a year ago, now I have no hope at all. It would need a miracle. It is a great pity that these two people with so much to give to the world can't give it together.'

A similar conclusion had been reached by a friend, who had discussed Diana's troubles with her at length. She said: 'If he had done the work in the early days and had the proper concern for his wife, they would have so much more going for them. However, they have now reached a point of no return.'

The words 'there is no hope' were often repeated when friends talked about the Waleses' life together. As one of her closest friends said: 'She has conquered all the challenges presented to her within the profession and got her public life down to a fine art. But the central issue is that she is not fulfilled as a woman because she doesn't have a relationship with her husband.' The continual conflict and suspicion in their private life inevitably coloured their public work. Nominally the Prince and Princess were a partnership, in reality they acted independently, rather like the managing directors of rival companies. As one former member of the Wales Household said: 'You very quickly learn to choose whose side you are on — his or hers. There is no middle course. There is a magic line that courtiers can cross once or twice. Cross it too often and you are out. That is not a basis for a stable career.'

Similar sentiments were expressed by the small army of executives who passed through Kensington Palace. In 1992 David Archibald, Prince Charles's financial director, known as the comptroller, abruptly resigned. Staff in both offices felt that the main reason why he was leaving was the difficulty of working in an atmosphere of mutual distrust and jealousy between the two antagonistic offices. As ever the Prince of Wales, who has been described as 'Britain's worst boss', blamed the departure on his wife. Archibald had good reason to throw in the towel. The rivalry between Charles and Diana ranged from the petty to the pathetic. The first sign of this in public was when both made important speeches, Charles about education, Diana about Aids, on the same day. One inevitably stole the thunder from the other and such behaviour was part of a continuing cycle. When the couple returned from a joint visit to Canada in 1991, the Princess wrote a number of thank-you letters to the various charities and government organizations who had arranged the trip. When they were passed to her husband to 'top and tail' with his own sentiments he went through each letter and crossed out every reference to 'we' and inserted 'I' before he was prepared to sign them.

This was not an unusual occurrence. In January 1992, when the Prince sent a bouquet of flowers to Mother Teresa of Calcutta, who was recovering from a heart condition, he ordered his private secretary Richard Aylard to make sure they were sent only from him, not jointly. It mattered little. Diana arranged a special meeting whereby she flew to the hospital in Rome to see the woman she so admired. Again, during a planning meeting for their joint visit to India in February 1992, it was felt that Diana should concentrate on promoting family planning issues. 'I think we will change your profile from Aids to family planning,' remarked a diplomat who was impressed by her performance in Pakistan. When Prince Charles was asked about the idea he complained that he wanted to spearhead that particular issue. For once Diana told staff to ignore 'the spoiled boy'. As one of her closest friends said: 'It's time he started seeing her as an asset, not as a threat, and accepted her as an equal partner. At the moment her position within the organization is a very lonely one.'

Consultation between the couple was invariably adversarial, taking place within an atmosphere of mutual recrimination. It was so unusual to have a calm discussion about problems that when the Prince approached Diana to consider a confidential report about staff abuses of the royal name, prepared by a senior courtier, the Princess, used to curt indifference, was genuinely surprised. There was concern that the royal name and royal notepaper were being used to acquire clothes discounts, theatre tickets and other perks. While the issue required delicate handling, the most surprising aspect of the episode was the liaison between the Prince and Princess.

While their normal working relations were pervaded by an atmosphere of intrigue and competitive resentment, Diana still felt a sense of responsibility towards her husband. When he returned to public duties in 1991, following a lengthy recuperation from his broken arm, he intended to make a bizarre 'statement' regarding the intense speculation surrounding his injury. He instructed his staff to find a false arm with a hook on the end so that he could appear in public like a real-life Captain Hook. Diana was consulted by senior courtiers who were worried that he would make a fool of himself. She suggested that a false arm should be obtained but then conveniently mislaid shortly before he was to attend a medical meeting in Harley Street, central London. While Charles was annoyed by the subterfuge, his staff were relieved that his dignity had been preserved thanks to Diana's timely intervention.

It would be a mistake to assume that the contest between the Prince and Princess of Wales was fought on even terms. The Princess may have been the bigger attraction to the press and the public but inside the palace walls she was dependent upon revenues from the Duchy of Cornwall, controlled by her husband, to fund her private office while her junior status within the royal hierarchy meant that Prince Charles always had the final say. Everything from her attendance at his planning meetings, to the composition of joint overseas tours and the office structure, was ultimately decided by the Prince of Wales. When she suggested she start a 'Princess of Wales Trust' to raise money for her various charities he refused to countenance the idea, knowing that it would take away kudos and cash from his own Prince's Trust charity.

During the Gulf crisis the Princess and her sister-in-law, the Princess Royal, independently came up with the idea of visiting British troops stationed in the Saudi Arabian theatre of operations. They planned to fly out together and were rather looking forward to driving round the desert in tanks and meeting the boys in khaki. However, the Queen's private secretary, Sir Robert Fellowes, intervened. The scheme was shelved as it was thought that it would be more appropriate if a more senior royal represented the family. So Prince Charles flew to the Gulf while the Princess of Wales was assigned the supporting task of travelling to Germany to meet the wives and families of troops.

The constant needle and edge in their working relationship was matched by a cloak of secrecy the warring offices threw around their rival operations. Diana had to use all her guile to tease out information from her husband's office before she flew to Pakistan on her first major solo overseas tour in 1991. She was due to stop over in Oman where Prince Charles was trying to woo the Sultan to win funding for an architectural college. Curious by nature, Diana wanted to know more but realized that a direct approach to Prince Charles or his senior advisers would receive a dusty response. Instead she penned a short memo to the Prince's private secretary, Commander Richard Aylard, and innocently asked if there was anything in the way of briefing notes she needed for the short stopover in Oman. The result was that, as she was travelling on official Foreign Office business, the Prince was forced to reveal his hand.

In this milieu of sullen suspicion, secrecy was a necessary and constant companion. Caution was her watchword. There were plenty of eyes and ears as well as police video cameras to catch the sound of a voice raised in anger or the sight of an unfamiliar visitor. Tongues wag and stories circulate with electrifying efficiency. This was why, when she was learning about her bulimic condition, she hid books on the subject from prying eyes. She dared not bring home tapes from her astrology readings nor read the satirical magazine *Private Eye* with its wickedly accurate portrayal of her husband in case it attracted unfavourable comment. The telephone was her lifeline and she spent hours chatting to friends: 'Sorry about the noise, I was trying to get my tiara on,' she told one disconcerted friend.

She was a hostage to fortune, held captive by her public image, bound by the constitutional circumstance of her unique position as the Princess of Wales and a prisoner of her day-to-day life. Her friends referred to the acronym POW as meaning 'prisoner of war'. Indeed the cloying claustrophobia of royal life merely served to exacerbate her genuine fear of confined spaces. This was brought home to her in 1991 when she went to the National Hospital for a body scan because her doctors feared she may have a cervical rib, a benign growth that often traps nerves below the shoulder blade. Like many patients, once she was inside the enclosed scanning machine, she felt very panicky and needed to be calmed down with a tranquillizer. It meant that an operation which should have lasted 15 minutes took two hours.

She began to send scented candles rather

than letters of thanks to those who supplied goods and services in case her well-meaning notes fell into the wrong hands. Again, before she went skiing in Austria in 1992 with her children and her friends Catherine Soames and David Linley, she agonized over inviting Major David Waterhouse. She had comforted him at his mother's funeral in January and felt a holiday would help ease the loss he felt over her death. However, Diana, who had been seen regularly in his company, worried that the wrong interpretation would be placed on his presence and his own life would come under undue scrutiny as a result. So she did not invite him. Although her children gave her immense joy, she also knew that they were her passport to the outside world. She could take them to the theatre, cinema and parks without exciting adverse comment from the media. There were drawbacks, however. When she took Prince Harry and a party of friends to see Jason Donovan in the musical *Joseph and the Amazing Technicolor Dreamcoat,* the Princess had to lurk outside the gentlemen's lavatory during the interval waiting for her charges.

She had to conduct her social life with caution. While her husband had been able to conduct his private life unnoticed for years, Diana was keenly and resentfully aware that every time she was seen with an unattached male, however innocently, it made headline news, as when she spent the weekend at the country home of Philip Dunne's parents. There was no respite. She had to cancel a lunch date with her friend Terence Stamp because she was made aware that his apartment in the Albany was being 'staked out' by newspaper photographers.

Diana's enemies within were the courtiers who watched and judged her every move. If Diana was the current star of the Windsor roadshow then senior courtiers were the producers who hovered in the background waiting to criticize her every slip. When she spent three days with her mother in Italy she was driven everywhere by Antonio Pezzo, a handsome member of the family who were her hosts. As she said goodbye she impulsively kissed him on the cheek. She was carpeted for that gesture just as she was ticked off for praising the way the Prime Minister, John Major, behaved during the Gulf crisis. It was a human reaction to his difficult position as a novice Prime Minister but the Queen's private secretary, Sir Robert Fellowes, felt it sufficiently political to be worthy of unfavourable comment.

The smallest breach of royal behaviour

was deserving of complaint. After a film première, the Princess attended a party where she enjoyed a long conversation with Liza Minnelli. The following morning it was pointed out to her that it was not done to attend these occasions. The party had one happy result, however. She enjoyed the rapport with the Hollywood star who talked at length about her difficult life and told her simply that when she felt down she thought of Diana and that helped her endure. It was a touching and very honest conversation between two women who had suffered much in life and which formed the basis of their long-distance friendship.

It was little wonder then that the Princess, trusting by nature, trusted very few in the royal organization. She opened much of her own mail when she returned from her morning swim at Buckingham Palace so that she could see at first hand what the general public were thinking. It meant that she did not have to rely on the cautious filter of her staff. There were several satisfying results of this policy. A letter from a father whose son was dying of Aids particularly touched her. Before he died, the young man's last request was to meet the Princess of Wales. His father wrote to Diana in June 1991 but with little hope of success. After reading his plea, Diana personally arranged for his son to attend an Aids hostel in London run by the Lighthouse Trust which she was scheduled to visit. Her thoughtful gesture made his dying wish come true. If the letter had been processed in the usual way the family would probably have received a sympathetic but non-committal reply from a lady-in-waiting.

Such was her lack of confidence in these traditional royal helpmates, whose duties were to accompany her on public engagements and undertake administrative tasks, that they were gradually being phased out. She took to employing her elder sister Sarah in this capacity — she accompanied the Princess to Budapest in Hungary on an official visit in March 1992 — or would go on what she called her 'Awaydays' on her own. As one friend remarked: 'She had these terrific run-ins with her ladies-in-waiting, particularly Anne Beckwith-Smith (her one-time private secretary). She felt they were holding her back, being too protective and too "in" with the system.'

Instead she preferred to consult those who were tangential to the system. From time to time she telephoned Major-General Sir Christopher Airey at his Devon home for advice. Airey, who had been abruptly dismissed as Prince Charles's private secretary in 1991, was sufficiently aware of the machinations within the system to guide her sensibly. For a time Jimmy Savile helped smooth her public image while Terence Stamp gave her general guidance on her speech-making. She also relied on a coterie of unofficial counsellors, who preferred to remain anonymous, to sound out ideas and problems. They polished her speeches, advised on ticklish staff problems and gave fair warning of possible publicity difficulties.

She was attracted to outsiders precisely because she felt so alienated from the royal system. As James Gilbey said: 'She gets on much better with them than the men in grey because they [the men in grey] are tied up with preserving a system which she feels is outdated. There is a natural built-in confrontation there. They are trying to uphold something and she is trying to get out.' Her astrologer Felix Lyle observed: 'She has a soaring spirit and optimism which is easily defeated. Dominated by those with strong character, she does not yet have enough self-confidence to take on the system.'

It was a view endorsed by another friend who said: 'The whole royal business terrified her. They gave her no confidence or support.' As her confidence developed she came to believe that she could not achieve her true potential within the existing royal restraints. She told friends: 'Inside the system I was treated very differently, as though I was an oddball. I felt I wasn't good enough. Now, thank God, I think it's okay to be different.'

Diana led a confusing double life where she was celebrated by the public but watched in doubtful and often jealous silence by her husband and the rest of his family. The world judged that she had dusted off the dowdy image of the House of Windsor but within the royal family, reared on values of control, distance and formality, she was seen as an outsider and as a problem. She was tactile, emotional, gently irreverent and spontaneous. For a white-gloved, stiff-upper-lip institution with a large 'Do not touch' sign hanging from its crown, the Princess of Wales was a threat. Experience had taught her not to trust or confide in members of the royal family. She realized that blood ties matter most. As a result she kept a deliberate distance from her in-laws, skirting round issues, avoiding confrontations and locking herself away in her ivory tower. It was a double-edged sword as she failed to build any bridges, so essential in a closed world infected by family and office politics. She had few allies within the royal family. 'I don't rattle their cages and they don't rattle mine,' she said.

So although she loved Scotland and had been brought up in Norfolk, she found the atmosphere at Balmoral and Sandringham totally draining of her spirit and vitality. It was during these family holidays that her bulimia was at its worst and when she would try any ploy to escape for a few days. Diana lived the reality behind the public impression of unshakeable unity the monarchy exudes. She knew that in private the contemporary Court was not so very different from previous reigns with its squabbling, feuds and infighting.

At the time, the heart of the royal family was the tightly knit and implacable troika of the Queen Mother and her daughters, the Queen and Princess Margaret. As author Douglas Keay perceptively observed in his profile of the Queen: 'Cross one and you cross them all.' Diana's relations with these three central characters were uneven. She had much time for Princess Margaret, a neighbour at Kensington Palace, whom she acknowledged as giving her the most help in acclimatizing herself to the rarefied royal world. 'I've always adored Margo,' she said.

'I love her to bits and she's been wonderful to me from day one.'

Her relations with the Queen Mother were much less cordial. Diana saw her London home, Clarence House, as the fount of all negative comment about herself and her mother. She kept a distrustful distance from this matriarchal figure, describing social occasions hosted by the Queen Mother as stiff and overly formal. It was, after all, Diana's grandmother, Ruth, Lady Fermoy, the Queen Mother's lady-in-waiting, who testified in court about her daughter's unsuitability to look after her four children. Her view of Frances Shand Kydd was accepted by the judge and the hostility and bitterness within the divided Spencer family remained for a long time. At the same time the Queen Mother, unfavourably predisposed to Diana and her mother, exercised an enormous influence over the Prince of Wales. It was a mutual adoration society from which Diana was effectively excluded. 'The Queen Mother drives a wedge between Diana and the others,' noted a friend. 'As a result she makes every excuse to avoid her.'

Diana's relationship with the Queen was much friendlier. However, it was governed by the fact that she was married to her eldest son and the future monarch. In the early days Diana was quite simply terrified of her mother-in-law. She kept to the formal obsequies — dropping a deep curtsy each time they met — but otherwise kept her distance. During their infrequent and rather brittle *tête-à-têtes* about the Waleses' floundering marriage the Queen indicated that Diana's persistent bulimia was a cause, not a symptom, of their difficulties.

The Sovereign also implied that the instability in their marriage was an overriding consideration in any musings she may have had about abdication. Naturally this did not please Prince Charles who refused to speak to his mother for several days following her 1991 Christmas broadcast when she spoke of her intention to serve the nation and the Commonwealth for 'some years to come'. For a man who holds his mother in total awe that silence was a measure of his anger. Once again he blamed the Princess of Wales. As he stalked along the corridors at Sandringham the Prince complained to anyone who would listen about the state of his marriage. Diana pointed out to him that he had already abdicated his regal responsibilities by allowing his brothers, Princes Andrew and Edward, to take over as counsellors of state, the official 'stand-ins' for the Sovereign when she is abroad on official business. If the Prince showed such indifference to these nominal constitutional duties, she asked sweetly, why should his mother give him the job?

Certainly the early 1990s saw the Queen and her daughter-in-law develop a more relaxed and cordial relationship. At a garden party in 1991 the Princess felt confident enough to essay a little joke about the Queen's black hat. She complimented her on the choice, remarking how it would come in useful for funerals. In a more serious vein they held confidential discussions about her eldest son's state of mind. At times the Queen found the direction of his life unfocused and his behaviour odd and erratic. It did not escape her notice that he was as unhappy with his lot as was his wife.

While Diana found the monarchy as then organized a crumbling institution, she had a deep respect for the manner in which the Queen had conducted herself during her reign. Indeed, much as she would like to have left her husband, Diana emphasized to the Queen: 'I will never let you down.' Before she attended a garden party on a stifling July afternoon in 1991, a friend offered Diana a fan to take with her. She refused saying: 'I can't do that. My mother-in-law is going to be standing there with her handbag, gloves, stockings and shoes.' It was a sentiment expressed in admiring tones for the Sovereign's complete self-control in every circumstance, however trying.

At the same time the Princess had to adjust to other cross-currents within the family. While Diana enjoyed an amicable association with Prince Philip, whom she regarded as a loner, she realized that her husband was intimidated by his father. She accepted that his relationship with his eldest son was 'tricky, very tricky'. Charles longed to be patted on the back by his father while Prince Philip would have liked his son to consult him more frequently and at least recognize his contribution to public debate. It rankled with Prince Philip, for instance, that he started the public discussion about the environment but it was Prince Charles who won the audience.

As with her father-in-law, Diana enjoyed a distant but perfectly friendly relationship with her royal sister-in-law, the Princess Royal. Diana appreciated at first hand the difficulties a royal woman faced within the organization and had nothing but admiration for her independence and endeavours, particularly on behalf of the Save the Children Fund of which she is president. While their children often played together, Diana would never have thought of confiding in the Princess or of telephoning her for lunch. She was pleased to see her when they met at family occasions but that was as far as it went. The media made a fuss at the time of Prince Harry's christening when Diana's decision not to choose Anne as a godparent was seen as a sign of their rancorous relations. The Princess was not asked simply because she was already an aunt to the boys and her role as godparent would merely duplicate matters. As with all the royal family, there was always a divide between the two Princesses. Diana is an outsider by birth and inclination; Anne was born into the system. From time to time the Princess Royal did show where her loyalties ultimately lay. A confrontation at Balmoral in 1991 revealed the isolation of the two commoners, the Princess of Wales and the Duchess of York.

That confrontation on a warm August evening, as the family enjoyed a barbecue in the grounds of Balmoral castle, brought to the surface the nascent tensions and conflicts within their ranks. There was concern about an incident when Diana and Fergie had raced each other around the private roads in the Queen Mother's Daimler and a four-wheel-drive estate vehicle. The argument became much more personal, focusing primarily on the Duchess of York. It resulted in her stalking off. Diana explained on Fergie's behalf that it was very difficult to marry into the royal family and that the Duchess was finding it harder the longer she stayed within their confines. She impressed upon the Queen the need to give the Duchess greater leeway, emphasizing that she was at the end of her tether. This was confirmed shortly afterwards by Fergie who told friends that 1991 was the last time she would visit Balmoral. She was as good as her word. Eight months later the separation between the Duke and Duchess was announced.

It was a vivid contrast with the Duchess of York's first holiday at the Queen's summer retreat five years earlier when she had so impressed the royal family with her enthusiasm and vigour. Over the years Diana had watched, often sympathetically, her sister-in-law being battered by the media and overwhelmed by the royal system which had gradually ground down her spirit. At times the floundering behaviour of the Duchess of York resembled not so much life imitating art but life imitating satire. As her clothes, her mothering instincts and her ill-chosen friends came in for caustic criticism, the Duchess turned to an assorted group of clairvoyants, tarot card readers, astrologers and other soothsayers to help her find a path through the royal maze. She was introduced to some by her friend Steve Wyatt, the adopted son of a Texan oil billionaire, but many she discovered for herself. Her frequent visits to Madame Vasso, a spiritualist who healed troubled minds and bodies by seating them under a blue plastic pyramid, were typical of the influences upon this increasingly restless and unhappy individual.

There were days when the Duchess had her fortune read and her astrological transits analysed every few hours. She tried to live her life by their predictions, her volatile spirit clinging to every scrap of solace in their musings. While Diana, like many members of the royal family, was interested and intrigued by the 'New Age' approach to life, she was not ruled by every prophecy.

The Duchess, however, was held in their thrall, earnestly discussing their conclusions with her friends. The result was that the Duchess played Iago to Diana's Othello. She was an insistent voice in her ear, whispering, beseeching and imploring, predicting disaster and doom for the royal family while urging Diana to escape from the royal institution. It was no exaggeration to state that barely a week passed without the Duchess of York discussing the latest portents with her sister-in-law and her close friends and advisers. In May 1991, when the marriage of the Prince and Princess of Wales came under renewed scrutiny, Fergie's 'spooks' — as her friends describe them — predicted that Prince Andrew would soon become King and she the Queen.

While the Duke was excited by the prospect, his wife became increasingly disillusioned with her role. For a woman used to catching planes like others hail taxis, the claustrophobia of the royal world was more than she could bear. In August her soothsayers forecast a problem involving a royal car; in September they said an imminent royal birth would create a crisis. Specific dates were mentioned but even when they passed without incident, the Duchess kept faith in her oracles. By November there was talk of a death in the family and as Diana prepared to spend Christmas at Sandringham with the royal family, she was warned by the Duchess that there would be a row between herself and Prince Charles. He would try to walk out but the Queen would stop him.

Interspersed with these dire portents was

the almost daily drip, drip, drip of pleading, reason and wish-fulfilment as the Duchess beseeched the Princess to join her and leave the royal family. Her invitation must have been an attractive prospect for a woman in an impossible position, but Diana had come to trust her own judgement.

In March 1992 the Duchess finally decided formally to separate from her husband and leave the royal family. The Princess watched the acrimonious collapse of her friend's marriage with sadness and alarm. She saw at first hand how quickly the Queen's courtiers could turn against her. They viciously attacked the Duchess, accusing her of behaving in a manner unbecoming the royal family and cited various incidents when she had tried to profit from her royal associations. Courtiers even claimed, falsely, that the Duchess had hired a public relations company to publicize her departure from the royal family. As a BBC correspondent said: 'The knives are out for the Duchess at Buckingham Palace.' It was a foretaste of what Diana would have to endure if she decided to travel along that same road.

8
'I Did My Best'

A few days before the Queen celebrated the 40th anniversary of her accession, the Duke and Duchess of York drove from Buckingham Palace to Sandringham to see the Sovereign. On that bleak Wednesday in late January 1992 the royal couple formally discussed an issue which had troubled them for many months: their marriage. They had agreed that, after five years of married life, it would be sensible if they separated. The Duchess had become increasingly disillusioned with her life within the royal family and was depressed by continual and hurtful criticism, both inside and outside the Palace, which showed no sign of abating. The final straw was the raucous discussion in the media about her relationship with Steve Wyatt, headlines provoked by the theft of photographs taken when the Duchess, Wyatt and others were on holiday in Morocco.

During that meeting at Sandringham the couple agreed to the Queen's suggestion that they should have a 'cooling off' period of two months to allow time to reflect. Consequently the Duchess undertook only a couple of official engagements, spending the rest of the time with her family at Sunninghill Park or discussing her options with lawyers, members of the royal family, including the Princess of Wales and the Princess Royal, and close friends.

One of the first to be given the news was the Prince of Wales who was then staying on the Norfolk estate. He spoke to her about his own marriage difficulties, emphasizing that his constitutional position as direct heir to the throne made any thought of separation from Diana almost unthinkable. In a ringing rebuke the Duchess replied: 'At least I've been true to myself.' It is a sentiment which lay at the heart of the dilemma facing the Princess of Wales and struck at the foundations of the modern monarchy.

The chronic instability of the marriage of the Prince and Princess of Wales and the collapse of the Duke and Duchess of York's marriage were far more than personal tragedies. It was a signal that a necessary experiment born of changed historical circumstances had failed. When George V granted permission for his son, the Duke of York, to marry a commoner, Lady Elizabeth Bowes-Lyon, he was recognizing the reality that the First World War had harvested European monarchies and dried up the supply of suitable royal brides and bridegrooms. The Yorks' wedding began the transition of a virtual royal caste, where royalty married royalty, to a class within society. But the grafting of commoners, however high born, onto the Hanoverian tree has been a disaster. Apart from the marriages of the present Queen and the Queen Mother, and more recently Prince William, every significant union between royalty and commoner has ended in divorce; Princess Margaret and Antony Armstrong-Jones, Princess Anne and Captain Mark Phillips, the Duke and Duchess of York and the Prince and Princess of Wales.

Is this state of affairs simply a reflection of the changing face of society or does it raise questions about the way the royal family relates to outsiders? Certainly when Lady Diana Spencer wed Prince Charles, it seemed to her — and later Sarah Ferguson — that she married into a family as welded to tradition and content in their insularity as any obscure South Sea island tribe. While their idiosyncrasies help shield them from the outside world, they also made the task of a newcomer, who did not know the unspoken rules of the game, virtually impossible. The royal family is testimony to playwright Alan Bennett's maxim: 'Every family has a secret and the secret is that it is not like any other family.' The Queen and her sister, Princess Margaret, were the last generation immunized from reality. From an early age they lived in palaces, absolutely cocooned from the outside world. The gilded cage was their home and their life. A walk down the street, an afternoon's solitary shopping, waiting in line and making ends meet; these freedoms, however dubious, were never part of their lives. When Princess Elizabeth secretly joined the throng celebrating VE Day outside Buckingham Palace it was seen as such an unusual event that it was eventually made into a Hollywood movie. For all their privileges, their legions of servants, their chauffeur-driven cars, private yachts and planes, they were prisoners of society's expectations and puppets of the system. Duty, obligation and sacrifice were the expected and accepted threads of their lives and the weft and weave of the fabric of the Crown. The pursuit of personal happiness, as Princess Margaret discovered when she attempted to marry a divorcee, Group Captain Peter Townsend, has been sacrificed on the altar of monarchy and its moral ethos.

The Queen, groomed for the role, has performed those traditional and expected functions of the Crown supremely well, so much so that she leaves an unattainable benchmark for her successor. The mould has been deliberately broken. As Elizabeth Longford, the Queen's friend and biographer, has argued, one of the central achievements of the reign has been to educate her children in the real world. It has meant that her children are a hybrid generation, enjoying a taste of freedom but anchored to the world of castles and royal protocol. The actions, particularly of the Prince of Wales, demonstrate the particular perils of allowing future sovereigns to breathe, even for a short time, the air of freedom. Unlike his predecessors, doubt, uncertainty and questioning have been added to his inherited faith in and acceptance of royal traditions.

Enter into this equation then, the expectations and values of the commoners who have come into the family. It has proved an impossible hurdle to overcome. Lord Snowdon and Captain Mark Phillips were the first to fall, even though they had careers, photography and equestrian pursuits respectively, which took them outside the royal routine. The Princess of Wales and Duchess of York enjoyed no such luxury. It was perhaps inevitable then that Diana, who watched the royal family from the inside, saw a yawning gap between the way the world was moving and how it was perceived by the royal family. She believed that they were caught in an emotional timewarp without the necessary vision to appreciate the changes that have taken place in society. It was forcibly demonstrated during the royal family's traditional Christmas at Sandringham in 1991. During dinner one evening, Diana tentatively raised the question of the future of the British monarchy in a federal Europe. The Queen, Prince Charles and the rest of the royal family looked at her as if she were mad and continued with their debate on who had shot the last pheasant of the day, a discussion which occupied the rest of the evening.

As a friend said: 'She finds the monarchy claustrophobic and completely outdated with no relevance to today's life and problems. She feels that it is a crumbling institution and believes that the family won't know what has hit it in a few years' time unless it changes too.'

Diana discussed with her counsellor Stephen Twigg these serious doubts about the existing foundations of the monarchy. He argued: 'If the royal family doesn't change and their relationships with the rest of Society don't change, it is on a hiding to nothing. It can only deteriorate as a useful organ of society. It must remain dynamic and respond to changes. It's not just the royal family who must change but society itself must examine the way it looks at the royal family. Do we want the royal family to be revered because of their position or in a modern society do we want to admire them because of the way they cope with the traumas and tribulations of everyday life and learn from them in the process?' One of the many ironies of her life is that Diana's impact on the royal family is measured by how much more accommodating the House of Windsor is now to newcomers. It is noticeable that the Queen frequently joined Prince William's bride Catherine Middleton, now the Duchess of Cambridge, in the early days of her royal career. Certainly lessons have been learned — but at a price.

Although Diana successfully shook off the traditional image of the fairytale princess concerned exclusively with shopping and fashion it still coloured the preconceptions of those she met for the first time. She was used to being patronized. As she told close friends: 'It happens a lot. It's interesting to see people's reactions to me. They have one impression in mind and then, as they talk to me, I can see it changing.' At the same time her struggles within the royal family made her realize that she must not hide behind the conventional mask of monarchy. The spontaneity, the tactile compassion and the generosity of spirit she displayed in public were very genuine. It was not an act for public consumption. The Princess, who appreciated how the royal world anaesthetizes individuals from reality, was fiercely determined that her boys were prepared for the outside world in a way unknown to previous royal generations. Normally royal children have been trained to hide their feelings and emotions from others, constructing a shield to deflect intrusive inquiry. Diana believed that William and Harry should be open and honest to the possibilities within themselves and the variety of approaches to understanding life. As she said: 'I want to bring them up with security. I hug my children to death and get into bed with them at night. I always feed them love and affection — it's so important.'

The cultural code of the stiff upper lip was not for her boys. She had been teaching them that it is not 'sissy' to show their feelings to others. When she took Prince William to watch the German tennis star Steffi Graf win the women's singles final at Wimbledon in 1991 they left the royal box to go backstage and congratulate her on her victory. As Graf walked off court down the dimly lit corridor to the dressing room, royal mother and son thought Steffi looked so alone and vulnerable out of the spotlight. So first Diana, then William, gave her a kiss and an affectionate hug.

The way the Princess introduced her boys to her dying friend, Adrian Ward-Jackson, was a practical lesson in seeing the reality of life and death. When Diana told her eldest son that Adrian had died, his instinctive response revealed his maturity. 'Now he's out of pain at last and really happy.' At the same time the Princess was acutely aware of the added burdens of rearing two boys who were popularly known as 'the heir and the spare'. Self-discipline was part of the training. Every night at six o'clock the boys would sit down and write thank-you notes or letters to friends and family. It was a discipline which Diana's father instilled in her, so much so that if she returned from a dinner party at midnight she could not sleep easily until she had written her letter of thanks.

William and Harry were aware of their destiny. On one occasion the boys were discussing their futures with Diana. 'When I grow up I want to be a policeman and look after you, Mummy,' said William lovingly. Quick as a flash Harry replied, with a note of triumph in his voice, 'Oh no you can't, you've got to be king.'

As their uncle Earl Spencer recalled, their characters were very different from the public image. 'The press have always written up William as the terror and Harry as a rather quiet second son. In fact William is a very self-possessed, intelligent and mature boy and quite shy. He is quite formal and stiff, sounding older than his years when he answers the phone.' It is Harry who is the mischievous imp of the family. Harry's puckish character manifested itself to his uncle during the return flight from Necker, the Caribbean island owned by Virgin airlines boss Richard Branson. He recalled: 'Harry was presented with his breakfast. He had his headphones on and a computer game in front of him but he was determined to eat his croissant. It took him about five minutes to manoeuvre all his electronic gear, his knife, his croissant and his butter. When he eventually managed to get a mouthful there was a look of such complete satisfaction on his face. It was a really wonderful moment.'

His godparent Carolyn Bartholomew has said, without an ounce of prejudice, that Harry was 'the most affectionate, demonstrative and huggable little boy' while William was very much like his mother, 'intuitive, switched on and highly perceptive'. At first she thought the future king was a 'little terror'. 'He was naughty and had tantrums,' she recalls. 'But when I had my two children I realized that they are all like that at some point. In fact William is kind-hearted, very much like Diana. He would give you his last Rolo sweet. In fact he did on one occasion. He was longing for this sweet, he only had one left and he gave it to me.' Further evidence of his generous heart occurred when he gathered together all his pocket money, which only amounted to a few pence, and solemnly handed it over to her.

But he was no angel, as Carolyn saw when she visited Highgrove. Diana had just finished a swim in the open-air pool and had changed into a white towelling dressing gown as she waited for William to follow her. Instead he splashed about as though he were drowning and slowly sank to the bottom. His mother, not knowing whether it was a fake or not, struggled to get out of her robe. Then, realizing the urgency, she dived in, still in her dressing gown. At that moment he resurfaced, shouting and laughing at the success of his ruse. Diana was not amused.

Generally William was a youngster who displayed qualities of responsibility and thoughtfulness beyond his years and enjoyed a close rapport with his younger brother whom friends believe will make an admirable adviser behind the scenes when William eventually becomes king. Diana felt that in some way they will share the burdens of monarchy in the years to come. Her approach was conditioned by her firmly held belief that she would never become Queen and that her husband would never become King Charles III.

The boys were always a loving lifeline for the Princess in her isolated position. 'They mean everything to me,' she was fond of saying. However, in September 1991, when Prince Harry joined his elder brother at Ludgrove preparatory school, Diana had to face the prospect of an empty nest at Kensington Palace. 'She realizes that they are going to develop and expand and that soon a chapter in her own life will be complete,' observed James Gilbey.

The loss of her boys, at least during term-time, only served to highlight her cruel predicament — especially as the Duchess of York had already left the royal scene. Diana's world may have been characterized as an unstable equilibrium: the unhappiness of her marriage balanced by the satisfaction she found in her royal work, particularly among the sick and the dying; and the suffocating certainties of the royal system matched by her growing self-confidence in using the organization for the benefit of her causes.

During 1991 and 1992 her thinking about her royal position changed by the month but the general trend was towards staying within rather than leaving the organization. She felt impatience with the creaking machinery of monarchy rather than despair, businesslike indifference towards Prince Charles as opposed to shrinking deference and cool disregard of Camilla Parker Bowles rather than jealous rage. It was by no means a consistent development but her growing interest in how to control and reform the system as well as her serious commitment to use her position to do good in the world pointed to staying rather than taking flight.

At the same time the Duchess's departure merely added another element of uncertainty in an already precarious position.

It was not an issue for complacency. The Princess could be a volatile, impatient young woman whose moods regularly swung from optimism to despair. As astrologer Felix Lyle said: 'She is prone to depression, a woman who is easily defeated and dominated by those with a strong character. Diana has a self-destructive side. At any moment she could say "to hell with the lot of you" and go off. The potential is there. She is a flower waiting to bud.'

One evening she could be immensely mature, discussing death and the after-life with George Carey, then the new Archbishop of Canterbury, the next night giggling away at a bridge party. 'Sometimes she is possessed by a different spirit in response to breaking free from the yoke of responsibility that binds her,' observed Rory Scott who continued to see the Princess socially.

As her brother said: 'She has done very well to keep her sense of humour; that is what relaxes people around her. She is not at all stuffy and will make a joke happily either about herself or about something ridiculous which everyone has noticed but is too embarrassed to talk about.' Royal tours, these outdated exercises in stultifying boredom and ancient ceremonial, were rich seams for her finely tuned sense of the ridiculous. After a day watching native dancers in unbearable humidity or sipping a cup of some foul-tasting liquid, she often telephoned her friends to regale them with the latest absurdities. 'The things I do for England,' was her favourite phrase. She was particularly tickled when she asked Pope John Paul II about his 'wounds' during a private audience in the Vatican shortly after he had been shot. He thought she was talking about her 'womb' and congratulated her on her impending new arrival. While her instinct and intuition were finely honed, 'she understands the essence of people, what a person is about rather than who they are', said her friend Angela Serota. Diana recognized that her intellectual hinterland needed development. The girl who left school without an O-level to her name now harboured a quiet ambition to study psychology and mental health. 'Anything to do with people,' she said.

Although she had a tendency to be overly impressed by those with academic qualifications, Diana admired people who performed rather than pontificated. Richard Branson, the head of Virgin airlines, Baron Jacob Rothschild, the millionaire banker who restored Spencer House, and her cousin Viscount Linley who is chairman of the auction house Christie's and runs a successful furniture business, were high on her list. 'She likes the fact that David has been able to break out of the royal mould and do something positive,' said a friend. 'She envies too his good fortune in being able to walk down a street without a detective.'

For years her low intellectual self-esteem manifested itself in instinctive deference towards the judgements of her husband and senior courtiers. Now that she was clearer herself about her direction, she was prepared to argue about policy in a way that would have been unthinkable several years earlier. The results were tangible. Foreign Office diplomats, notoriously hidebound in their perceptions, were beginning to realize her true worth. They were impressed by the way she handled her first solo visit to Pakistan and subsequently discussed trips to Egypt and Iran. That was, as she would have said, a 'very grown-up' part of her royal life.

The speeches she was making with almost weekly regularity at this stage were a further satisfying feature of her royal life. Some she wrote herself, others were written by a small coterie of advisers, including her private secretary, Patrick Jephson, a firm ally in the royal camp as she personally appointed him in November 1991. It was a flexible, informal group who discussed with the Princess the points she wanted to make, researched the statistics and then constructed the speech.

The contrast between her real interests and the role assigned for her by her Palace 'minders' was amply demonstrated in March 1992 when, on the same day, she was guest of honour at the Ideal Home Exhibition and then in the evening, made a passionate and revelatory speech about Aids. There was an interesting symbolism to these engagements, separated only by a matter of hours but by a generation in personal philosophy. Her exhibition visit was organized by the Palace bureaucracy. They arranged everything from photo opportunities to guests lists while the subsequent media coverage concentrated on an off-the-cuff remark the Princess made about how she couldn't comment on her plans for National Bed Week because this was 'a family show'. It was light, bright and trite, the usual offering served up by the Palace to the media day in day out. The Princess performed her role impeccably, chatting to the various organizers and smiling for the cameras. However, her performance was just that, a role which the Palace, the media and public had come to expect.

A glimpse of the real Diana was on show later that evening when in the company of Professor Michael Adler and Margaret Jay, both Aids experts, she spoke to an audience of media executives at a dinner held at Claridge's. Her speech clearly came from the heart and her own experience. Afterwards she answered several rather long-winded questions from the floor, the first occasion in her royal life where she had subjected herself to this particular ordeal. This episode passed without a murmur in the media even though it represented a significant milestone in her life. It illustrated the considerable difficulties she faced in shifting perceptions of her job as a Princess, both inside and outside the Palace walls.

Her family, particularly her sisters, Jane and Sarah, and brother Charles, were aware of the appalling problems she was enduring. Jane had always given sensible advice and Sarah, from being dubious of her kid sister's success, was now very protective. 'You never criticize Diana in front of her,' noted a friend. Her relations with her mother and her father, when he was alive, were patchier. While Diana enjoyed a sporadic but affectionate relationship with her mother, she was robust in her reaction to news that her second husband, Peter Shand Kydd, had left her for another woman. In the summer of 1991 her bond with her father went through a difficult period following publicity surrounding the secret sale of treasures from Althorp House. The children, including the Princess, had written to their father objecting to the trade in family heirlooms. There were bitter exchanges, subsequently regretted, which deeply hurt the Princess of Wales. Even the Prince of Wales intervened, voicing his concern to Raine Spencer, who was typically forceful in her response. In the autumn a reconciliation between father and daughter was effected. During a leisurely tour around the world the late Earl Spencer was deeply touched by the affection shown towards his youngest daughter by so many strangers. He telephoned from America to tell her just how proud of her that made him feel.

The support of her family was matched by the encouragement of the small group of friends and counsellors who saw the real Diana, not the glowing image presented for public consumption. They were under no illusions that, while the Princess was a woman of considerable virtues, her character was prone to pessimism and despair, qualities which increased the likelihood of her leaving the system. The departure of the Duchess of York from the royal scene had exacerbated that defeatist side of her personality.

As she admitted to friends: 'Everyone said I was the Marilyn Monroe of the 1980s and I was adoring every minute of it. Actually I've never sat down and said: "Hooray, how wonderful." Never. The day I do we're in trouble. I am performing a duty as the Princess of Wales as long as my time is allocated but I don't see it being any longer than 15 years.'

While she had the right to feel sorry for herself, all too often this spilled over into self-imposed martyrdom. As James Gilbey said: 'When she is confident she extends herself and pushes out the barriers. As soon as there is a chink in the armour she immediately retreats away from the fray.' At times it was almost as though she wanted to engineer a hurt or a rejection before she was deserted by those she trusted and loved. This resulted in her blocking out her allies at crucial periods in her royal life when she most needed support.

As the Princess performed the impossible

balancing act which her life required at this stage, she drifted inexorably into obsession, continually discussing her problems. Her friend Carolyn Bartholomew argued that it was difficult not to be self-absorbed while the world was watching everything she did. 'How can you not be self-obsessed when half the world is watching everything you do; the high-pitched laugh when someone is talking to somebody famous must make you very, very cynical.' She endlessly debated the problems she faced in dealing with her husband, the royal family and their system. James Gilbey summed up Diana's dilemma: 'She can never be happy unless she breaks away but she won't break away unless Prince Charles does it. He won't do it because of his mother so they are never going to be happy. They will continue under the farcical umbrella of the royal family yet they will both lead completely separate lives.'

Her friend Carolyn Bartholomew, a sensible sounding-board throughout Diana's adult life, saw how that fundamental issue had clouded her character. 'She is kind, generous, sad and, in some ways, rather desperate. Yet she has maintained her self-deprecating sense of humour. A very shrewd but immensely sorrowful lady.'

Her royal future was by no means well defined. If she could have written her own script the Princess would have liked to have seen her husband go off with Camilla and attempt to discover the happiness he had not found with her, leaving Diana free to groom Prince William for his eventual destiny as the Sovereign. She even idly pondered the possibility of remarrying, intriguingly, to a foreigner. It was an idle pipe dream, at the time, as impossible as Prince Charles's wish to relinquish his regal position and run a farm in Italy. She had other more modest ambitions: to spend a weekend in Paris, take a course in psychology, learn the piano to concert grade and start painting again. The pace of her life made even these hopes seem grandiose, never mind her oft-repeated vision of the future where she saw herself one day settling abroad, probably in Italy or France. A more likely avenue was the unfolding vista of charity, community and social work which gave her a sense of self-worth and fulfilment. As her brother said: 'She has got a strong character. She does know what she wants and I think that after ten years she has got to a plateau now which she will continue to occupy for many years.'

As a child she sensed her special destiny,

as an adult she remained true to her instincts. Diana continued to carry the burden of public expectations while enduring considerable personal problems. Her achievement was to find her true self in the face of overwhelming odds. She continued to tread a different path from her husband, the royal family and their system and yet still conformed to their traditions. As she said: 'When I go home and turn my light off at night, I know I did my best.'

■ ■ ■ ■

DIANA: HER TRUE STORY — THE AFTERMATH

■ ■ ■ ■

9
'WE'D RUN OUT OF STEAM'

During the rush to deify Diana, Princess of Wales, following her tragic death on 31 August 1997, it could be difficult to remember that she was not always regarded as the epitome of everything a modern princess should be. After the initial, brutal, shock at her death and the demonstrations of love and regret, not just across Britain, but throughout the world, it was conveniently forgotten that she was for a time widely seen as a destructive influence upon the whole fabric of the British monarchy, and spoken of in terms a good deal less kind than the cliché 'loose cannon'. Even before her official separation from Prince Charles in December 1992, the Establishment, and her husband's supporters, swung into action. If there was much that was both self-interested and misogynistic about the pronouncements that filtered out, they nevertheless had the effect of inducing in the public a cynical view of her actions and intentions, and in the media something generally rather less than benevolent.

The starting gun for the full-scale 'War of the Waleses' was fired following the publication of my book *Diana: Her True Story* in June 1992. As far as the beleaguered Princess was concerned it was both a lifeboat and a passport. The book, written with her secret co-operation and complicity, was her testament, the evidence of her determination that she was no longer prepared to live a lie, to put up with the misery of her life within the royal family. Here was the chance both to escape from the prison of her marriage and to give her own version. While she dreaded its publication, it was nevertheless something she also badly wanted: a chance to put her case, to speak to the people over the heads of the Palace.

In the event, however, the effect of the book's appearance was even more shattering than anyone had predicted. The Palace were horrified, the media outraged and the public profoundly shocked. What followed was not always edifying, let alone fair.

The *Sunday Times* began serializing the original edition of *Diana: Her True Story* on 7 June 1992, under the front-page headline 'Diana driven to five suicide bids by "uncaring" Charles'. The extracts the paper printed made three sensational assertions: that the Princess of Wales had suffered from an eating disorder, bulimia nervosa; that she had several times, albeit half-heartedly, attempted suicide; and that her husband, Prince Charles, had enjoyed a secret relationship with another woman, Camilla Parker Bowles, throughout his marriage to Diana.

On the following day, the royal couple met at Kensington Palace to discuss the future of that marriage. If their mood was sombre, at least the Prince and Princess were for once able to sit down together and talk through the repercussions of a separation coolly and calmly. It was then that they took the decision to end the charade by formally separating. Diana said later that she felt 'deep, deep, profound sadness. Because we had struggled to keep it going, but obviously we'd both run out of steam.'

But with the first hurdle — her confrontation with Prince Charles — successfully cleared, she also felt a deep inner peace. That night, for the first time in many, many months, she slept soundly. There was, too, a sense of relief among her circle of friends, knowing that she had finally embarked on a difficult journey, but one which at least brought her the hope of a happy ending. However, there was also anxiety that Diana would not have the stamina to stand up to the intense pressure to come, both from inside and outside the royal family.

Unknown to the Princess, her husband had already made the first move. The previous day he had seen the Queen at Windsor Castle and had discussed with her the consequences of a divorce. The Queen had long been aware of the breakdown of her son's relationship with his wife, but was above all things concerned about the impact of a divorce upon her grandchildren, Prince Charles's public image and the monarchy.

As the public absorbed the twists and turns of the marriage crisis, events moved inexorably to a climax within Palace circles. On the day the *Sunday Times* serialization began, the Queen was the guest of honour at Windsor Great Park for a polo match in which Prince Charles was playing. Her gesture in inviting Camilla Parker Bowles and her husband, Andrew, to join her in the Royal Enclosure on the very day when the nation was digesting the implications of the Waleses' unhappy marriage was seen by Diana's circle as a graphic remonstration against the Princess.

At the same time, the Establishment and

their media allies were in full cry. Lord McGregor, then Chairman of the Press Complaints Commission, issued a statement condemning the hysteria that the book immediately generated as 'An odious exhibition of journalists dabbling their fingers in the stuff of other people's souls.' In fact, this criticism was never made of the book itself; indeed, Lord McGregor later told me that the issue had been the 'most difficult' of his tenure. The Archbishop of Canterbury worried publicly about the effects of the publicity on Princes William and Harry; Lord St John of Fawsley condemned the book's publication, while a potpourri of MPs were keen to see me locked away in the Tower; it was, too, a torrid time for Diana's supporters.

As loyalists rallied to the flag, ignoring the message while deriding the messenger, the public gradually began to accept the book's veracity through statements by Diana's friends, further confirmed when she visited her old friend Carolyn Bartholomew, who had spoken about the Princess's bulimia. While the visit helped establish the dawning realization that *Diana: Her True Story* was what it said in the title, senior courtiers, including the Queen's private secretary, Sir Robert Fellowes, pointed accusing fingers at Diana when they saw the front-page coverage of the visit.

Hours after that confrontation the Princess flew by helicopter to Merseyside for a visit to a hospice, her first official engagement since *Diana: Her True Story* hit the headlines. It proved to be an emotional meeting between Diana and her public. She was so touched by the show of affection from waiting well-wishers that she burst into tears, overcome by the distressing echoes of her morning meeting with Palace officials, and by the underlying strain of the decision she and Prince Charles had taken. As she later told a friend: 'An old lady in the crowd stroked my face and that triggered something inside me. I simply couldn't stop myself crying.' The public tears did not surprise her close friends, who knew only too well the private anguish of her lonely position, the strain she had borne for 18 months. As one remarked: 'She is a brilliant actress who has disguised her private sorrow.'

But although Diana was buoyed by public sympathy for her plight, she realized that she alone must face the royal family at a traditional series of summer engagements, beginning with Trooping the Colour. If that most formal of engagements proved to be a day of tension and anxiety, she approached with far greater trepidation the week-long stay at Windsor Castle for the Royal Ascot race meeting. She and Prince Charles had arranged, while there, to discuss the marriage situation with the Queen and the Duke of Edinburgh. Diana's anxiety about this meeting was shared by her corps of loyal friends, who had known for years of the difficulties she had faced within the royal family, and who were well aware of the pressure that would be brought to bear upon her in the coming days and weeks. They knew, too, that she was neither as streetwise nor as manipulative as some of her detractors claimed, and that she would need all her fighting spirit and all her inner strength for the many battles that lay ahead.

That confrontation with the Queen, Prince Philip and Prince Charles in the private apartments at Windsor Castle gave Diana a vivid glimpse of the prospect before her. She was greeted with a flat refusal to countenance even the idea of separation, in any form, before she and her husband had at least tried for a period — thought to be around three months — to resolve their differences. In the meantime, the façade of normality — or of what passes for normality in a royal marriage — was to be maintained.

But if the rift between the Prince and Princess of Wales had now been made only too apparent to press and public alike, signs of the division within the royal family itself now spilled over into the traditional Ascot ceremonial. In a faintly ridiculous, if not demeaning, tableau, the Duchess of York, now separated from Prince Andrew, stood with her two daughters and other spectators to watch the procession of royal carriages from the sidelines. Twice the Prince and Princess of Wales left the racecourse together in his Aston Martin, only to part a few miles down the road where Diana's own car was waiting for her. More obviously, the Duke of Edinburgh was seen pointedly to ignore her when she walked past him in the royal box at Ascot. For once the imperturbable mask of monarchy was allowed to slip in public, a measure of the confusion and conflict within the royal family as it struggled to cope with the crisis.

As the royal system absorbed the gravity of the situation, the views of the Queen and her immediate family gradually filtered through the Palace hierarchy and spread like ripples to the outer ring of royalty. The chill towards the Princess of Wales and those loyal to her was now all too apparent. Although she was not actually greeted with silence by courtiers, there could be no mistaking their lack of warmth or approval.

For her father-in-law, however, a withering silence at Ascot was not, it seems, sufficient mark of his disapproval. Over the next few weeks Diana received four stinging letters from the Duke of Edinburgh, by turns angry, reproachful, conciliatory and ultimately gruffly affectionate. These missives, which were initially accusatory, left her shocked and numb, but where once she would have been reduced to tears and shrunk back into her shell, she was no longer prepared to accept such an onslaught from the royal family. For once she was determined to argue her case. Through a friend, she contacted a lawyer; then, with the help of her private secretary, Patrick Jephson, one of her few trusted allies, she dispatched formal replies to Prince Philip, effectively spelling out the way she felt she had been treated by her husband, his family, and their courtiers, and including her demand that, as a condition of her staying within the royal family, Prince Charles should quit Kensington Palace.

The letters were the opening salvo in what proved to be a long hot summer of intrigue and innuendo. The image of the House of Windsor as a dutiful, sober and industrious family had for years captured the public imagination. Now the sudden and dramatic disclosure that their behaviour was no better than any other family's — and often a good deal worse — came as an unpleasant surprise to many who had once unquestioningly accepted the sanitized Palace version as it was transmitted through trusted editors, writers, interviewers and programmemakers. Of the many shocks inaugurated by the publication of *Diana: Her True Story,* and confirmed within only a few weeks of its appearance, this contrast between the public royal family and the private Windsors was one of the most dramatic.

Within the Palace, a whispering campaign against the Princess now began in earnest as the royal family closed ranks against her. Both she and the Duchess of York became convinced that there were numerous plots and conspiracies against them, as often as not aimed at reducing the public's support for them. At times they fell victim to wild and ludicrous exaggerations; at others, however, their suspicions proved all too well founded. Meanwhile, a climate of paranoia prevailed within the royal family itself. Bitter accusations, witch-hunting inquests and acrimonious investigations — the latter occasionally involving officers from the Royal Protection Squad — became routine occurrences. It is little wonder, therefore, that coded conversations, the scrambler telephone and the paper-shredder came to figure daily in Diana's life. At Kensington Palace she had the rooms swept for listening devices and destroyed every scrap of paper she wrote on, knowing that there were those who would secretly rummage through the waste-paper baskets for anything that might be used against her.

As the summer dragged on, Prince Charles's allies began to rally round in earnest. Friends who, a dozen years earlier, had warned him against marrying Diana now questioned her mental stability, advising him to 'dump her immediately' and seek a divorce. Describing *Diana: Her True Story* as 'the longest divorce petition in history', they urged the Prince to authorize an assault on his estranged wife's integrity. While Prince Charles himself made it clear that he would take no part in any such campaign against Diana, his sympathizers gradually took it upon themselves to contact the media and give his side of the story. Diana, as the rumoured source of my book, would be painted as a sick woman barely maintaining a tenuous grasp on reality. This offensive, rooted in disdain, if not derision, for the Princess, enjoyed the willing collusion of numerous newspaper executives. (One senior editorial figure even faxed a sympathetic piece to Prince Charles at Highgrove. Though he initially vetoed it, that did not prevent its appearance a few weeks later.) As the daily drip of critical, often downright abusive, articles about her turned into a downpour, the Princess gradually learned who was trying to blacken her name and poison the public against her. At first she was disbelieving, but eventually she was forced to accept, albeit reluctantly, that close friends of her husband's — friends whom she had thought sympathetic to her — were briefing the media almost every day. If she was sickened, however, she was not about to give in to the pressure: 'Why don't you save yourself a phone call and ring the papers direct?' she demanded of Prince Charles during one terse conversation.

As effective as the smear campaign undoubtedly was, it could not amount to a vindication of the Prince of Wales. That task largely fell to his private secretary, Richard Aylard, who in late June convened a meeting of the Prince's friends to try to salvage his reputation. Again, several newspaper executives were used as conduits for positive stories about Prince Charles and his valuable contribution to national life; he was, too, portrayed as a doting father to his sons, a by-word for unassuming parental devotion, in sharp contrast to his wife's suffocating affection for her children. Indeed, Diana was accused of thwarting the Prince's attempts to see the two boys so effectively that he was forced to act like a divorced father seeking access. One royal writer, Penny Junor (a biographer of the Prince), described Diana's conduct as 'irrational, unreasonable and hysterical'; other newspapers were told by Charles's friends that his wife was a 'megalomaniac who wants to be at the top of the pile. She wants to be seen as the greatest woman in the world. Her behaviour is endangering the future of her marriage, the country and the monarchy itself.'

With open warfare declared between the Waleses, Buckingham Palace in turmoil and separation discussions under way, the grotesque charade of normality was still maintained. A summer cruise, foolishly billed as a 'second honeymoon' for the Prince and Princess, was announced. For Diana it was the holiday from hell. She had too many painful memories of previous holidays on board the *Alexander,* one of 11 luxury yachts owned by the Greek billionaire John Latsis. The distance between the couple was all too evident to the other members of the party, who included Princess Alexandra and her husband, the Honourable Sir Angus Ogilvy, and Lord and Lady Romsey. Diana kept herself to herself, having little contact with her husband, sleeping in a separate cabin and preferring to take her meals with the children. The underlying tension was not helped when she picked up a ship-to-shore telephone and overheard her husband speaking to Camilla Parker Bowles. She was not surprised, though her misgivings about the relationship had been derided as the fantasies of a sick woman. 'Why don't you go off with your lady and have an end to it?' she asked Prince Charles wearily. 'The marriage is all over bar the statement,' one of those on the yacht remarked after the royal party had left. For the Princess, the holiday had simply been yet another example of royal duplicity and self-serving hypocrisy.

Meanwhile, the summer suddenly became uncomfortably hot for the Duchess of York, on holiday in the South of France with her daughters and her 'financial adviser', John Bryan. Long-distance photographs of Bryan sucking a topless Fergie's toes and kissing her made headlines around the world. The episode was devastating for the Duchess's public image, and effectively ended any chance of a reconciliation between her and Prince Andrew. The presence of her children heightened the scandal, angering MPs, press and public alike, and there were calls for her to be stripped of her title and expelled from the royal family.

The repercussions of this episode were still being felt when, in August 1992, Diana found herself caught up in a similar scandal. Under the headline 'My life is just torture', the *Sun* newspaper ran a transcript of a tape-recorded telephone conversation between a woman alleged to be the Princess of Wales and a mystery admirer, later revealed as James Gilbey. It would prove to be one of the most embarrassing episodes of Diana's royal career.

There were, in fact, two tapes, both recorded illicitly — indeed, illegally — by radio hams, who had then contacted the *Sun,* though there was a year between their approaches to the newspaper. The conversations were similar; the first had been recorded on New Year's Eve 1989, when the Princess had been at Sandringham. Her ostensible lover had spoken from his car while parked by a roadside in Oxfordshire;

in the course of a long conversation in which the woman emerged as a deeply troubled, lonely and vulnerable person, almost pathetically grateful for her caller's attentions, he called her 'Darling' 53 times and 'Squidgy' or 'Squidge' 14 times. Inevitably, the scandal came to be known as 'Squidgygate'.

During the racy, if rambling and rather juvenile, conversation, the Princess was heard telling Gilbey about her impossible life with Prince Charles and her isolation inside the royal family which, she felt, was increasingly 'distancing' itself from her. She spoke of her fear of becoming pregnant (though this part of the tape was not published until five months later, on the eve of her solo visit to Nepal), her anxiety about a clandestine meeting with her admirer, and her dreams for the future: 'I'll go out and conquer the world . . . do my bit in the way I know how and leave him behind,' she says significantly — if not prophetically — having complained that her husband made her life 'real, real torture'.

Amid much chatter about mutual friends, horoscopes, and fashion — Diana admitted that she dressed another lover, Captain James Hewitt of the Life Guards, 'from head to foot' — she went on to discuss the royal family. She dismissed the Duchess of York's attempts to mend her tarnished image, and recalled the 'strange look' the Queen Mother had turned upon her during lunch — 'It's not hatred, it's sort of interest and pity . . . I was very bad at lunch and I nearly started blubbing. I just felt really sad and empty and thought: "Bloody hell, after all I've done for this fucking family" . . . It is just so desperate. Always being innuendo, the fact that I'm going to do something dramatic because I can't stand the confines of this marriage.'

The Princess, so obviously lonely, despondent and neglected, derived much comfort from her besotted admirer. Their long-distance dalliance, at a time when she was only just beginning to fight her bulimia, and to come to terms with her husband's relationship with Camilla Parker Bowles, vividly demonstrated her chronically low self-esteem as well as an embryonic ambition to use her undoubted abilities outside the confines of the royal system.

The front-page treatment given to the Squidgy tape 'devastated' Diana, while Gilbey became for a time Britain's most wanted man, hunted day and night by teams of journalists; he has, however, resolutely refused to comment, either publicly or privately, on the conversation. The Princess was certain that the tape's publication was part of the campaign to discredit her: 'It was done to harm me in a serious manner, and that was the first time I'd experienced what it was like to be outside the net, so to speak, and not be in the family.' She tried to show a brave face in front of the royal family, but her moods swung wildly. 'I ain't going anywhere. I haven't got a single supporter in this family but they are not going to break me,' she told anxious friends. Her sense of isolation in this hostile climate was complete; indeed, at the height of the scandal she even seriously considered packing her bags and leaving the royal family and public life for ever. Sometimes, too, that courageous façade would slip. Several friends confirmed that she felt 'destroyed' by the coverage, telling one of her circle that 'If this is the price of public life then it is a price I am no longer willing to pay.' According to the same friend, the Princess had never sounded so depressed or hopelessly forlorn. She did, however, find one, perhaps rather unlikely, ally at the Palace in the Queen, whose understanding and helpful attitude did much to encourage Diana to soldier on. Even so, the Princess had few illusions about the royal family, its courtiers and supporters: as one of her closest friends remarked, 'Even if they have not managed to kill the golden goose that laid the golden eggs for the media, they have certainly succeeded in wounding her.'

It would seem that the royal family was unwilling to learn that lesson, wholly unable to see that an orchestrated campaign to discredit the Princess of Wales was intrinsically self-defeating, and ultimately deeply damaging to the monarchy. For now the coverage ranged from the hysterical to the sinister, as every day seemed to bring its own new royal scandal. Amid such frenzied speculation, a suspicion developed within Diana's circle that there was a conspiracy among Prince Charles's closest friends, the Palace Establishment, or even the security service, MI5, to discredit the Princess of Wales.

Yet black propaganda can only achieve so much. The issue of the Waleses's marriage had still to be addressed, and to this end a deal was discussed during a closed meeting at Balmoral between the Queen, Prince Philip and the Prince and Princess of Wales. The central issue discussed was an informal separation, a course the Queen had long favoured, and under which Diana could lead a separate life within the royal family, joining her husband only for formal engagements such as Trooping the Colour. Prince Charles agreed to move out of Kensington Palace and Diana, determined to achieve a working relationship with his family on her terms, tacitly accepted. For a time, an unstable equilibrium was established.

Ultimately, the Princess was always loyal to the Crown, and almost always ready to defer to the Queen. She was, too, especially sensitive to the Queen's difficulties in a year the Sovereign herself would later describe as her *annus horribilis:* her solicitor, Sir Matthew Farrer, was negotiating with Downing Street over secret proposals to pay income tax; senior Church figures were criticizing the royal family for not providing a healthy example of family life; and opinion polls were charting the general public's growing disaffection with the monarchy.

Now, in the autumn of 1992 and against this background of public and private disquiet, the Princess of Wales embarked on a series of meetings with her private secretary, Patrick Jephson, and her lawyer, Paul Butner, to discuss an official separation from her husband and to plan her own future within the royal family. Those involved in these delicate negotiations recalled her evident vulnerability. 'She was terrified that the family were going to take the children away and drive her into exile,' said one adviser. 'It was her greatest anxiety and she was prepared to give up everything, do anything to keep the boys.' Diana needed no reminding of her own parents' acrimonious divorce, during which her mother, Frances Shand Kydd, lost custody of her four children to Diana's father, Earl Spencer.

Meetings between the Waleses to discuss the issues involved in a formal separation were invariably emotional and highly strung, ending, and sometimes starting, with slammed doors, raised voices and moist eyes. A venerable legal figure in the considerable shape of Lord Goodman was brought in to arbitrate on the constitutional questions raised by the prospect of a formal separation. At various stages the Prime Minister, John Major, was consulted and asked what effect, if any, a separation would have on the governance of the country. He indicated that it would have none.

For the most part, the discussion centred on the children, the couple's homes and their offices. At the same time as asking Charles to leave Kensington Palace, Diana also wanted to divorce her office staff from his, which were both based at St James's

Palace, and move her employees to quarters at Buckingham Palace. This demand was unacceptable to Charles. As one of his advisers recalled: 'The Prince was reluctant to go down the road of a formal separation and divorce, not only for the sake of the children, but also for the constitutional mess which would arise from that.'

The meetings continued, each with its highly charged content of argument and anger. Tried beyond endurance, during one of these discussions Diana desperately played her ace. Her frustration with the royal system was such that she threatened to take her children and live with them abroad, making a new life in Australia. To no avail — she was reminded very forcibly that the boys were second and third in line to the throne and as such had to be raised inside the royal court in order to learn their royal duties. She was also made chillingly aware of the stark legal realities underlying her predicament. Laws which apply exclusively to the royal family effectively deny a royal mother any real say in the upbringing of her children. Her ace was comprehensively trumped.

All through that tense autumn of 1992 the steady drizzle of pro-Charles stories continued, heightened when it was announced that he had commissioned the broadcaster Jonathan Dimbleby to write his biography, described as the 'complete riposte' to *Diana: Her True Story.* The image of a loyal employer, a loving, if thwarted father, and a misunderstood public figure who was there for the duration — all this was beginning to emerge.

As the preparations were completed for a joint visit to Korea in November, Prince Charles's private secretary briefed several newspaper editors that it would be the 'togetherness tour'. By this time the separation negotiations had reached a critical stage and the Princess was in no mood to continue the hollow charade. Earlier in the year, on an unhappy trip to India, Diana had used her body language to devastating effect when she posed alone by the Taj Mahal, that monument to lost love, while Charles addressed a business meeting. The distance between the couple was underlined when the Princess deliberately turned away as the Prince tried to kiss her after a polo match in Jaipur. She used the same tactics in Korea, determined to show the world what was really going on, a decision which several friends, including Rosa Monckton, then the President of Tiffany's, questioned. Headlines like 'The Glums' and 'How much longer can this tragedy go on?' signalled that the ploy had been successful.

The tour was also dogged by exaggerated reports of the contents of the paperback edition of *Diana: Her True Story,* which briefly mentioned the angry letters she had received from Prince Philip. When all this had been embroidered by the tabloids, there seemed to be the makings of yet another 'Diana' scandal, and in the end she was forced to make a brief public statement in explanation of her relationship with the Queen and the Duke of Edinburgh. 'The suggestion that they have been anything other than sympathetic and supportive is untrue and particularly hurtful,' she said.

It was, in any case, now only a matter of time before the official separation was announced by the Prime Minister. The Princess had asked that the statement be made while the boys were still protected at school, and the date was set for 9 December 1992. The week before, Diana had been to see Princes William and Harry at Ludgrove School in Berkshire so that she could break the news to them herself and try to reassure them about the future.

During that tearful encounter Diana steadfastly refrained from mentioning the name of the woman who had, to her mind, destroyed her marriage. She was acutely aware of the distress caused to children when 'the other woman' is given as a reason for the collapse of a marriage. For the Princess, her boys came first — whatever the cost.

The announcement itself was, Diana said, 'very, very sad. Really sad. The fairytale had come to an end . . .'

It was not only the Princess's personal fairytale that had ended. The events of 1992, the Queen's *annus horribilis,* had effectively shattered the myth of the royal family. The year saw the collision of fantasy and reality, as unadorned facts triumphed over homely fiction. 'The symbolism of the fire at Windsor Castle was not lost on anyone inside the family,' Diana told her friends.

A mortal blow had been struck at the royal family's image as the 'perfect' family. For too many years Diana had been an unwilling party to the hypocrisy surrounding her life within the royal clan. It had left her emotionally drained and physically exhausted. Now the true story was out in the open, and there was no more need to go on lying or hiding from the truth.

Only a year before it had seemed an impossible dream, but now the Princess was

471

ready to leave the past behind her. A new life beckoned, a freer existence without the shackles of a desperately unhappy marriage. She was making a fresh start alone, although she would still be part of the royal family and living under the constraints of the royal system she had come to despise and distrust. It was an uneasy compromise, and it would not be long before Diana rattled once more at the bars of her gilded cage. As she told her friends: 'I have contracted, I've agreed to pay the piper for now. The fun is to come, maybe in two or three years.

'I'm learning to be patient.'

10
'MY ACTING CAREER IS OVER'

For many years, there had been little laughter and even fewer smiles in the apartments at Kensington Palace where the Prince and Princess of Wales had made their London home. Visitors were quick to sense the cheerless atmosphere, and words like 'dead energy', 'gloomy' and 'tense' became the commonplaces of their descriptions. 'I feel I have died in that house many, many times,' Diana told friends. Even her bedroom gave out an air of sadness. 'I can imagine her lying in bed at night cuddling her teddy and crying,' one former member of staff remarked of this little-girl's bedroom, with its population of staring toy animals left over from an equally unhappy childhood.

Now she was separated, not only from her husband, but from much of the misery in which her marriage had plunged her. Perhaps symbolically, her first decision was to throw out the mahogany double bed she had slept in at Kensington Palace since her wedding 11 years before. Then she had the bedroom painted and new locks fitted, and changed her private telephone number. Her new life alone had begun.

During the winter of 1992 there was much to-ing and fro-ing between Highgrove, Kensington Palace and St James's Palace as the couple's personal possessions were ferried back to them in their now bachelor homes. 'It was,' said one Palace official, 'an undignified and very sad finale to the fairytale.' The Prince and Princess, who had received an Aladdin's Cave of gifts during their marriage, unsentimentally consigned unwanted possessions to the flames. A bonfire of their vanities was made in the grounds of Highgrove; valuable items were sent for storage at Windsor Castle or given to charity. At Kensington Palace, only a few items were left as reminders of Prince Charles's tenure there.

For Prince Charles, his wife was not even permitted that small remembrance. Over the next few months every sign that she had ever lived at Highgrove was systematically wiped away. A designer was then hired to redecorate the house completely, as well as the Prince's new home at St James's Palace. Visitors to Highgrove could not fail to notice that, among the scores of family photographs, there was not a single one of the Prince of Wales's estranged wife.

In the months following the separation, frequent visitors to Kensington Palace began to notice a change in the previously forlorn Apartments Eight and Nine. The staff seemed friendlier, less formal, the atmosphere lighter and more relaxed. There were, too, small decorative changes: walls were repainted, terracotta pots appeared, filled with arrangements of mosses and twigs, and Prince Charles's stark military and architectural pictures were replaced with gentle landscapes and dance paintings. Guests were greeted by the sound of loud music and the scent of freesias or white Casablanca lilies. The prevailing mood was inevitably more feminine, although Diana never quite made up her mind to follow her initial impulse and completely redecorate her house.

The truth was that the Princess had a love-hate relationship with her home in Kensington Palace, as hostages are said to do with their captors. To her, the Palace represented so much accumulated misery and heartache, and yet, as she told friends, 'I feel secure here.' Throughout her marriage her first-floor sitting room had been, in her words, 'My retreat, my empire and my nest.' In truth, it was a shrine to the two men in her life, Princes William and Harry. In front of the fireplace was a five-foot leather rhino cushion for them to lie on as they watched television, while on every conceivable surface there were photographs in wooden or silver frames of the boys go-karting, in tanks, on horseback, cycling, fishing, on police bikes or in school uniform. More framed photographs, this time of her late father, Earl Spencer, her sisters Jane and Sarah, and her brother Charles, the present Earl, adorned the mantelpiece. In this gallery, too, were pictures of the Princess herself: a signed black-and-white photograph of her dancing with the film director Richard Attenborough, another with singer Elton John, a third with Liza Minnelli, and privately taken pictures of her imitating Audrey Hepburn in outfits from the film *Breakfast at Tiffany's.*

Crowded with comforting groups of pottery animals, enamel boxes and porcelain figurines, the room gave the impression of belonging to a woman trying to protect herself from the incursions of the outside world. 'It is like an old lady's room,' a girlfriend observed, 'packed to the gunwales with knick-knacks . . . You can hardly move.'

Another close friend explained something of the mentality behind this profusion: 'It's very common for people coming from a broken home to want material possessions around them. They are building their own nests.' The general air of claustrophobia was, however, lightened by evidence of Diana's gentle, occasionally self-deprecating sense of humour. On every chair were silk cushions embroidered with humorous motifs such as 'Good girls go to heaven, bad girls go everywhere', 'You have to kiss a lot of frogs before you find a prince', and 'I feel sorry for people who don't drink because when they wake up in the morning that is the best they are going to feel all day.' Her bathroom and lavatory were decorated with newspaper cartoons depicting Prince Charles talking to his plants and their visit to the Pope in the Vatican; these, too, give another glimpse of what she found amusing.

But even these light touches could not conceal her general feeling of dissatisfaction, manifested in her ambivalent attitude towards her home. For months following the separation she vacillated between wanting to stay at Kensington Palace and feeling she would like to move into a place of her own in the country. The sensation of living inside an open prison at Kensington Palace, constantly under the eye of staff and police, gnawed at her spirit. She longed to break free, yet at the same time realized the interpretation that press and public alike would put on her buying a house of her own; it would seem such a very obvious break with all that had gone before since her marriage had started in 1981. A friend recalled: 'One thing which concerns her above all else is a deep fear of censure and condemnation. So, as ever, she drew back.'

By the spring of 1993 Diana had become increasingly unhappy with having to live in Kensington Palace. So she was 'excited and delighted' when, in April, her brother Charles, Earl Spencer, offered her the Garden House, a four-bedroomed property on the estate at Althorp. It was an offer that also neatly sidestepped the problem of her being thought to be extravagant. 'At long last I can make a cosy nest of my own,' she told friends, filled with enthusiasm at the idea of furnishing and decorating her own place; indeed, the desire to make the place 'cosy' became her constant refrain. For the first time she would be able to express herself without having to look over her shoulder or be reminded of sad events. She contacted a family friend, Dudley Poplak, a

South African-born designer who had organized the interior decoration of the apartments she had shared with Prince Charles
in Kensington Palace. Together they discussed colour schemes, fabrics and wall-
papers — pale blues and yellows were
provisionally chosen. The exciting vista of a
new life opened up before her. Moreover,
the Garden House had another advantage.
It was not overlooked by any other build-
ings on the estate, allowing her absolute
privacy, and, best of all, the ubiquitous
armed bodyguard would not have to intrude
on her new home, since there was a small
house nearby in which he could be based.

Just three weeks later Diana's brave new
world collapsed around her. Earl Spencer
telephoned her and said that he no longer
felt comfortable with the idea. He argued
that the extra police presence, the inevitable
cameras and other surveillance would involve unacceptable levels of intrusion. With
Althorp open to the public, various restric-
tions would have to be placed on her freedom of movement. Diana was stunned, for
once absolutely lost for words. While her
brother's arguments were perfectly valid,
for her his decision constituted much more
than simply the loss of a house. Her 'cosy
nest' had represented both a challenge and

a new beginning; more than that, however, the Garden House had literally been the home of her dreams. For several months there was a coolness between the Princess and her brother.

Relationships within the Spencer clan had never been easy. Her parents' divorce and her father's subsequent remarriage to Raine, Countess of Dartford, daughter of the romantic novelist Barbara Cartland, had left the family bitter and divided. Diana had never forgiven her grandmother, Ruth, Lady Fermoy, one of the Queen Mother's ladies-in-waiting, for her decision to give evidence against her own daughter — and Diana's mother — Frances, during the bitter divorce case. When Prince Charles and her granddaughter separated, Lady Fermoy once again failed to side with her own flesh and blood. It was therefore with a surprise bordering on astonishment that the family heard of two visits Diana made to see Lady Fermoy at her Eaton Square apartment in June 1993, just three weeks before the latter's death. Rather than allow her feelings of resentment to simmer, the Princess simply decided to confront the woman who had hurt her so badly. They were understandably difficult, and at times frosty, encounters, Lady Fermoy visibly taken aback by Diana's courageous decision to raise the problems which had driven them apart, instead of — as is the royal way — engaging in meaningless small talk while the real issues remain unspoken. It would be an exaggeration to say that these meetings brought about a reconciliation, but they did lead to a truce between the two warring relations.

Her willingness to build bridges was a sign of Diana's determination to lay the ghosts of her past. This new-found resolve was at the heart of her reconciliation with her stepmother in May 1993. It was no secret that Diana, her sisters and brother had little love for the woman they called 'Acid Raine'. When her father died, the Princess could have been excused for consigning her stepmother to the dustbin of her life, but she chose not to do so, inviting Raine and her new husband, a French aristocrat, Count Jean-François de Chambrun, to lunch. It was an emotional encounter, and one that marked a turning point in their relationship, although their frequent meetings subsequently were frostily received by the rest of the Spencers, and led on one occasion to an angry confrontation with her mother, Frances Shand Kydd. During this exchange Diana pointed out that as she had hated Raine the most, and yet had been able to forgive and forget, then so should the rest of the family.

Diana's success in clearing away some of the emotional brushwood of the past left her free to begin laying the foundations of a new life. A new home had been the keystone of her dream, and the collapse of that ambition dealt her a grievous blow. Her hopes dashed, the Princess spent many months licking her wounds, enduring, though not enjoying, life at Kensington Palace, which by now possessed an atmosphere that led one royal employee to dub it 'Bleak House'. She had become, in a sense, a prisoner of her own making, a captive of her psyche. She had won a measure of freedom, even if not full emancipation. The door of the gilded cage was open. Now she had to find the will to make a new life for herself. Instead, she seemed to half live the old.

It was, in truth, a quiet, almost monastic, life. The Princess's daily routine rarely varied. Her day started promptly at 7 a.m. After a light breakfast of pink grapefruit, home-made muesli or granary toast, or fresh fruit and yoghurt and coffee, she departed for her daily workout at the exclusive Chelsea Harbour Club. She never showered at the club, preferring to change at home, away from curious eyes — and possible camera lenses. Around 9 a.m. her flamboyant hairdresser, Sam McKnight, put in an appearance. He was one of the few men in her life who could keep the Princess waiting — and still keep her smiling. While he attended to her hair (a change of style invariably signalled a change in the direction of her life), the Princess was busy on her bedroom phone, for friends knew that early morning was a good time to catch her. At that time of day she was usually chatty and lighthearted. By evening, however, when the events of the day had exhausted her and left her emotional batteries depleted, making conversation could be, as one friend noted, 'like pushing glue uphill'.

There was a mound of correspondence to be dealt with every day, with the help of her private secretary, Patrick Jephson, and her secretaries. Diana insisted on opening much of the mail herself. As well as letters from her charities, there were others from members of the public. These, usually diffident in style, contained homilies, felicitations and accounts of difficult personal experiences. The Princess was deeply touched by many of them and would often write personal replies. She was, in any case, an assiduous correspondent, one who remembered dozens of birthdays every year and who, in her friend Rosa Monckton's words, 'wrote thank-you letters more promptly than anyone else I know'. Jephson recalled: 'After a tour she might write to your wife and say sorry for taking him away. She could be an inspiring boss as well as a demanding one, and often displayed great acts of kindness to those who worked for her.'

From about 10 a.m., she liked to telephone friends. Regular callers included Lord Palumbo, her lawyer, Lord Mishcon, the Duchess of York and, following their reconciliation, her stepmother, Raine. If she was feeling depressed or bored or lonely, she would go shopping to cheer herself up. There were also weekly trips to see her therapist, Susie Orbach, at her North London home, and what the Princess herself called 'Pamper Diana' days, where she enjoyed a variety of New Age therapies.

At lunchtime she might meet friends at a restaurant or occasionally host a business lunch at home. Most of the time, however, she ate a modest meal alone at Kensington Palace. After lunch, she might receive official visitors connected with her charities or the regiments she was involved with, or spend an hour or so catching up with correspondence, leaving her butlers to field the constant telephone enquiries. Sometimes she would visit her offices at St James's Palace, or drive to the boys' schools, watching them play in their sports teams. On summer afternoons she would spend hours sitting in the garden, engrossed in the latest blockbuster novel.

In her Kensington Palace fastness, Diana knew that every time she ventured out from behind the safety of her front door she made herself a hostage to fortune. Occasionally she would go to the cinema with a couple of girlfriends, but she cancelled a trip to see *What's Love Got to Do With It?* — about Tina Turner's violent relationship with her husband — in case her choice of film was misconstrued. She often spent her evenings alone, retiring to bed to eat a light supper from a tray and watch television.

Her increasingly solitary existence became a matter of concern to her circle of friends. 'Such loneliness, she doesn't know who she can trust,' said her friend Lucia Flecha de Lima. The Princess's global celebrity only heightened this sense of emotional isolation. 'She feels that she is in a prison, not just a goldfish bowl but within her own experience, a prison with no way out and no shoulder to cry on. It is a terrible space to be in,' said an adviser.

She missed her children badly, particularly at traditional times of family celebration. On Christmas Day 1993, a little over a year after the separation was announced, the Princess stayed with the boys at Sandringham, the Queen's Norfolk retreat, on Christmas Eve, but left, smiling bravely, for Kensington Palace on the morning of Christmas Day. Back in London she ate her Christmas lunch alone before going for a swim, again alone, at Buckingham Palace. The next day she flew to Washington to spend a week with Lucia Flecha de Lima. As Diana herself recalled: 'I cried all the way out and all the way back, I felt so sorry for myself.'

Her weekends were, if anything, even quieter than her weekdays, except when the boys came to stay. Under the terms of the separation, the Princess saw the boys on alternate weekends when school holidays allowed. Diana would pick them up from Ludgrove and, later, Eton, and drive them back to London for tea in the nursery. Like most youngsters, they sat glued to the latest action movies on satellite television, which the Princess had installed so they wouldn't miss their favourites. After supper, the boys watched a rented video like *Rambo* — Arnold Schwarzenegger was something of a hero — or played a Nintendo computer game before going to bed.

On Saturday and Sunday mornings, at around 8.30, William and Harry had breakfast with their nanny. The Princess kept to her own schedule even when the young Princes were there, and it was left to the nanny to supervise dressing. When they were ready, they might join their mother at her gym, where they were learning to play tennis, or stay at home, riding their BMX bikes in the Kensington Palace grounds, or let off steam in vigorous water-pistol fights, spraying each other with hosepipes, or have pitched water-bomb battles with schoolfriends. There were other diversions, too, especially when their mother's schedule allowed her to take them on outings. Harry's favourite pastime then was go-karting at a circuit in Berkshire. As a sportsman he was quite fearless, eager to run William into the ground. The older prince preferred to go riding or shooting with his friends, where he was not constantly frustrated by his inability to better his younger brother. He was, in any case, the more serious of the two, Harry the more nimble and impish, both in sport and conversation. Yet while Harry teased his elder brother mercilessly, he needed him desperately.

When the boys were with their father, or had gone back to school, the apartments in Kensington Palace returned to their customary quiet. The cloistered atmosphere was disturbed only by the shrill sound of the telephone, an instrument which was at once the Princess's confessional, her best friend and her occasional doom. The publication of the Squidgy tape had caused Diana grave embarrassment and distress. Now, however, it was Prince Charles's turn to rue the telephone's invention.

The Prince's public image had been seriously harmed in the months before the separation, and in January 1993 it was dealt a further blow when tabloid newspapers published the transcripts of a tape-recorded telephone conversation allegedly between the Prince and Camilla Parker Bowles, said to have taken place on 18 December 1989. Its content, which was both intimate and distasteful, forced many leading Establishment figures traditionally loyal to the Crown — notably members of the Church, the military and Parliament — to question Prince Charles's fitness to rule.

The late-night call made plain the couple's undying affection for one another, not least by its sometimes childishly lewd intimacy. After various words of endearment from the woman, the man says: 'Your great achievement is to love me,' adding, 'You suffer all these indignities and tortures and calumnies.' The woman responds: 'I'd suffer anything for you. That's love. It's the strength of love.' The man makes a coarse joke about being turned into a tampon so that he might be constantly joined with his lover who, if this were indeed Camilla Parker Bowles, was then the wife of one of his oldest friends. Just before he rings off he says he will 'press the tit', meaning one of the buttons on the telephone. The woman replies: 'I wish you were pressing mine.' He answers: 'I love you, I adore you', and the woman answers in kind: 'I do love you.' Significantly, neither the Prince of Wales nor Camilla has ever denied that the tape was genuine.

For some time friends of Prince Charles had been trying to explain away the whispered telephone calls, the clandestine meetings and the secret gifts between Charles and Camilla in terms of friendship. Diana, however, had always preferred to trust her observations and her instincts. Although she was in no doubt that the taped conversation was genuine, she was still shocked to see the sordid details written down in black and white. Appalled and sickened, she read the transcript with mounting anger as she recognized the names of so many friends, people she had known and trusted for years, who had conspired to deceive her by providing cover stories or safe houses where the Prince and Camilla could meet in secret.

The tape fuelled the Princess's continuing obsession with the relationship which had cast such a shadow over her marriage. While she pretended indifference to the fate of Prince Charles and Camilla Parker Bowles, she watched their every move like a hawk. With her astrologer she pored over Camilla's chart — she is Cancerian, like Diana — brooding over the couple's fate with a fascination that was at once morbid and unhealthy.

In public, the Princess put a brave face on her troubles, but privately she was a woman in grief, mourning her lost innocence, a failed relationship and the wasted years of her adult life. At moments of optimism Diana felt she could beat the royal system and use her position in a more positive way. At other times she would suddenly find herself in tears, unexpectedly moved by a sentimental film, or some innocent remark that brought back all the misery of the past. It was noticeable, too, that she took to wearing sombre colours, especially black, a striking habit in someone who set such great store by colours. Isolated and lonely within her cocoon at Kensington Palace, she fell prey to drift and indecision.

The collapse of her marriage, her awareness of the hostility directed towards her by many in royal — and especially Prince Charles's — circles, her obsession with her husband's affair, and her often rather meaningless life within the depressing atmosphere of her home, all contributed to a deep loneliness and a destructive lowering of her self-esteem. There was, however, another factor in the Princess's profound and growing isolation, for she was still struggling to find a fulfilling public role. In March 1993 she flew to Nepal for five days on her first official overseas visit since the separation. The media dwelt on the signs that she was being treated as a second-class royal, quite failing to realize that the low-key, informal nature of the visit was something that Diana herself had requested.

Unwittingly, the Princess had established for herself a persona that would, in time, become a phenomenon. Almost uniquely among leading members of the royal family, she had recognized the public's desire for a more modest and relevant monarchy, a wish that neatly coincided with her objectives of reshaping her royal public life to her own design. Overseas work she found stimulating, not only because it gave her a different stage from that occupied by her husband, but also because it took her out from under the gimlet eye of Buckingham Palace. In these early days of her separation, both the Princess and the Palace were uncertain about her future plans. Her constitutional position was simply that of the mother to the future king; that, at least, nobody could take away from her. But her public role was unclear. As she herself said: 'People's agendas changed overnight. I was now the separated wife of the Prince of Wales, I was a problem, I was a liability. "How are we going to deal with her? This hasn't happened before." '

Whatever the personal feelings of the Queen's men towards Diana, their primary task was to serve the Sovereign and her son, and to maintain the status quo. To this end they too, like the Prince of Wales's friends, attempted the difficult task of resurrecting his public image at the price of reducing the status of the Princess, whom they readily acknowledged was still the shining star in a fading royal firmament. If their vision of a role for the Prince cut across the undefined ambitions of his estranged wife, then so be it. Now Diana began to find that visits abroad were being blocked and letters going mysteriously astray. When, for instance, she expressed a wish to visit British troops and refugees in Bosnia under the auspices of the Red Cross, she was told that Prince Charles's plans to go there took precedence. Then, in September 1993, she was told that, for 'security reasons', she could not undertake a private visit to Dublin to meet the Irish President, Mary Robinson — yet two months later she attended the Remembrance Day service in Enniskillen, Northern Ireland, potentially an infinitely more hazardous trip.

Privately, Diana suspected that the Establishment did not want her to enjoy such a high public profile, and thus inevitably overshadow her estranged husband. Moreover, she was in no doubt that a campaign was being waged against her by people she termed 'the enemy'. 'The enemy was my husband's department, because I always got more publicity,' she said. Yet the Princess was no royal rebel. She had learned enough during her decade inside the Firm to toe the party line. She recognized that her popularity was seen as a threat to the Prince of Wales by the 'men in grey' at the Palace, 'But I wanted to do good things. I was never going to hurt anyone. I was never going to let anyone down.'

It was a frustrating situation, and one exacerbated by her exasperation with a system which subtly straitjacketed or side-lined her proposals and ambitions. Her frustration came to a head that autumn after a series of sympathetic newspaper articles about the changing face of the monarchy, which were based on briefings to journalists by Sir Robert Fellowes and other Palace officials. In one piece, an unnamed courtier was quoted as commenting patronizingly: 'Diana is headstrong but we must show her love and understanding and bend over backwards to avoid a chasm in the early stages because, if she became bitter and twisted, it would be impossible for the children.' Furious at her portrayal as a foolish child, she spoke angrily to Fellowes, her brother-in-law, telling him that not only was she sick of being used by the Palace as newspaper fodder, but that this kind of story merely fanned the flames of speculation about her life.

It was in any case true that during 1993 the battle of the Waleses was fought out as much in the media as behind the scenes, Prince and Princess alike attempting to win the hearts and minds of the public. By the summer there were nine officials working directly or indirectly either on Prince Charles's portfolio of well-publicized interests, or on improving his image. By contrast, the Princess, whose staff were paid from the Prince's estate of the Duchy of Cornwall, made do with a part-time press officer. Yet she found herself accused of being a media junkie, lurching from one photocall to another: a holiday in the Caribbean, riding a log flume at Thorpe Park leisure centre, or skiing with her children. For a princess used to an adoring media, this change in fortunes undermined still further her precarious self-esteem and fed her existing anxieties. Her belief, at times all-consuming, in the predictions of her astrologer shows how little value she placed on her own instincts and judgement.

It was, for Diana, a miserable summer. She had started the year with a burst of energy, but as the months went by the constant criticism, both inside and outside the Palace, wore her down, something which showed in her stale response to bread-and-butter royal duties. The continual round of handshaking, tree-planting, small talk and smaller children was, to her mind, both repetitive and pointless. At the end of June the Princess decided that her 'Awaydays', her visits outside London, should end. A photocall in the course of a visit to Zimbabwe in July, during which she was pictured doling out food to children, symbolized her deep dissatisfaction with the inane circus. She felt the exercise patronized the children and reinforced the 'begging-bowl' image of Africa. She vowed that it would never happen again.

During an extended summer break, first in Bali and then with her boys in America, Diana thought long and hard about her future. She returned home, refreshed, to hostile headlines and disturbing news from the Palace. Prince Charles had hired a 'surrogate mother' to take her place when the boys were staying with him.

Diana could hardly contain her anger. Already edged to the margins of royal life, she was now being undermined in her most fulfilling role. She watched in simmering silence as Alexandra 'Tiggy' Legge-Bourke organized outings for the boys, took them shopping and kept them entertained. She winced when she saw newspaper photographs of Harry sitting on Tiggy's knee and shuddered at the idea of Tiggy calling the boys 'my babies'. Tiggy was all the more of a threat because she was similar in age and social status to Diana and mixed easily with

Prince Charles's friends.

The long-standing resentment was to come to a head more than three years later at a Christmas party when Diana made a remark to the boys' nanny about the relationship that she enjoyed with Prince Charles. Tiggy was left in tears, and subsequently sent a solicitor's letter to the Princess, demanding an apology for the 'false allegations'. It was an unpleasant incident. Quite innocently, Tiggy seemed to represent in Diana's mind all that she resented about the royal system and what she saw as its attempts to wrest her children from her. Fortunately, before her death, Diana became reconciled to Tiggy's active involvement in the lives of her boys. At the time, though, she felt that the wolves were circling for the kill. Her enemies had undermined her status, her personality and her position. Now they wanted the one thing in her life she held most dear: her motherhood.

During the autumn Diana began to plan her withdrawal from public life. Confused by the hostility of the media which had once lauded her, battered by the Palace machine and constantly looking over her shoulder at Prince Charles's camp, the Princess was at the end of her tether. Her private misery spilled over into public anger. 'You make my life hell,' she shouted at a photographer as he took pictures of her and her children leaving a West End cinema. She prodded his chest and jabbed her finger in his face before stalking back to William and Harry. The incident was only one of many ill-tempered spats with professional cameramen.

It was, however, an amateur photographer who proved to be the last straw. If she had been hesitant before about retiring from the public gaze, her mind was made up when she looked at the front page of the *Sunday Mirror* early in November and saw a full-page picture of herself working out at her former health club. She had long suspected that these photographs existed, but it was still a shock to see herself, dressed in a leotard, exploited in this way. The pictures had been taken secretly by the gym's manager, New Zealand businessman Bryce Taylor. Their publication constituted a flagrant invasion of privacy, but it was one for which Taylor was paid a six-figure sum. Buckingham Palace, MPs, other newspaper editors, and Lord McGregor, the Chairman of the Press Complaints Commission, howled their fury at the offending newspaper group. The Princess felt betrayed and violated. 'Bryce Taylor pushed me into the decision to go,' she said. 'The pictures were horrid, simply horrid.'

She was further infuriated when Taylor had the gall to claim that she had secretly wanted the pictures taken. Such was the hostility towards her among the Establishment that several influential columnists and politicians took to implying that there was a grain of truth in Taylor's accusations that the Princess was manipulating the press. Nor did the fact that she had taken the rare step of instructing her lawyers to sue Taylor and Mirror Group Newspapers still her critics. It was a further signal to her that however hard she tried, however innocent her actions, a cancer of cynicism was gradually corrupting the public's perception of her. All of which hardened her in her fierce determination to break free from the fickle and gloating media who had for so long held her in their power. Months later her stand was vindicated, the newspaper paying a large sum to charity.

On Friday, 3 December 1993, at a charity luncheon in aid of the Headway National Head Injuries Association, the Princess announced her withdrawal from public life for a period. In a sometimes quavering, yet defiant, voice, she appealed for 'time and space' after more than a decade in the spotlight.

During her five-minute speech she made a particular point concerning the unrelenting media exposure: 'When I started my public life 12 years ago, I understood that the media might be interested in what I did. I realized then that their attention would inevitably focus on both our private and public lives. But I was not aware of how overwhelming that attention would become; nor the extent to which it would affect both my public duties and my personal life, in a manner that has been hard to bear.'

As she later said: 'The pressure was intolerable then, and my job, my work was being affected. I wanted to give 110 per cent to my work, and I could only give 50 . . . I owed it to the public to say "Thank you, I'm disappearing for a bit, but I'll come back." '

Indicating that she would continue to support a small number of charities while she set about rebuilding her private life, the Princess emphasized: 'My first priority will continue to be our children, William and Harry, who deserve as much love, care and attention as I am able to give, as well as an appreciation of the tradition into which they were born.'

While she singled out the Queen and the Duke of Edinburgh for their 'kindness and support', Diana never once mentioned her estranged husband. In private, she was unequivocal about where the blame lay for her departure from the stage. 'My husband's side have made my life hell for the last year,' she told a friend.

When she reached the relative sanctuary of Kensington Palace that afternoon, Diana was relieved, saddened but quietly elated. Her retirement would give her a much-needed chance to reflect and refocus. If the separation had brought her the hope of a new life, her withdrawal from royal duties would give her the opportunity to translate that hope into a vibrant new career, one that would employ to the full her undoubted gifts of compassion and caring on a wider, international stage.

A few months later, at a reception at the Serpentine Gallery, of which she was patron, the Princess was in fine form. She was relaxed, witty and happy among friends. The events of 1993 seemed a dim and dismal memory. As she chatted to the movie star Jeremy Irons he told her: 'I've taken a year off acting.'

Diana smiled and replied: 'So have I.'

11
'I Am Going to Be Me'

Throughout her life, Diana was dominated by men; Prince Charles shaped her private life, the 'men in grey' her public life and newspaper editors her international image. Nowhere was this ambiguous relationship more apparent than with her personal bodyguards. They were at once her gaolers and her friends, protecting her not just from the unwelcome attentions of the paparazzi but acting as lookouts in her continual battles with the Palace.

They told her the latest Palace gossip, covered her tracks and kept her supplied with *risqué* jokes. Over the years several, like Barry Mannakee, Graham Smith and Ken Wharfe, became father figures, listening to her problems and giving advice — friendly faces in a hostile world. It was no coincidence that she went to see the Kevin Costner film *The Bodyguard* as soon as it was released.

While they were allies, they were also part of the system, a club she was trying to resign from. If she were to define her own life, exercise her freedom, she had to do it on her own. Quite simply, she wanted the right to grow up, to learn from her mistakes, to achieve something for herself. At the same time she wanted to enjoy the simple pleasures most people take for granted. As she once said: 'I like to live as normally as possible. Walking along the pavement without a bodyguard gives me such a thrill.'

Now that she was semi-detached from the royal family, she believed that she had the right to be treated like a private citizen. It was no easy task. The Metropolitan Police, who guard the royal family, were horrified at the idea of leaving the Princess, one of the world's most famous faces, on her own, prey to the attentions of terrorists, aggressive photographers and lone madmen. While they agreed, albeit with the greatest reluctance, to withdraw her personal protection, they continued to monitor her movements — but from a discreet distance.

It was not going to be an easy option, but then again, nothing in Diana's life was straightforward. The paparazzi who dogged her footsteps were not slow to see their opportunity. 'Why don't you rape someone else?' she shouted at several cameramen during a private shopping trip. They quickly got used to her avoidance tactics — the sour expression, the averted head and the handbag strategically placed in front of her face — and dubbed her the 'royal baglady'. She had to prove to the many Doubting Thomases in the Metropolitan Police that she could survive without a permanent shadow. More than that, however, she also wanted, quite simply, to be left alone.

Behind the scenes, away from the prying eyes of the media, the Princess was quietly pursuing her charity work. For a long time she had been secretly exploring royal visits that brought her as close to the people as possible without the need for smiling officials and the ubiquitous photographers. During the summer of 1992, when public attention on her marriage was at its most intense, she had begun a series of private visits to hospices, visits that resulted in her plan to one day open hundreds of such institutions around the world. At the same time she toured refuges for battered women and shelters for the homeless, as well as entertaining charity officials at Kensington Palace or joining them in a variety of discussion groups.

For years the Princess had been celebrated

simply for being. Now she wanted to be judged for doing, in words and deeds, an idea that powerfully drove her desire to do more in the way of private charity work. It was an ambition which, however worthy, still required her to make adjustments, even sacrifices, to learn new skills, to adapt to circumstances, sometimes at a moment's notice. In all these, however, she persevered, using friends and contacts to help her build a firm foundation from which to launch her new career. Determined to polish her speech-making, Diana enlisted the help at various times of the film director Lord Richard Attenborough, the actor Terence Stamp and the voice coach Peter Settelen. Her speeches, though initially hesitant, gradually earned her both recognition and praise, her sincerity and courage in dealing with difficult emotional issues shining through. For a girl who hated speaking in public, her speech-making gave her a real sense of control. Her audience was not always sympathetic, however. The agony aunt Claire Rayner, accused her of 'glamorizing' eating disorders, and in June 1993 the conservative columnist Mary Kenny, a Roman Catholic, criticized her 'self-indulgent psychobabble' after she had made a speech highlighting the problems faced by women dependent upon tranquillizers and other drugs. Diana was shocked and upset by the hostility. The issues she was addressing — Aids, battered women, drug addiction, alienation and loneliness — were challenging ones, not only for herself but also for society. She was learning that this was a school of hard knocks.

The unhappiness she had suffered in her own life gave her a genuine empathy with people in difficulties. Her friend Rosa Monckton has described her 'intuitive genius', and Diana herself spoke of her own instinctive ability almost to 'see inside someone's soul' when she first met them. In this she believed she was watched over from the spirit world by her grandmother, Cynthia Spencer. Her psychic abilities and uncanny empathy with those making their last spiritual journey strengthened her conviction that in another existence she had been a nun. It may be for this reason that she felt so drawn to — indeed, adored — the late Mother Teresa who once said to Diana: 'To heal other people you have to suffer yourself', a sentiment with which the Princess wholeheartedly agreed. She herself once said: 'Death doesn't frighten me.' Father Alexander Sherbrooke, who saw Diana going about her work in Mother Teresa's

House for the Dying in Calcutta, was one of many people who were impressed by the Princess's ability to cope gracefully with suffering, to look with clear eyes and an open heart upon the diseased and the dying. He observed that the majority of people found that dealing with the severely disabled and afflicted required a special kind of courage, one that does not come easily to most. 'But the Princess was completely intuitive, and saw something special in every human being,' he said.

Examples abound. When friends asked her to visit a pensioner who was dying of a brain tumour she was pleased to help. There was also a guileless joy in being able to assist a friend in trouble. Again, when her lady-in-waiting Laura Lonsdale lost her 11-month-old son, Louis, through cot-death syndrome, the Princess spent many months counselling her through her grief. Her sensitivity and understanding were much appreciated by the family. 'The Princess of Wales is the nearest thing to an angel on earth,' said one relative. 'She has a unique quality of being able to comfort someone without being pushy or over the top. She has a magic touch all of her own.' A few weeks after the tragic death of the Labour Party leader, John Smith, she invited his widow and three daughters to Kensington Palace for a private lunch so that she could personally express her sympathy, and she took time to write to the parents of baby Debbie Humphries who was kidnapped from hospital when just four hours old. As Oonagh Toffolo, one of Diana's friends, said: 'Her public image is one of beauty, grace and caring. Her private life is one of simplicity and humility. She has time for everyone, the old, the sick and the deprived.'

In truth, Diana moved effortlessly into the role of ministering angel. As Rosa Monckton said: 'She had a unique ability to spot the broken-hearted, and she could zero in on them, excluding all hangers-on and spectators.' It was a view wholeheartedly endorsed by her brother, who observed of her work: 'She strikes me as an immensely Christian figure and she has the strength which I think true Christians have and the direction in her life which others can envy; that sureness of her purpose and the strength of her character and position to do an enormous amount of good.'

The many private visits she made, undertaken without fuss or formality, could not have been in greater contrast to the carefully contrived and stage-managed artificiality of a traditional royal visit. At last Diana had the chance to perform meaningful and satisfying work. 'I want to walk into a room, be it a hospice for the dying or a hospital for sick children, and feel that I am needed. I want to do, not just to be,' she said. Her difficulty was that her position provided her with a role in which she was effective — the presence of a princess was guaranteed to raise money — but which also left her feeling personally unfulfilled. By contrast, her private work was fulfilling, but ultimately ineffectual without the wider audience of the world stage. It was a dilemma for which she had yet to find a solution.

The Princess was anxious that her sons should also see something of the real world beyond boarding schools and palaces. As she said in a speech on Aids: 'I am only too aware of the temptation of avoiding harsh reality; not just for myself but for my own children too. Am I doing them a favour if I hide suffering and unpleasantness from them until the last possible minute? The last minutes which I choose for them may be too late. I can only face them with a choice based on what I know. The rest is up to them.'

She felt this was especially important for William, the future king. As she once said: 'Through learning what I do, and his father to a certain extent, he has got an insight into what's coming his way. He's not hidden upstairs with the governess.' Over the years she took both boys on visits to hostels for the homeless and to see seriously ill people in hospital. When she took William on a secret visit to the Passage day centre for the homeless in Central London, accompanied by the late Cardinal Basil Hume, her pride was evident as she introduced him to what many would consider the flotsam and jetsam of society. 'He loves it and that really rattles people,' she proudly told friends. The Catholic Primate of All England was equally effusive. 'What an extraordinary child,' he told her. 'He has such dignity at such a young age.' This upbringing helped William cope when a group of children with special needs joined fellow school pupils for a Christmas party. Diana watched with delight as the future king gallantly helped these youngsters join in the fun. 'I was so thrilled and proud. A lot of adults couldn't handle it,' she told friends.

Again, during one Ascot week, a time of champagne, smoked salmon and fashionable frivolity for High Society, the Princess took her boys to the Refuge night shelter for down-and-outs. William played chess while Harry joined in a card game. Two hours later the boys were on their way back to Kensington Palace, a little older and a little wiser. 'They have a knowledge,' she once said. 'They may never use it, but the seed is there, and I hope it will grow because knowledge is power. I want them to have an understanding of people's emotions, people's insecurities, people's distress and people's hopes and dreams.'

Her quiet endeavours gradually won back many of the doubters who had come to see her as a threat to the monarchy, or as a talentless and embittered woman seeking to make trouble, especially by upstaging or embarrassing her husband and his family. The sight of the woman who was still then technically the future Queen, unadorned and virtually unaccompanied, mixing with society's poorest or most distressed or most threatened, confounded many of her critics.

There was, too, another advantage, equally undesigned but no less beneficial. The peeling away of the layers of protocol surrounding the Princess meant that she became far more involved in the day-to-day running of her life than ever before. Her staff of 12 gradually dwindled as Diana reduced her royal duties and adopted a more hands-on approach. She and her private secretary, Patrick Jephson, began discreetly lobbying her many influential contacts on behalf of her charities. For a time, the Princess handled her own press relations, with mixed success.

None of this, however, not even the most fulfilling charity work or the most successful appeal, could hide the fact that Diana's life was in limbo — officially separated, yet not divorced, officially a member of the royal family, yet no longer either a willing or a welcome part of it. She had left one world without a clear idea of where she was going next. For all the praise her charity work earned her, there was impatience that she should return to the fold, or forge a clearly defined new life for herself, or failing either, that she should fall from grace. Many were uneasy with, and intolerant of, this continuing hiatus as she quietly but sincerely endeavoured to carve a new lifestyle. Now everything from her fashions — she was accused of looking like a suburban housewife by *Tatler* magazine — to her battles with photographers began to come under hostile scrutiny.

It was the unfairness that hurt her most. Accustomed to an adoring press, she was startled by how quickly reverence and respect had evaporated since discarding the invisible but protective cloak of royalty.

Meanwhile she watched with growing concern as her husband's star gradually grew brighter. His was a much easier task. Unlike the Princess, Prince Charles was not rocking the boat, but merely waiting his turn to be captain of the 'good ship Windsor'. With the voluble support of the Prime Minister, the Cabinet, the Church, the rest of the royal family, Establishment newspapers and the Great and the Good, and backed by a professional office staff, he was by definition able to play the waiting game.

The centrepiece of Prince Charles's long haul back to credibility, following the collapse of his marriage and the 'Camillagate' tapes affair, was a documentary by TV star Jonathan Dimbleby to mark the 25th anniversary of his investiture as Prince of Wales. From the moment the Prince informed Diana of the project, in the summer of 1992, she had been on tenterhooks, concerned that her role as a mother would be questioned, and that her estranged husband might use their children as innocent props in the exercise.

In the event, the Princess herself hardly featured in the programme, broadcast in June 1994, which focused on Prince Charles's working life. It was, however, her husband's anguished confirmation that he had been unfaithful which hit the headlines next day. In response to Dimbleby's question, 'Were you, did you try to be faithful and honourable to your wife when you took on the vow of marriage?' the Prince replied: 'Yes, absolutely.' Dimbleby continued, 'And were you?' 'Yes,' Prince Charles answered, but after a brief pause added, 'until it became irretrievably broken down, us both having tried.' Asked about his relationship with Camilla Parker Bowles, the Prince confirmed that she remained the mainstay of his life, and would continue to do so in spite of her perceived role in the break-up of his marriage. She was, he said, 'a great friend of mine . . . she has been a friend for a very long time and will continue to be a friend for a very long time'.

Diana had decided against seeing an advance viewing of the film, and on the evening of the broadcast, which was watched by 13 million people, she set out not merely to enjoy herself, but to be seen doing so. She had a long-standing engagement at the Serpentine Gallery. The dinner was a sophisticated international event, and one where she found herself among friends. Her flirty little black dress designed by Christina Stambolian could not have been a more appropriate choice, its style shouting the message, 'Whatever Charles may do, I'm having a ball.' It was immediately dubbed 'The Revenge Dress'. Yet in private she was not so calm. Her initial response to the programme was: 'My first concern was for the children. I wanted to protect them.' Then she added: 'I was pretty devastated myself. But then I admired the honesty.'

If the Prince had been candid about his affair with Camilla, what was less clear was the question of divorce. In the Dimbleby interview he was evasive, saying that it was 'very much in the future' and 'not a consideration in my mind'. But his public admission of adultery — in effect, an admission that he was to blame — undoubtedly broke the stalemate surrounding divorce discussions.

From the beginning Diana was adamant that she would not be the one to initiate proceedings, and this had formed the basis of any dialogue about what she called 'the D-word'. As far as she was concerned it was Charles who had asked her to marry him, and it was Charles who must request a divorce. 'I'm not going anywhere, I'm staying put,' she emphasized, insisting that the initiative had to come from her husband's side. It was a view she would later reiterate during her famous *Panorama* interview.

A friend who regularly discussed the issue with the Princess explained her thinking: 'She always operated on the basis that it was not going to be her that caused the crisis because she felt that it would reflect badly on her. She had a pathological fear of being blamed. At the same time she would have felt cheated out of all the effort and good work that she had been doing. At the end of the day she wanted to leave her mark and if she just walked away she would be the loser. Everyone would say that she had not been able to take the pressure. The royal family would be sitting there and she would have endured 13 years for nothing before opting out.'

Yet her understandable caution, especially regarding access to the children, worried some of her friends, who watched with concern as she slipped on the familiar psychological garb of the victim, a helpless pawn unable to shape the course of events rather than one of the central characters in the unfolding drama. If, they argued, she was genuinely searching for a new role and a new life then there was little point in marking time on the fringes of the royal family. The 'pack-your-bags-and-leave' school felt that the longer she vacillated the more she compromised the freedom for which she so clearly longed. Other friends and advisers, in particular her legal team headed by Lord Mishcon, took the view that tactically she would obtain a fair financial settlement — there was much discussion about suitable houses — but that overriding all other concerns were her demands in relation to the children, who were her first concern, and her royal status, particularly her right to use the title of honour 'Her Royal Highness', an appellation in the sole gift of the Sovereign.

In many respects she was ambivalent about keeping this 'handle', and at times even talked about reverting to her maiden name, Lady Diana Spencer. Not only did she feel that a royal title got in the way of her relationship with the public — the modest manner in which she conducted her engagements without an accompanying retinue underlined her lack of interest in outward show — but she was also far prouder of her own family heritage, the Spencers being a good deal more English than the Windsors, than she was of the royal family. While she had little truck with the style that goes with royalty, she knew that the position lent a status which allowed her to promote causes she believed in. A divorce implied that she would no longer be dusted with that special magic royalty confers, at a stroke radically diminishing both her prestige and her chance to perform effectively on the world stage.

Perhaps Diana's true feelings came to the surface the day she took Prince William for lunch at a fashionable family restaurant, Smollensky's Balloon in Central London, where magician John Styles took her wedding ring, placed it in a silk handkerchief and, with a flourish, made it vanish. Diana collapsed into a fit of laughter and cried: 'Good.' Sadly, though, she knew all too well that there was no magic wand which could erase the hurt of the last decade, or easily resolve the constitutional and financial consequences of a royal divorce.

Worse than that, while the issue remained unsettled, she was open to criticism from her enemies inside and outside the Palace. For instance, when Prince Charles privately complained about Diana's £3,000-a-week grooming bill, his grievance conveniently found its way into two national newspapers known to be hostile to her. The criticism, which conveyed an image of frivolity and excess, perplexed the Princess who, while ridiculing the assertion, noted that a similar whispering campaign had been waged against the Duchess of York when she, too, was in the throes of divorce negotiations.

This was the downside of playing the waiting game. Not only did it put off the day when she could strike out on her own, leaving behind the royal family and all its trappings of prestige and privilege, but it made her a hostage to fortune, prey to continual hostile sniping. As she later acknowledged: 'I was the separated wife of the Prince of Wales. I was a problem. She won't go quietly, that's the problem. I'll fight to the end, because I believe that I have a role to fulfil and I've got two children to bring up.'

It was a lonely struggle. Thwarted by what she called 'the men in grey' in her attempt to redefine her role as a 'princess for the world' rather than as the Princess of Wales, frustrated by the prevarication over the divorce and continually judged by a fickle jury of the press and public, Diana once again felt a deep need to state her case. In 1992 she had used me as the means of articulating the true nature of her life inside the royal family. Three years later she decided to drop the pretence and speak to her public in person. This was both a courageous decision, and one which showed the extent to which she had grown up in the intervening period. For the first time she was prepared to take responsibility for her own words, her own actions, her own life.

That, however, proved to be easier said than done. While every other member of the royal family, most notoriously her husband, had used television to promote their causes and latterly to talk about their private lives, Diana knew that she would never be allowed that freedom by the Palace. She had enjoyed countless approaches from the world's most prominent broadcasters, including Barbara Walters and Oprah Winfrey, while in 1994 she was in detailed secret discussions about an ITV documentary of her life. In the end she reluctantly decided against co-operation, not only because Prince Charles was then working with Jonathan Dimbleby for his own programme, but also because of antagonism from courtiers. 'It was the right pitch at the wrong time,' recalled the producer, Mike Brennan. 'It didn't help that the Palace continually tried to shunt the project into a siding.'

A year on, the increasingly beleaguered Princess decided to take matters into her own hands, secretly agreeing to be interviewed by Martin Bashir, a journalist then attached to the BBC's flagship current-affairs programme, *Panorama*. Ironically, Bashir was the latest in a long line of *Panorama* reporters who had for some time been unenthusiastically trying to cobble together a broadcast about the monarchy. This time, however, he cracked the code. Like me, he soon realized that secrecy was essential if the project was to be a success — at any moment the Palace could have killed the proposed interview with a single telephone call. Only by elaborate subterfuge would Bashir and his crew be able to record Diana's words. They used special compact cameras so as not to attract attention when they arrived at Kensington Palace on a quiet Sunday in early November 1995. As a precaution Diana had dismissed her staff for the day, knowing that she could not trust a soul. Even when the programme had been completed, BBC executives, fearing censorship from on high, kept the Corporation's governors in the dark. The fact that the Princess of Wales, a major international figure, and the BBC, a leading public broadcasting company, had to go to such extraordinary lengths to record an interview makes a mockery of the notion that we live in an open society. Indeed, if the programme had been the smuggled testimony of a Middle Eastern princess there would have been outraged protests about a repressive regime.

This very British television coup, broadcast in November 1995, was a sensation, in every meaning of the word. The Princess, wearing striking black eye make-up, discussed her life, her children, her husband and her hopes for the future with remarkable frankness. Inevitably her interview retraced many aspects of *Diana: Her True Story,* as she talked openly about her eating disorders, her depression, her cries for help, the enemy inside the Palace, and her husband's relationship with Camilla Parker Bowles. In a phrase that pithily captured the problems of her relationship with Prince Charles she said: 'There were three of us in this marriage so it was a bit crowded.' At the same time she admitted her own infidelity with the former Life Guards officer James Hewitt, who had previously told the story of their affair in a book. 'Yes, I adored him, yes, I was in love with him,' she said, adding that she had felt 'absolutely devastated' by his betrayal when news of the book he had coauthored reached her ears. While casting doubts on her husband's fitness to rule, and thus his eventual accession to the throne, she spoke of her own ambitions not just for herself but for her children and the monarchy. 'I would like to be a Queen in people's hearts . . . someone's got to go out there and love people and show it.' The programme attracted the largest audience for any television documentary in broadcasting history.

In the ensuing furore over her admission of infidelity and her comments about Camilla Parker Bowles, less was made of Diana's desire to be an ambassador for Britain than she had hoped. It was a failure of emphasis she came to regret. At first, however, it seemed that before the Princess could take on any new role as a goodwill ambassador, both she and the Palace had to learn that diplomacy begins at home. The state of open warfare between the Waleses, immensely damaging to the monarchy, could not be allowed to continue, and it therefore surprised no one when, just four weeks after the interview, the Queen, after consultation with the Prime Minister and the Archbishop of Canterbury, wrote personally to both the Prince and Princess of Wales requesting that they divorce sooner rather than later.

The Sovereign's intervention finally got negotiations started, both sets of lawyers working their way through labyrinthine divorce details. Late on Wednesday, 28 February 1996, a date Diana described as 'the saddest day of my life', the Princess announced her decision to agree to an uncontested divorce. It followed a 45-minute meeting at St James's Palace with Prince Charles, who was dismayed when Diana took it upon herself to announce the news to the world. In a statement she said: 'The Princess of Wales has agreed to Prince Charles's request for a divorce. The Princess will continue to be involved in all decisions relating to the children and will remain at Kensington Palace, with offices in St James's Palace. The Princess of Wales will retain the title and be known as Diana, Princess of Wales.'

Her statement was one presumption too many as far as the Queen was concerned. She authorized her courtiers to issue a rare and icy public rebuke to her daughter-in-law, saying that she was 'most interested' to hear that the Princess of Wales had agreed to the divorce. According to Her Majesty, details concerning the settlement, the Princess's future role and her title remained to be addressed. 'This will take time,' a Buckingham Palace spokesman announced ominously.

Diana was understandably distressed, telling friends: 'I did not want this divorce but I have agreed to it. Now they are playing Ping-Pong with me.' It seemed that the sticking points with her estranged husband were her demand for offices at St James's Palace, now his London residence — Prince Charles preferred her to be based at Kensington Palace — and her desire to have a lump-sum payment rather than staggered amounts from the Duchy of Cornwall. At the same time his camp indicated that they had no objection to Diana retaining the style 'Her Royal Highness'. Negotiations were to continue for another four months until finally, on 15 July 1996, the Prince of Wales was granted a decree nisi. Six weeks later, on 28 August, the fairytale marriage ended with the issue of the decree absolute. While the Princess won her demands for offices at St James's Palace and a lump-sum payment, estimated at £17 million, she was stripped of her title of honour, a move which was judged mean and spiteful by the public.

While Diana made light of the matter, her friend Rosa Monckton echoed the views of many when she said: 'I think it was a petty thing to have removed from her. It always seemed strange to me that the royal family said she was still very much part of their family but were not allowing the nation to recognize her as part of that family. She didn't resent it at all because she wasn't somebody who stood on ceremony.' However, her eldest son consoled her with the promise that he would reinstate her title of 'Her Royal Highness' on the day he became king.

Of rather more personal significance was the fact that the divorce finally allowed her to spring-clean her life. For a long time she had discussed dropping most of her huge raft of charities so as to be able to concentrate on those which really mattered to her. Even before the separation she had become dismayed that her endless round of charity dinners and balls was preventing her from meeting, and thus learning and understanding more about the people who really mattered, those suffering from Aids, cancer, leprosy, and alienation from society. It was no surprise that Diana, who had always seen herself as an outsider, chose to retain five charities — the Leprosy Mission, Centrepoint (a charity for the homeless), the National Aids Trust, the Royal Marsden NHS Trust (a cancer hospital) and the Great Ormond Street Children's Hospital — charities devoted to helping those on the margins both of society and of life itself. With the exception of the English National Ballet, more than a hundred other charities, including the British Red Cross, were pruned from her portfolio.

While some observers argued acidly that her decision was a vindictive rejoinder to the Queen's decision to strip her of her title of honour, the real reason went to the heart of her personality. For years she had searched for a role which allowed her to contribute to national life while fulfilling her yearning to use her unique gifts of compassion and empathy to help needy individuals, as well as experiencing for herself the most challenging aspects of charity work. By focusing on a handful of charities, Diana hoped to make a difference both to herself and to those genuinely in need of her special abilities.

In many ways, the finality of the divorce gave Diana permission to free herself. Not only did it end her marriage, it cut her loose from the yoke of royalty, for in the years following the separation she had remained inextricably linked to Prince Charles and his family. The divorce closed that unhappy chapter in her life, the hard choices she had made during the turbulent 1990s giving her the one thing she had never dared dream of — hope. At last she could be herself; more than that, for the first time in her life she had the opportunity to explore fully the talents she had been born with.

Yet while she hovered tantalizingly on the

brink of a new life, her thoughts were often tinged with all too understandable anger and the sense of betrayal she felt at the wasted years spent suffocating inside a miserable marriage and a stultifying system.

Since her separation she had slowly, cautiously — perhaps even unconsciously — performed a kind of striptease, unpeeling the veils of convention which had surrounded her. During the 1980s she had been defined only by her fashions, seen merely as a glamorous clothes horse, a royal adjunct, a wife and mother. Since the separation, however, her regal wardrobe, which defined her royal mystique, had been left in the closet. Indeed, her decision, inspired by Prince William, to hold an auction of her royal wardrobe for Aids charities in New York in the summer of 1997 was a very public farewell to that old life. She no longer wanted to be seen as just a beautiful model for expensive clothes. Moreover, during her sensational days as a semi-detached royal she had deliberately stripped away other trappings of monarchy, her servants, her ladies-in-waiting, her limousines and, most controversially, her bodyguards. The casting off of her royal title was one giant step on that journey.

She had spent much time grieving over a

failed relationship, lost hopes and broken ambitions. She had once said: 'I had so many dreams as a young girl. I hoped for a husband to look after me, he would be a father figure to me, he would support me, encourage me, say "Well done" or "That wasn't good enough." I didn't get any of that. I couldn't believe it.'

The days of betrayal, anguish and hurt lay in the past. Now it was time to move on, to make the most of her position and her personality. Opportunity beckoned. As the Princess admitted: 'I have learned much over the last years. From now on I am going to own myself and be true to myself. I no longer want to live someone else's idea of what and who I should be.

'I am going to be me.'

12
'TELL ME YES'

Like so many crucial events in Diana's life, it began by chance. A casual conversation with her divorce solicitor Maggie Rae resulted in a secret meeting with the then Opposition leader, Tony Blair, and finally the resolution of the issue which had dominated her thinking for months, namely her determination to become a humanitarian ambassador.

It was an ambition which had burned within her long before she publicly gave vent to her wishes during her only television interview in 1995. Her long-standing commitment to finding a role as a princess for the world rather than the Princess of Wales said much about her feelings towards duty to the nation, as well as graphically illustrating her development as a woman and, perhaps surprisingly, as a feminist. During her early years in public life she was happy to conform to society's — and the monarchy's — expectations of a princess. Essentially royal men are judged by what they say, royal women by how they look. As she blossomed into a natural beauty, Diana was defined by her appearance, not by her achievements. For a long time she accepted the role of the docile helpmate to her husband. She was praised for simply existing. For being, not for doing. As one of her friends remarked: 'She was only expected by the royal system to be a clothes horse and an obedient wife.'

The separation in December 1992 changed everything. Unlike Prince Charles, whose constitutional position as the future king is clearly defined, the Princess had no preordained role, no lodestar to guide her. Semi-detached from the monarchy, for the first time in her adult life she was flying solo and was aware that it would be a tricky ride. 'I will make mistakes,' she said, 'but that will not stop me from doing what I feel is right.'

It was a process which embraced a liberation from her royal past as well as a recognition of her own abilities and limitations.

One of the many perplexing contradictions about Diana was that while she did not value herself highly as an individual she did understand her worth on the public stage, seeing that her standing in society, both at home and abroad, gave her a unique springboard to support the causes and issues she cherished. Yet she was deeply disenchanted with the protocol, the flummery and the artifice which inevitably surrounded royalty. Her challenge was to reinvent her public persona, to discard the robes of her office while retaining her authority. As a close friend noted: 'She felt she was being held back by the system and unable to fulfil her true potential.'

Essentially the fount of her discontent lay in the manner and style of the British monarchy, the brittle formality and mind-numbing irrelevance of so much of royal life. The Princess felt instinctively that if she could change the style of her public life she could enhance the substance of her contribution to the nation. 'I want to help the man in the street,' she once said, a sentiment which reflected the fact that in her heart she was a woman happier with the people rather than with her people. 'I feel much closer to people at the bottom than to people at the top and they [the royal family] don't forgive me for it,' she said shortly before her death.

Her skill in public life was the intuitive ability to use her office to promote her causes, while her inherent nature drew her to the dying, diseased and dispossessed. It was a potent combination. 'I will never complain again,' she said as she emerged from a one-room airless hut in one mountain village in Nepal during her first solo overseas visit in 1993.

She aspired towards a more informal, relaxed and approachable royal style; 'This needs a woman's touch', was her common refrain. Her view in essence was that so many issues and problems in a male-dominated world derive from the aggressive, secretive and often insensitive masculine ego. Problems could be more effectively addressed, she felt, when female qualities, as she saw them, of intuition, compassion, compromise and harmony were added to the equation. Her thinking, influenced by New Age advisers, was also rooted in her jaded view of the monarchy as a male-dominated institution, and in her undoubted cynicism towards the opposite sex following the failure of her marriage, views reinforced by her frequent private visits to the refuges for battered women.

Her interest in women's issues was matched by her growing awareness that she could play a genuine solo role on her own upon the world stage. It was exciting and exhilarating. Her work for Aids and leprosy proved that she could cut across national boundaries while her courage in admitting her eating disorders had prompted thousands of sufferers around the world to seek help. Many sent her letters of gratitude for helping them face problems in their own lives, a response which she found as embarrassing as it was pleasing.

It was against this developing philosophy that the Princess discussed with the Prime Minister, John Major, and Foreign Secretary, Douglas Hurd, her ideas for a future role. She wanted a roving ambassadorial position with a humanitarian rather than political emphasis. Diana's thinking was that so many conflicts arise from stalled communications between warring parties. Her solution was that the female touch can pour oil on troubled waters and help unblock choked lines of discussion. Simplistic certainly, grandiose possibly, but the notion of the Princess acting as a humanitarian ambassador did win a constructive response from the Prime Minister, who referred the proposal to Buckingham Palace for their consideration. They politely informed Downing Street that this was the kind of role tailor-made for the Prince of Wales. 'We want the heir not her', was the all too familiar cry from the 'men in grey'.

Little wonder, then, that when Diana watched Nigel Short play Garry Kasparov in the World Chess Championship she saw in the game a parable of her own position. 'I adored the game, it's my life. I'm just a pawn pushed around by the powers that be,' she observed. Even though she felt that her ambitions were thwarted by the British Establishment, her work did not go unnoticed elsewhere. In December 1996 Dr Henry Kissinger presented her with the 'Humanitarian of the Year' award at a ceremony in New York, the veteran diplomat acknowledging her strength and 'luminous personality' and praising the way she had 'aligned herself with the ill, the suffering and the downtrodden'.

Lauded abroad but sidelined at home, Diana, like others before her, saw herself as a prophet without honour in her own country. This frustration had earlier spilled over in her famous *Panorama* television interview when she appealed to the public over the heads of the Palace. She said plaintively: 'I'd like to be an ambassador for this country. As I have all this media interest, let's not just sit in this country and be battered by it. Let's take them, these people, out to represent this country and the good qualities of it abroad . . . I've been in a privileged position for 15 years. I've got tremendous knowledge about people and how to communicate and I want to use it.'

While her words may have fallen on deaf ears inside the government and the Palace, others were listening. During her earlier divorce negotiations Diana inevitably spent much time with her lawyers, building a strong bond with Maggie Rae. By co-incidence, Maggie was a great friend of fellow lawyer Cherie Blair and her politician husband, Tony. Encouraged by Diana, Rae agreed to act as an informal conduit between the Princess and the Labour Party politician. Tony Blair instinctively realized that Diana had outstanding potential as someone to represent Britain on the world stage. 'She was the face of the youthful New Britain he wanted to build,' recalls a Blair aide. However, great care had to be exercised in arranging face-to-face contacts as any leak would have been politically embarrassing both for Tony Blair and Diana. Several meetings were arranged, Blair impressed more and more by her humanitarian instincts and her international appeal.

On becoming Prime Minister in May 1997, Blair had the opportunity to employ

Diana's obvious talents officially, organizing a weekend summit at Chequers, the Prime Minister's official country retreat, in the summer. While Prince William played football with the Blair boys on the lawn, the Princess and the Prime Minister talked through the details of her informal ambassadorial role. Diana was delighted, remarking afterwards: 'I think at last I will have someone who will know how to use me. He's told me he wants me to go on some missions. I'd really like to go to China. I'm very good at sorting people's heads out.'

Indeed, what impressed the youthful Prime Minister more than anything was her uncanny gift for going to the heart of a difficult issue without unduly raising political hackles. As he commented after her death: 'She had a tremendous ability, as we saw over the landmines issue, to enter into an area that could have been one of controversy and suddenly just clarify for people what was the right thing to do. That in itself was an extraordinary attribute and I felt there were all sorts of ways that could have been harnessed and used for the good of people.'

More than anything in the last few weeks of her life, the Prime Minister's ardent approval and encouragement of her work as well as the success of her campaign against the evil of landmines gave her a renewed sense of self-worth, as well as a more sharply focused direction in her public life. Her staff were the first to notice the change of mood. 'Her enthusiasm was permanent and contagious,' recalled her secretary Louise Reid-Carr.

As with her compact with Blair, her involvement with the landmine issue was a case of the right pitch at the right time. By happy coincidence her friend, the film director Lord Attenborough, invited Diana to a charity première of his film *In Love and War,* a moving documentary about the havoc wreaked by landmines on civilians, particularly women and children, at the same time as Mike Whitlam, then Director-General of the British Red Cross, was visiting Kensington Palace to try to secure a renewed commitment to the charity.

The film, which focused on the work of the Red Cross, captured Diana's imagination and she agreed with alacrity to help raise funds in the campaign to rid the world of landmines. Furthermore she decided to accompany Red Cross officials and a BBC film crew to publicize the work of the charity in war-torn Angola. It was, as Diana would have put it, a 'very grown-up' assignment.

At a meeting at Kensington Palace before she flew to Africa the Princess expressed her concern that her actions could be seen as political. Lord Attenborough recalled: 'She was aware that there were possible political pitfalls but decided to take the risk on the grounds that the suffering caused by landmines should be brought to the public's attention.' Inevitably, by championing the fight to ban landmines, Diana did raise political hackles — one junior minister in the then Conservative government described her as a 'loose cannon', while the objections of Tory MPs prevented her from attending a meeting of the all-party landmines eradication group in the House of Commons. Typically the Princess remained quizzically aloof from her accusers. 'I'm a humanitarian. I always have been, and I always will be,' she said simply.

More than that, by adding her weight to the campaign she clearly was making a difference. Pictures of her walking through a minefield in Angola forced the world to sit up and take notice — 'The impact she had was absolutely phenomenal,' said the British Red Cross. It became one of the most iconic photographs of her career.

Enthused by this initial success — the new British government responded by banning the export and use of landmines while the Clinton administration was pressurized into a similar policy rethink — the Princess discussed visits to other countries, notably Cambodia, Thailand, Afghanistan, northern Iraq and Bosnia. In the end, after advice from the Foreign Office, she decided to make a three-day visit to Bosnia, still slowly recovering from civil war, in the company of the distinguished journalist Lord Deedes. He recalled not only her gentle sense of humour but her ability to listen and to communicate the uncommunicable. When she walked around Sarajevo's largest cemetery she encountered a mother tending her son's grave. 'There was no language barrier,' he wrote. 'The two women gently embraced. Watching this scene from a distance, I sought in my mind who else could have done this. Nobody.'

However, the 40-odd cameramen and journalists who trailed around the ruins of a once-proud nation were not so much concerned with the sober issues surrounding landmines as with the explosion of interest in the new man in Diana's life, Dodi Fayed, the playboy son of the controversial owner of Harrods department store, Mohamed al-Fayed. It was a telling reminder to Diana, if she needed one, that while she might have escaped the suffocating embrace of the royal family and managed to reinvent her public persona, she could never free herself of her enduring and overarching image as a beautiful, single and available young woman. Whether she liked it or not, who she was going to marry was a question of more abiding fascination than what she was going to say.

More than that, since her separation in December 1992, the Princess had had to learn to deal with a society uneasy with strong, determined women. More than one commentator observed that Charles and Diana's separation released 'a backlash of misogynistic indignation that was truly shocking'. She knew that if she were caught in a careless caress or innocent embrace with another man, the whispering campaign would begin. This was no exaggeration, as was illustrated by the quasi-ritual humiliation faced by the separated Duchess of York when pictures of her having her toes sucked by her financial adviser John Bryan were released.

Until the divorce was finalized and the terms of settlement clarified, it was Diana's greatest concern that her children would be taken away from her by the most influential and feared family in Britain. So she was

541

forced to exercise extreme caution, for example, never having dinner parties at Kensington Palace because they would be misconstrued, any unattached men present becoming fair game for an ever-watchful media. Indeed, when she wanted to see a male visitor at Kensington Palace, like as not she would insist that they travel in the trunk of her car to avoid the waiting paparazzi. As she frequently complained: 'Who would take me on? I have so much baggage. Anyone who takes me out to dinner has to accept the fact that their business will be raked over in the papers. I think I am safer alone.'

She was acutely and often angrily aware that her tracks were dogged by paparazzi photographers hungry for that jackpot first picture of the Princess with the new man in her life. Her caution was therefore understandable. However innocent her friendships, she knew from bitter experience that male companions experienced lengthy, if not eternal, misery through the attentions of the media. She had almost lost count of the number of men — and often their wives — who had found themselves front-page news because they had spent a casual evening with her at a cinema, theatre or restaurant.

It was an unhealthy situation compounded by her emotional nature. The Princess was a tactile, affectionate and needy woman who craved the warmth and companionship that a loving relationship could bring but which she had been so long denied. Locked into a cool and distant marriage for most of her adult life, she was forced to channel her affections elsewhere, buying generous presents for friends and surrounding herself with material possessions to cushion her isolation. So she was fiercely protective of her boys, overly familiar with her staff because she was lonely, and unnervingly open with total strangers in her charity work. As a friend observed: 'She is always doing everything for everybody else; she needs to start doing things for herself. She wants the praise and adulation for being a martyr because of her great insecurity.'

Her image of sophisticated glamour and unapproachable sexuality merely masked her innermost need for a man to cherish her, to nurture her and to love her. Unwanted as a baby, unloved as a wife, she simply desired a man whom she could rely on, a companion she could trust. Yet all Diana had known was a romantic life of betrayal, either through circumstance or design, and disloyalty. When she had trusted, she had been let down, when she had loved, she had been cruelly exposed. She was rejected by Prince Charles for another woman; her former bodyguard Barry Mannakee, whom she adored, was tragically killed; her relationship with James Gilbey was viciously and publicly exposed in the Squidgygate tapes, while her lover, Captain James Hewitt, sold his story. Her friendship with former England rugby captain Will Carling ended when his wife Julia, a TV personality, blamed her for the break-up of their marriage, while her relationship with art dealer Oliver Hoare ended abruptly after a police investigation into a series of nuisance telephone calls to his home. Her subsequent love affair with heart surgeon Dr Hasnat Khan ended because he was not comfortable in the public spotlight.

For in spite of the hurt and betrayal, the Princess, who was at heart a guileless, rather naïve young woman, retained a romantic vision of her future, dreaming of a knight in shining armour who would whisk her away to a new life. 'Her head tells her that she would like to be the ambassador to the world, her heart tells her that she would like to be wooed by an adoring billionaire,' commented a friend presciently. For a time billionaire Teddy Forstmann as well as reality

TV personality, property mogul and now President of the United States, Donald Trump attempted, unsuccessfully to woo her. She was all too aware of the turbulence a fresh union would create, both inside the royal family and with her two boys. As she once told her husband: 'If I fall in love with somebody else the sparks will fly and God help us.' Uppermost in her mind was her consideration for her sons. Any future suitor for her hand had to earn their approval before he could truly win her heart. Indeed, one of the attractions of James Hewitt was that he got on so well with William and Harry. While she wanted two more children, preferably girls — she was excited when her astrologer predicted that she would have another baby in 1995 — her desires were balanced by her sensitivity to the impact this would have on her existing family.

Thus her eternal hope that she could find a man to share her life was steadied by a caution born out of her experience, her position and her existing family. 'I haven't taken such a long time to get out of one poor marriage to get into another,' she told Taki Theodoracopulos, a gossip writer. This tension in her heart manifested itself in her frequent consultations with astrologers, seeking some kind of sign, some sense of where her future lay. She constantly asked them to predict the kind of man she would one day marry. 'Whoever you are, come here,' she used to say lightheartedly. While many prophecies were wildly off the mark, the central predictions, those she truly believed, now have an eerie, cock-eyed accuracy. A consistent theme among these prophecies was that she would marry a foreigner or at least a man of foreign blood. France appeared time and again in her private astrological prophecies both as a future home and as the birthplace of the new man in her life. Indeed, one of the reasons why she considered living in France, South Africa or America was not just unwelcome media attention at home, but also because her astrologers descried a beckoning vista of new love, new happiness and hope away from her home shores.

Her ruminations about the future were matched by her brooding on the past. With her friends she endlessly discussed the questions that vexed her; whether Charles and Camilla would ever find happiness together or if he would ever have the courage to give up the throne for the woman he loves. Her moods of obsessional curiosity were matched by a sympathy for their plight. 'He won't give her up and I wish him well,' she once told a friend. 'I would like to say that to his face one day.' As the years passed she became reconciled to Camilla as the châtelaine at Highgrove and began to appreciate that her loyalty and discretion should be rewarded by the Prince's public acknowledgement of their relationship. Yet that mood all too easily turned to reproach or self-pity as she mourned a lost youth and innocence. So when the Prince made it known that he was to host Camilla's 50th-birthday party at Highgrove in July 1997, Diana decided to make herself scarce. While she put a brave face on the event — 'Wouldn't it be funny if I suddenly came out of the birthday cake?' she joked — she knew that the media coverage would only reopen old wounds and reawaken old pains.

It was in this mood that she decided to accept a standing invitation from Mohamed al-Fayed, the owner of Harrods department store, for her and the boys to join him, his wife Heini and their four children at his holiday villa in St-Tropez in the South of France. Even though Fayed, a controversial figure whose payments to certain Members of Parliament had helped topple the Conservative administration, had known the Spencer family for years, several of her friends, including Rosa Monckton, wife of the then editor of the *Sunday Telegraph,* advised against accepting. The Egyptian multi-millionaire, who has been denied British citizenship, despite frequent protestations at what he regards as the unfairness of this exclusion, employed Diana's stepmother, the Countess de Chambrun, in his store and had become so close to the late Earl, Diana's father, that he would boast that they were like brothers. While he is ruthless and dictatorial in his business life, as those who have tangled with him will attest, Diana only saw the warm, generous and affectionate side of his character. She was happy to be photographed with his arm around her when they stood on the deck of one of his yachts near St-Tropez. For once Diana seemed relaxed and carefree, seemingly oblivious to the watching press as she jet-skied or swam off the beach in front of Fayed's villa.

However, media censure that the Princess had chosen a dubious and inappropriate holiday host needled her. She motored over to a boatload of British journalists and complained that they had been cruel to Fayed, whom she considered a long-standing family friend, and unfair to her and the boys, asking if they could leave them all in peace. In a parting shot she said:

'Expect a big surprise in the next two weeks.' Given subsequent tragic events, there has been much speculation about what she meant. It seems that she was going to announce the launch of a campaign to establish a chain of hospices around the world.

At the time it was interpreted as something more sensational. It was an incident that seemed to symbolize her unworldly innocence as well as her constant vulnerability. She was naïve to expect anonymity in the company of a man who was a thorn in the flesh of the British Establishment, at the most fashionable resort in southern France, and at the height of summer. At the same time, she was always on the lookout for a safe haven, particularly during school holidays, where she and her boys could enjoy some time together before the Princes journeyed back to their father at Balmoral. Perhaps if she had bought her own country seat — for a time she hunted for properties in Berkshire near William's public school, Eton — or achieved her dream of living on the Althorp estate she would have treated holiday invitations from well-meaning friends more cautiously. The ultimate irony was that, before the Fayed offer, she had already been invited to stay at a holiday home at Southampton in the Hamptons on the east coast of America by her billionaire friend Teddy Forstmann. However, for some unknown reason, the security services did not feel that the place offered sufficient security for the Princess and her boys, and the offer was declined.

Four days into that fateful July holiday, the party was joined by Fayed's eldest son, Emad, known as Dodi, who had first met the Princess ten years before when he played alongside Prince Charles in a polo match. There was little sign of their later intimacy when he was introduced to Diana. Crew members noted that he bowed and called her 'Ma'am', treating her with the deference due her station. Indeed, Dodi had his own yacht moored near *Jonikal,* his father's boat, and it was on that vessel that he was staying with his then fiancée, the Californian model Kelly Fisher.

At first sight the 41-year-old playboy, a Hollywood film producer, was an unlikely suitor for the hand of a princess, a woman who had spent her life stripping away the bogus glamour of royalty so that she could spend time with and truly understand people on the margins of existence. Born into unashamed luxury, Dodi, the only son of Mohamed al-Fayed and his first wife, the late Samira Khashoggi, whose brother Adnan is the billionaire arms dealer, was given his own Rolls-Royce complete with chauffeur and bodyguard when he was just 15. Educated at a series of exclusive schools in Switzerland, France and Egypt, his training was rounded off by a period at the Sandhurst Royal Military Academy, to 'toughen him up' before he joined the United Arab Emirates Air Force.

As a young man with a predilection for fast cars and beautiful women, it was inevitable that he should be drawn to the shiny glamour of Hollywood where he became a film producer involved most notably with the Oscar-winning *Chariots of Fire*. Following the failure of his eight-month marriage to the model Suzanne Gregard, he was linked to a series of glittering girlfriends including Brooke Shields, Joanne Whalley, Cathy Lee Crosby and Julia Roberts. His holiday companion, Kelly Fisher, was the latest in a long line of loves. Though he once said that his first marriage had put him off the institution for life, it seemed he was ready to settle down with the Californian model. Kelly Fisher later claimed that they were engaged at the time; he had bought her a $200,000 ring, presented her with a cheque for the same amount — it subsequently bounced — and picked out a sea-front property in Malibu where he and Kelly would live after their marriage.

Outwardly, then, Dodi Fayed was the archetypal frivolous playboy, skimming across the surface of life, buying fame and friendship as he bought his five Ferraris, with the reputed $100,000-a-month allowance he received from his father. Yet Diana was able to plumb beneath the shallows of his personality to discover several attributes which may have reminded her of her first love, Prince Charles.

Apart from a mutual love of polo, both men had other striking similarities, living as they did in the shadow of strong, dominating fathers. Those who knew Dodi well say that underneath the veneer of gentlemanly charm and courtesy, qualities which Diana admired in Prince Charles, was a man with sadness in his soul. His sensitivity was attributed to the calamities he had experienced in his life, namely the deaths of his mother, whom he adored, and of several other close relatives. This combination of suffering and sensitivity was attractive to Diana, who reacted with an intuitive reflex when she saw pain in others.

As important as their personal chemistry was Dodi's relationship with the boys. He rented a disco for two nights so that Diana and her children could dance in private, while those who watched him with William and Harry at La Renaissance bistro in St-Tropez noticed that they seemed at ease in his company. Later on they all drove to an amusement park where they played on the bumper cars.

By now the formality and distance which had characterized their first couple of days together had changed to a smiling intimacy, the couple chatting amicably and easily together. 'They were relaxed, full of knowing looks and obviously comfortable together,' observed a crew member. Diana's verdict, before flying to Milan to join Elton John and other celebrities at the funeral of Gianni Versace, was simple and direct: 'It was the best holiday of my life.'

As their friendship gathered strength, Mohamed al-Fayed encouraged his son's budding relationship, unashamedly making clear his ambitions for his eldest son and the world's most famous woman. 'I did give them my blessing,' he said, as the possibility of the linkage between his family dynasty and the upper echelons of British society became tantalizingly close.

All the while Prince Charles's shadow loomed in the background. In a curious way his decision to 'come out' in public with Camilla by hosting her 50th-birthday party seemed to have given Diana permission to be open about her love life as well. Just as her animosity towards Camilla was draining away, so the friendly equilibrium she had reached with Prince Charles, together with the new direction and success of her public life, all pointed one way — Diana was not only beginning to find inner peace but was prepared for the man she so keenly awaited to enter her life. In short, she was ready for romance.

Like a thunderstorm on a peaceful summer's day, the sudden eruption of this love affair took everyone by surprise. 'Don't worry, I'm not going to elope,' she told a friend as she flew off in a Harrods jet for a cruise off the Sardinian coast alone with the new man in her life. For the first time since her separation Diana no longer felt the need to hide, to conduct her love affair under cover, viewing with equanimity the news that trailing paparazzi had taken long-range pictures showing the couple hugging and kissing. She told friends that she felt that in Dodi, so warm, affectionate and endlessly attentive, she had at last found a man who appreciated her for herself, and wanted nothing from her but her own happiness.

Even the tearfully televised claims of Kelly Fisher that Dodi had jilted her for Diana, which should have set alarm bells ringing, did little to dim her affections. There were soon further worrying reports from America as Dodi's former lovers told of his idiosyncrasies, one even claiming that he had threatened her with a gun. Diana was unruffled. All the while shadowy figures, seemingly in the Fayed camp, were providing help to journalists, giving quotes, attributed to 'friends', that emphasized the couple's growing closeness. Dodi's father could barely contain his glee.

When she flew to Bosnia, once again courtesy of a Harrods jet, on her landmines campaign, the couple kept in touch via their satellite telephones. 'She laughed and laughed with him,' said Sandra Mott, who was hostess to the Princess for her three-day visit. As Dodi told his ex-wife Suzanne Gregard: 'Diana and I are having a romance, a true romance.' These sentiments were underscored by a change in his character. His long-standing friends noted that Dodi seemed more settled and serious, determined that he and Diana should make their relationship work. 'I'll never ever have another girlfriend,' he told Fayed's spokesman Michael Cole, who duly released that nugget of conversation.

What had started as a silly-season story was now taken more seriously, a fact underlined when the couple flew in Dodi's helicopter to see her psychic, Rita Rogers, a key adviser to Diana and the Duchess of York. Her closest friends found it perplexing that she was revealing such intimate aspects of her life to a man she had known for such a short time. While Dodi flew out to Los Angeles to settle the Kelly Fisher fiasco she secretly travelled to the Greek islands with her friend Rosa Monckton, once again courtesy of a Harrods jet. Even though she had not made any decisions about her future it was clear to her friend that for the first time in years Diana was happy, enjoying herself with a man who obviously and publicly cared for her.

Yet Diana felt distinctly unhappy about the way he lavished presents on her. 'That's not what I want, Rosa, it makes me uneasy. I don't want to be bought, I have everything I want. I just want someone to be there for me, to make me feel safe and secure.' It doubtless provoked painful memories of a childhood in which she wanted for nothing materially but everything emotionally.

Whatever anxiety Dodi's extravagant behaviour may have caused her, the Princess, herself famously generous with her friends, bought her boyfriend a cigar-cutter from Aspreys, the London jewellers, inscribed with the words: 'With love from Diana'. As a further sign of her affection she gave him a pair of cufflinks which had belonged to her father. 'She said that she knew that it would give him joy to know they were in such safe and special hands,' said a Fayed spokesman the day before her funeral.

As whirlwind romances go, this was a tornado. The couple had spent barely a week alone in each other's company but already the mass media, their appetites fuelled once again by judicious leaks from unnamed sources, were talking about marriage. It was by no means one-sided, Diana's instinctive caution and disapproval of conspicuous consumption was overwhelmed by Dodi's obvious affection, his consideration and his sensitivity. With him she didn't feel lonely any more. 'Elsa, I adore him. I have never been so happy,' the Princess told her friend Lady Elsa Bowker. She even called her answering machine from her mobile phone simply to hear his 'wonderful voice'. On 21 August the couple flew to the Mediterranean where they boarded Fayed's yacht, the *Jonikal,* for their second holiday alone that month. Once again, certain journalists obtained details of their approximate arrival and departure times, photographers capturing Diana and Dodi walking across the beach at St-Tropez.

As they larked about on a jet-ski in the bay, Diana swinging her leg over Dodi's shoulder, the intimacy and warmth of their body language clearly indicated the closeness of their relationship. More importantly, they managed to evade the media to go window shopping in Monte Carlo. Diana was said to be impressed with a diamond ring in the window of Alberto Repossi's jewellery store in Place Beaumarchais. The ring, a large diamond surrounded by a cluster of smaller stones and valued at £130,000, was from a collection of engagement rings called 'Tell Me Yes'. 'That's the one I want,' Diana was reported to have said, though those close to her dispute this. It was unclear if the ring symbolized a more lasting union, a signal that yes, at last she had found true peace and happiness. The purchase, or non-purchase, of the ring was at the centre of numerous claims and counter claims at the subsequent official investigations into her death.

While she may have been content, peace was more elusive. As the couple cruised off Portofino, the dark outriders of journalism, the notorious paparazzi, photographed the couple at long range carousing on the deck of the 195-foot *Jonikal.* Their intrusions provoked alarm but that did not prevent pictures of the Princess sunbathing on the yacht's diving platform being published around the world. 'Just tell me, is it bliss?' asked Rosa Monckton when she phoned Diana on her mobile phone on 27 August, just days before her death. Her reply said it all: 'Yes, bliss. Bye-bye.'

She seemed to have it all. Humanitarian success on the world stage, contentment and love in her private life. As she lazed on the deck of the *Jonikal,* for once the barometer of her heart was set fair. By some curious alchemy the public sensed this transformation, that this lonely, vulnerable and rudderless vessel had at last found a comforting anchor in life, a safe harbour to run to from the perils of the deep.

For a few short days she enjoyed that state of grace in a stormy existence. Then the heavens cracked open — and claimed her.

13
'THE PEOPLE'S PRINCESS'

To live in the hearts of those we leave behind is not to die.
Thomas Campbell 1777–1844

Inscription on the gates of Kensington Palace in the days of mourning before the funeral of Diana, Princess of Wales

She was at peace now, her face serene, almost angelic. Plainly and elegantly dressed, she looked beautiful. On her wrists were several bracelets, on her fingers a couple of simple rings.

At the very end her butler, Paul Burrell, stayed by her side so that, in the hours before she was taken for her final journey, she would not be alone. As he prayed and shed silent tears beside her coffin which lay in Kensington Palace, the world wept with him, still disbelieving, still uncomprehending of the stark and shocking fact that Diana, Princess of Wales was dead.

Only days before, the public had enjoyed seeing pictures of her relaxing on her Mediterranean holiday with the new man in her life, Dodi Fayed. She seemed at ease with herself, the public fascinated to see that a woman who had suffered so much seemed to have achieved a measure of personal happiness and contentment — at least for a time. Her enthusiastic focus on her humanitarian causes, notably her campaign against landmines, and the sense that she had resolved many of the difficulties that had assailed her since her departure from the royal family, were sources of quiet pleasure for many of her supporters. Earlier that summer, her decision to sell her royal wardrobe at a charity auction in New York was a very public sign that the Princess was about to move on, that her new life, her real life, was just beginning. Indeed, buoyed by the success of the auction, she had written to several girlfriends asking them to return clothes she had given them. Some received her request the morning after her death.

The public sensed this sea change, an awareness which made the suddenness of her death all the more difficult to bear. It was a mood captured by the writer Adam Nicolson: 'The clutching dragging sadness felt by the world was the knowledge that this long hard struggle, so bravely and in some way blindly fought, like a drowning person struggling for air, for the surface, for the light, should be cut off and shut down by the grim banality of a car crash. It is a disproportionate end to everything that went before. That is why it hurts.'

There was little consolation in the knowledge that the last few days of her life had been truly idyllic, enjoying her second holiday alone with Dodi Fayed cruising off the coast of Sardinia on his father's yacht *Jonikal.* They planned to round off their holiday with a night in Paris before Diana flew back to Britain to see her boys. While the trailing paparazzi had been a nuisance, arguing openly with the yacht's crew, the couple's departure for Paris was anticipated. None the less, when they arrived at Le Bourget airport outside Paris on a warm Saturday afternoon, paparazzi were waiting as, too, were drivers and security men from the Ritz hotel, owned by Mohamed al-Fayed.

On the way to the five-star hotel they stopped at what was once the Paris home of the Duke and Duchess of Windsor, another jewel in Fayed's crown, so that Dodi could show the Princess around the lovingly restored mansion and its magnificent gardens. During that journey from the airport they were trailed by a number of photographers on motorcycles who buzzed her Mercedes in their desire to get snatched pictures of the couple. The bodyguard, Kes Wingfield, travelling in a backup security vehicle together with Henri Paul, who played a fateful part in their deaths, recalls that the Princess, though irritated by the attentions of photographers, had been more concerned lest one of the trailing cameramen should fall and hurt himself, such was the recklessness of their pursuit.

The behaviour of the paparazzi was not the only matter on her mind that fateful afternoon. Once they had arrived at the Ritz the Princess received a phone call from an anxious Prince William who had been asked to appear in a photocall at Eton, where he was due to start his third year. While the Buckingham Palace request was part of the compact between the press and the Palace that, in return for leaving the young princes in peace, the media would be given occasional official photo opportunities, William was worried that there was a danger that his younger brother, Prince Harry, was being overshadowed. It was a concern shared by Diana.

As she had her hair done at the Ritz she

doubtless pondered on this conversation, her last with her eldest son. In the meantime, at around 6.30, Dodi visited the nearby jewellery store of Alberto Repossi, which had altered the 'Tell Me Yes' ring Diana had chosen while the couple were shopping in Monte Carlo during their Mediterranean cruise. Later that evening they planned to visit Dodi's splendid apartment on the Champs-Élysées before having supper at Le Benoît restaurant near the Pompidou Centre.

Was it here that Dodi planned to make a declaration of love, present the ring, which was later found in his apartment, and ask for Diana's hand in marriage? Certainly their last conversations with confidants that night suggested that their brief affair was about to take a significant and perhaps permanent course. Earlier Diana telephoned Richard Kay, a *Daily Mail* reporter who had got to know her well since her first solo foreign visit to Nepal in 1993. As she talked he got the impression that she was in love with Dodi and he was in love with her. They were, he surmised, 'blissfully happy'. That same evening Dodi spoke to the Saudi Arabian millionaire, Hassan Yassin, the brother of Dodi's stepfather, who was staying at the Ritz at the same time, and told him: 'It's serious. We're going to get married.' Hassan later recalled: 'I was very happy for him, for both of them.'

At just after 7 p.m. the couple made the short journey to Dodi's apartment where they stayed for a couple of hours. Again photographers snapped them coming out of the hotel and entering his apartment, where later her tokens of affection, the cigar-cutter and her father's cufflinks, were found. The presence of lurking photographers made them decide to cancel their restaurant booking and return instead to the Ritz for dinner. When they arrived at 9.50 p.m., Diana, dressed in a black blazer and white jeans, and Dodi, in a brown suede jacket, looked ill at ease, a mood aggravated by the stares of fellow diners when they sat down for dinner in the hotel's two-star Espadon restaurant. Instead they returned to the £6,000-a-night Imperial Suite where Diana ate scrambled eggs with asparagus followed by sole. In the meantime Henri Paul, the hotel's deputy head of security, who had been off duty for three hours, was called in to organize the couple's return to Dodi's apartment where they were due to spend the night. Waiting for her in his apartment was a love poem written by Dodi which he had had inscribed on a silver plaque. He had carefully placed it under her pillow. She never saw it.

Meanwhile the gaggle of photographers waiting outside the hotel for the couple to emerge was growing by the hour and from time to time Henri Paul, who knew several by name, went outside to chat and tease them about when the couple would emerge. His boss, Dodi Fayed, had other ideas. According to bodyguard Kes Wingfield, Dodi had come up with a plan to mount an operation which would leave the photographers empty-handed. It was a simple enough plan: decoy cars were to leave from the front of the Ritz and lure the paparazzi away and so allow Dodi and Diana to escape from the rear and return unhindered to his apartment. At 12.20 a.m. the Mercedes S280, containing Diana, Dodi, Henri Paul as driver and another bodyguard, Trevor Rees-Jones, roared away from the rear service entrance of the hotel. While Henri Paul was alleged to have shouted to the handful of paparazzi, 'Don't bother following, you won't catch us', photographers on foot did manage to snatch shots of the Princess, hiding her face in her arms, as the car left the hotel precincts.

Details of the next few minutes remain murky, with spokesmen from all corners twisting every scrap of available evidence in their attempts to avoid responsibility for the fatal events of that night. What is in no doubt was that the driver, Henri Paul, was drunk, in fact so drunk that he was three times over the legal limit for drinking and driving. He had also taken a mixture of drugs, one an antidepressant, another used to treat alcoholism.

From the amount of alcohol in his bloodstream he was 600 times more likely to have a fatal car crash than if sober. High on drink, drugs and adrenalin, desperate to ensure that Dodi's decoy ruse worked successfully, Henri Paul drove like a maniac, roaring through a heavily built-up area at reckless speeds. As Dominic Lawson, former editor of the *Sunday Telegraph* and a friend of the Princess, has observed: 'Drunk or sober, no chauffeur would travel at over 100 miles per hour in a tunnel with a 30 miles per hour limit, unless ordered to do so by his boss.'

At the Place de la Concorde, Paul was seen by one trailing photographer to have jumped the Mercedes through a red light and to be hurtling towards the Place de l'Alma underpass on the north bank of the Seine at high speed. At around 12.24 a.m. the Mercedes, travelling at between 85 to

95 miles an hour, entered the dimly lit tunnel. Henri Paul lost control, the car colliding head-on with an unprotected concrete pillar dividing the carriageways, skidding around and coming to a halt facing the wrong way.

The driver and Dodi were killed instantly while the bodyguard, the only occupant wearing a seatbelt, was critically injured, regaining consciousness two weeks later. The Princess was trapped in the well between the front and back seats, fatally injured and unconscious. First on the scene were the pursuing photographers, travelling about 300 metres behind, who said that they heard a bang so loud that they thought Diana had been the victim of an assassin's bomb.

A passing French doctor, Frédéric Maillez, administered emergency aid, failing to recognize the barely breathing woman who was, in his words, 'unconscious, moaning and gesturing in every direction'.

Once other medical help arrived several of the paparazzi milled around the car taking pictures. A photographer, Romuald Rat, a trained first-aider, opened the rear door, allegedly to check Diana's pulse, and comforted her in English. Others were less charitable, claiming that the door was opened so that he and his colleagues could take clearer pictures of the bloody scene. What repulsed many, as the first incomplete accounts filtered out, was that the cameramen had failed to comfort the dying Princess or to phone for medical assistance. Initial police reports described a scene of mayhem with 'camera flashes going off like machine-gun fire around the back right-hand side of the vehicle where the door was open'. The first police on the scene even had to call for reinforcements to deal with the truculent paparazzi, whose actions in pursuing Diana at first indicated that she had literally been hounded to death. Seven photographers were subsequently arrested and placed under formal investigation for manslaughter and for failing to assist the accident victims.

It is one of the many savage ironies in a life suffused with tragedy that, when she was still married to Prince Charles, one of Diana's most cherished ambitions was to spend a weekend in Paris without bodyguards or photographers, losing herself in the crowd. Instead, as life slipped from her, with the Mercedes horn mournfully blaring into the night like a macabre 'Last Post', her adult life ended as it had begun, in the brazen, staccato embrace of the camera flash. Even in the city of dreams she could not escape her past.

It took rescue crews an hour to stabilize her and pull her from the mangled wreckage before she was slowly driven to the nearby La Pitié-Salpêtrière hospital for emergency surgery. By then it was much too late. She had suffered massive head and chest injuries and although the medical team did everything they could they knew it was a lost cause. At 4 a.m., 3 a.m. in London, she was pronounced dead. A post-mortem report indicated that the Princess, who never regained consciousness, was probably dead some 20 minutes after the crash. As her mother, Frances Shand Kydd, said days later: 'I know the extent of her injuries and I promise everyone that she knew nothing. She did not suffer at all.' She added: 'My knowledge comes first hand', seen as a rebuke to Mohamed al-Fayed who, the night before the funeral, publicized the fact that he had passed on Diana's alleged last words and instructions to her elder sister, Lady Sarah McCorquodale, during a meeting at Harrods. Mrs Shand Kydd's dismissal of the 'last words' was backed up by a statement from the first doctor to arrive at the scene of the crash.

Shortly after the accident the Queen and Prince Charles, who were at Balmoral, were woken by aides and told that Diana had been seriously injured. The Prince listened to radio bulletins all night but did not wake the boys until later in the morning when he told them the awful news. 'I knew something was wrong, I kept waking up all night,' Prince William was reported to have said. The news, likewise, was relayed to the Prime Minister, Tony Blair, and Diana's sisters, Lady Sarah McCorquodale and Lady Jane Fellowes. At 4.41 a.m. the world was told the dreadful news in a brief news-flash. 'Diana, Princess of Wales has died, according to British sources, the Press Association learned this morning.'

As the nation groped to understand the enormity of its loss, the need to apportion blame was the inevitable handmaiden of its grief. Before it was discovered that the driver was drunk and speeding, it was the notorious paparazzi who were in the dock. Speaking from South Africa, Earl Spencer was the first to point a finger. Visibly angered by the waste of his sister's life he said: 'I always believed the press would kill her in the end. But not even I could imagine that they would take such a direct hand in her death as seems to be the case. It would appear that every proprietor and editor of every publication that has paid for intrusive and exploitative photographs of her, encouraging greedy and ruthless individuals to risk everything in pursuit of Diana's image, has blood on their hands today.'

He went on: 'Finally the one consolation is that Diana is now in a place where no human being can ever touch her again. I pray that she rests in peace.'

The Fayed family, too, were moved to action, lawyers acting for the family taking out a civil suit against the photographers who had been arrested at the scene. Their spokesman now denounced their activities. 'There is no doubt in Mr Fayed's mind that this tragedy would not have occurred but for the press photographers who have dogged Mr Fayed and the Princess for weeks.' The paparazzi, he said, behaved like 'Apache Indians swarming around a Wells Fargo stage-coach firing not arrows but flashlights into the driver's eyes'. Central to the discussion was whether the paparazzi had caused the crash as a direct result of their actions or obliquely, as a result of their unwelcome presence.

While the recriminations continued throughout a week that has proved to be a watershed in British history, in the first hours there were the practical matters of organizing Diana's funeral and the sad task of bringing her body back from France. As a divorced Princess of Wales without a royal title, Palace courtiers were initially confused about her style and status, as unsure about how to treat her in death as in life. Certainly she could not be treated as any private citizen who had been killed abroad. The Queen and the Prince of Wales and their advisers were in full agreement, contrary to some reports, that she must be accorded full royal status.

Before he and Diana's sisters flew to Paris, the Prince joined the rest of the royal family, including Princes William and Harry, at Sunday service at Crathie church close to the Balmoral estate. The boys, who had been given the option of attending or not, insisted on taking part in the service. Although this lasted an hour, no mention was made of Diana's death nor were prayers spoken in remembrance. Instead, the minister stuck to his original sermon about the dubious joys of moving house, replete with jokes by the Scottish comedian Billy Connolly. This was the first of many differences of tone and emphasis between the people and the Palace which at first jarred and then led to open resentment.

While the royal family were at prayer, Diana's butler, Paul Burrell, was one of a number of royal officials who flew to Paris to organize her homecoming. He carried a small suitcase containing her clothes and make-up, spending a long time preparing the body for the imminent arrival of the Prince of Wales and Diana's two sisters. When the royal party flew in, late in the afternoon, they were led to the first-floor casualty room where Diana's coffin lay. Each of the group spent a few minutes alone saying their private farewells, the Prince of Wales remaining with his former wife for 30 minutes. It was clear when they emerged that many tears had been shed.

On a day when millions of people around the world literally couldn't or wouldn't believe that their princess was dead, it was only when the BAe 146 of the Queen's Flight made its final approach to RAF Northolt at 7 p.m. on Sunday evening, 31 August, that the enormity of her loss began to sink in. Her coffin, draped with the Royal Standard and topped with a single wreath of white lilies from her family, was borne in silence across the tarmac by eight RAF pall-bearers, watched by the Prime Minister and a number of other military and government dignitaries. While her body was taken first to a private mortuary and then to St James's Palace, the body of her companion, Dodi

Fayed, was buried at Brookwood Cemetery in Woking following a service at the Regent's Park mosque.

The Prime Minister, Tony Blair, who was in close contact with the Queen and Prince Charles, captured the feelings of loss and despair when he spoke to the nation earlier in the day from his Sedgefield constituency. Speaking without notes, his voice breaking with emotion, he described Diana as a 'wonderful and warm human being'.

'She touched the lives of so many others in Britain and throughout the world with joy and with comfort. How difficult things were for her from time to time, I'm sure we can only guess at. But people everywhere, not just here in Britain, kept faith with Princess Diana. They liked her, they loved her, they regarded her as one of the people. She was the People's Princess and that is how she will stay, how she will remain in all our hearts and memories for ever.'

While his was the first of many tributes which poured in from world figures, it perfectly captured the mood of the nation in a historic week which saw the British people, with sober intensity and angry dignity, place on trial the *ancien régime*, notably an elitist, exploitative and male-dominated mass media and an unresponsive monarchy. For a week Britain succumbed to flower power, the scent and sight of millions of bouquets a mute and telling testimony to the love people felt towards a woman who was scorned by the Establishment during her lifetime.

So it was entirely appropriate when Buckingham Palace announced that her funeral would be 'a unique service for a unique person'. The posies, the poems, the candles and the cards that were placed at Kensington Palace, Buckingham Palace and elsewhere spoke volumes about the mood of the nation and the state of modern Britain. 'The royal family never respected you, but the people did', said one message, as thousands of people, most of whom had never met her, made their way in quiet homage to Kensington Palace to express their grief, their sorrow, their guilt and their regret. Total strangers hugged and comforted each other, others waited patiently to lay their tributes, some prayed silently. When darkness fell, the gardens were bathed in an ethereal glow from the thousands of candles, becoming a place of dignified pilgrimage that Chaucer would have recognized. All were welcome and all came, a rainbow coalition of young and old of every colour and nationality, East Enders and West

Enders, refugees, the disabled, the lonely, the curious, and, inevitably, droves of tourists. She was the one person in the land who could connect with those Britons who had been pushed to the edges of society as well as with those who governed it.

In some way Diana's life, her vulnerability, her strength, her frailty, her beauty, her compassion and her search for fulfilment, had touched them, inspired them and in the end moved them, perhaps more than anything else in their lives. Not only did she capture the spirit of the age, mirroring society as the monarchy once did, but the manner of her life and death seemed at the time to form part of a religious cycle of sin and redemption, a genuinely good and Christian woman who was martyred for our sins, epitomizing our strange appetite for celebrity. The singer Madonna confessed: 'As much as I want to blame the press we all have blood on our hands. All of us, even myself, bought these magazines and read them.' Even the T-shirts hastily printed with the mawkish sentiment: 'Born a princess, died a saint' had an accurate sense of the popular mood less than a thousand days before the new millennium.

Those few days after her death captured for ever the contrast between the Princess and the House of Windsor: her openness, their distance; her affection, their frigidity; her spontaneity, their inflexibility; her glamour, their dullness; her modernity, their stale ritual; her emotional generosity, their aloofness; her rainbow coalition, their court of aristocrats. As the commentator Polly Toynbee wrote: 'Diana the Difficult was a problem the Palace could tackle but St Diana is something the Palace can never contend with . . . If some day the monarchy finally draws peacefully to a close, Diana's ghostly spirit will have played its part.'

As the royal family spent the week in seclusion at Balmoral, they seemed a troubled clan bewildered by events, retreating from the nation rather than leading them in mourning. While this was a wholly unfair presumption, the nation's growing irritation with their behaviour was nothing new. During the late 1980s when Britain suffered a series of appalling disasters, notably the Hillsborough football stadium tragedy, the Pan Am aeroplane crash at Lockerbie, and the sinking of the *Marchioness* pleasure cruiser, the royal family were conspicuous in their absence, preferring to remain on holiday rather than attend memorial services. At that time there was much criticism of them, though it was anger which soon abated. This time the strength of feeling threatened to overwhelm. It was perhaps fortunate that a deer-stalking party, planned for that week on the Balmoral estate, did not go ahead.

While the church service at Crathie jarred, resentment built up as the Palace appeared more concerned with protocol than the people's wishes. The public were irritated in a number of small ways; the police at first refused to allow bouquets to be placed outside Buckingham Palace where the Union Flag, unlike those on almost every other public building in Britain, was not even flying at half mast. Those wishing to pay tribute were waiting for up to 12 hours to sign one of the 5 books of condolences at St James's Palace — these were increased to 43 only after public complaints. More important than the royal family's inadequate response to the outpouring of public grief was the impression that they were turning their backs on the nation when the nation most needed them. The Queen's decision to arrive in London on the Saturday morning of the funeral even provoked the historian Lord Blake into criticizing courtiers for sticking too rigidly to the royal rule book. 'There will never be another Princess Diana,' he said. The *Sun* newspaper was characteristically blunt: 'Where is the Queen when the country needs her? She is 550 miles from London, the focal point of the nation's grief.'

For once this was not merely a tabloid rant. In a way that went to the heart of the purpose of a monarchy in a modern democratic state, the people wished to see the Head of State unify and console, taking her position at the centre of the national stage rather than watching from the wings. So there was a ripple of applause among the throng outside Buckingham Palace when it was announced that the Queen would be returning to the capital and would address the nation on the eve of the funeral. 'Our mother is coming home,' said one middle-aged man, barely able to contain his tears. The sensitivity, warmth and generosity of the Queen's tribute, made from the first-floor balcony overlooking the Mall, stilled many carping tongues. She told her TV audience: 'What I say to you now as your Queen and as a grandmother, I say from my heart. First, I want to pay tribute to Diana, myself. She was an exceptional and gifted human being. In good times and bad, she never lost her capacity to smile and laugh, to inspire others with her warmth and kindness. I admired and respected her for her energy and commitment to others, especially for her devotion to her two boys.' She went on to explain that at Balmoral that week the royal family had been trying to help Princes William and Harry to come to terms with the 'devastating loss' they had suffered.

The unprecedented decision to allow the Union Flag to fly at half mast over Buckingham Palace after the Queen had left to attend the funeral service, the agreement to double the length of the funeral route, and the walkabouts by the Queen and Prince Philip outside Buckingham Palace and by the Prince of Wales and his children outside Kensington Palace demonstrated that the Sovereign, her heir and the Prime Minister were sensitive to what the Queen called the 'extraordinary and moving reaction' to Diana's death, and had responded to it.

While the Queen had emerged splendidly from the shadows, it was the presence of Prince William, the standard bearer of Diana's legacy, who was the true focus of affection. When he joined his father and brother outside the gates of Kensington Palace, this shyly smiling, dignified young man was treated with the kind of genuflecting ecstasy more in keeping with a Papal visit, some women bursting into tears when they kissed his hand.

This devout mood was reflected in the manner of Diana's departure. Her funeral was, in sight and sound, more medieval than modern; there was the doleful sound of the tenor bell which tolled every minute as Diana's coffin, borne on a horse-drawn gun carriage, made its sombre way from Kensington Palace to Westminster Abbey; the straining silence of the crowd; the ancient solemnity of the Christian service; and the strewing of flowers along the road as Diana's body was taken to Althorp where, after a private ceremony, she was laid to rest on an island called the Round Oval in a lake on the family's ancestral estate.

Even Earl Spencer's rapier thrusts at the royal family during his funeral oration, sentiments which drew growls of approval from the crowds outside, were reminiscent of an impudent Earl of Essex daring to challenge Elizabeth I in full view of her Court. The sight of Princes William and Harry following the rumbling gun carriage vividly expressed the intimacy of their loss, revealing the Spencers and the Windsors not as remote, shimmering figures but as two families grieving together.

While the style was ancient, almost tribal, the substance on that day, 6 September

1997, will be seen by historians as marking the crumbling of the old hierarchical regime and the coming of a more egalitarian era. When the Queen bowed to the Princess's coffin as it passed Buckingham Palace she was paying obeisance not only to Diana but to everything she represented, values which express so much of modern Britain — 'The stiff upper lip versus the trembling lower lip', as one wag put it.

If Elton John's emotional rendition of 'Candle in the Wind', rewritten to incorporate a tribute to Diana, expressed everyone's feelings, Earl Spencer gave vent to the nation's thoughts with a cutting and remorseless honesty. He threw down the gauntlet to the Sovereign and her family as well as the massed ranks of the Fourth Estate, implicitly rebuking the royal family for taking away Diana's title and for the way they brought up their children. Diana, he said, 'needed no royal title to continue to generate her particular brand of magic', a reference to the fact that the Queen had stripped the Princess of her right to be styled 'Her Royal Highness' when she divorced. It was no surprise that when his brother-in-law, Sir Robert Fellowes, then the Queen's private secretary, transmitted later that day the offer to reinstate her title of honour, her brother turned it down flat.

Nor did Earl Spencer spare the Windsors their record on child rearing. 'On behalf of your mother and sisters, I pledge that we, your blood family, will do all we can to continue the imaginative and loving way in which you were steering these two exceptional young men, so that their souls are not simply immersed by duty and tradition, but can sing openly as you planned.'

Having effortlessly skewered the Windsors as a dysfunctional family, he went on to bludgeon the mass media. 'My own and only explanation [for her treatment by the media] is that genuine goodness is threatening to those at the opposite end of the moral spectrum. It is a point to remember that of all the ironies about Diana, perhaps the greatest was this — a girl given the name of the ancient goddess of hunting was, in the end, the most hunted person of the modern age.'

While it was these sentiments which provoked spontaneous applause from the congregation, he spoke with insight about the character of his sister, whom he called, 'the unique, the complex, the extraordinary and irreplaceable Diana whose beauty, both internal and external, will never be extinguished from our minds'. He praised her compassion, her style, her gifts of intuition and sensitivity, while admitting that her underlying feelings of insecurity and unworthiness had provoked her eating disorders.

Her brother, like the royal family and her friends and advisers, was astonished by the outpouring of overwhelming grief at her death, and he cautioned against canonizing her memory. 'You stand tall enough as a human being of unique qualities not to need to be seen as a saint,' he said.

It proved a vain hope. As a memorial fund in her memory attracted hundreds of millions of pounds, as Elton John's Diana tribute became the fastest- and biggest-selling record of all time, as the books, videos, magazines and other memorabilia emerged, Diana joined the pantheon of the immortals. Like Graceland, the home of Elvis Presley, her final resting place at Althorp has become a place of pilgrimage and homage. She has been garlanded with numerous posthumous awards — the Nobel Peace Prize would have been particularly appropriate — her name has been lent to hospitals, hospices and other charitable causes around the world, while her work and memory continue to inspire many among this generation to live worthier and more fulfilled lives.

It is clear that there are two Dianas, the individual known to her friends and family, and now the venerated icon, the projection of millions of fantasies, hopes and dreams. Many of those who knew her as a young girl, a troubled princess and a divorcee searching for happiness still remain baffled by the global outpourings of grief. For her death did not provoke the kind of mass hysteria which is often seen at pop concerts but something much deeper. Many doctors started talking of 'the Diana Syndrome' as they dealt with troubled members of the public who had come to them for help because the Princess's death had awakened painful memories buried deep inside themselves.

How then do we explain Diana the individual and Diana the phenomenon? In her life Diana was a complex web of contradictions; fearless yet frail, unloved but adored, needy but generous, self-obsessed yet selfless, inspirational yet despairing, demanding of advice but disliking criticism, honest yet disingenuous, intuitive yet unworldly, supremely sophisticated yet constantly uncertain, and manipulative but naïve. She could be wilful, exasperating, a flawed perfectionist who would disarm with a self-deprecating witticism; her penetrating, cornflower-blue eyes seduced with a glance. Her language knew no boundaries; her lexicon was that of the smile, the caress, the hug and the kiss, not the statement or the speech. She was endlessly fascinating and will remain eternally enigmatic.

All through her life she was guided, not by argument or debate, but by instinct and intuition. It was a river which took her on a journey into the worlds of astrologers, psychics, soothsayers and therapists. Here lies the key that unlocks the doors between her personality and her universal appeal. This is why if Diana had lived for ever, the media would never have understood or appreciated her. When she looked at a rose she savoured its beauty, they counted the petals.

In her work Diana embraced those who were on the margins of society — lepers, Aids victims and others. Hers was an appeal to our emotional rather than intellectual intelligence, our intuitive and nurturing nature, as well as to the way she had been used and exploited by men in her life, be they princes or photographers, reflecting how many women saw their own lives. At heart she was a woman who championed feminine values rather than simply craving acceptance in a male-dominated world. Her importance now lies not just in what she did during her lifetime but in the meaning of her life, the inspiration she gave to others, particularly women, to search for their own truth.

AFTERWORD: 'WE THINK OF HER EVERY DAY'

It was quiet now. Peaceful. Her apartment at Kensington Palace which had once rung to the sound of laughter and conversation now stood empty and silent. It was as though Diana had never existed. Her bedroom, sitting room, nursery and elsewhere had all been stripped bare, right down to the wallpaper. Her furniture was taken to St James's Palace for William and Harry or to the Royal Collection at Windsor Castle. Her clothes, letters and other papers were burned, shredded or packed up and sent to Althorp, the Spencer family home. Fifteen years of her correspondence — letters to charities and government departments — disappeared without a trace, leaving her former private secretary Patrick Jephson utterly bemused. Even the ink blotter on her desk was cut into tiny pieces.

The fear of souvenir hunters taking Diana's belongings and selling them meant that everything — the carpets, the silk wallpaper, the plants and even the light bulbs — was removed, leaving apartments eight and nine empty and anonymous. Her butler Paul Burrell was given formal notice; the sackfuls of mail sent to her home were all opened, answered and filed away. Then, to tie everything up, around the first anniversary of her death, the sign outside her former home indicating the Waleses' residence was painted over.

Certainly there were those inside and outside the royal palaces who wished that her memory could be expunged so easily, enabling the spotlight once more to focus on the Queen and her family. Her brother Charles caught the mood: 'I think there is a feeling among those who were never Diana supporters of "Let's try and marginalize her and tell people she never mattered." ' It was easier said than done. Her death had induced the birth of a remarkable charity, the Diana Memorial Fund, which arose from the extraordinary outpouring of grief, expectation and hope in the days following her death. In a spontaneous gesture by her public, thousands of pounds were sent to Kensington Palace, temporarily turning the royal garages into a makeshift sorting office. The tears of grief grew into a tsunami of giving as every day 6,000 letters arrived containing cheques, cash, pocket money and postal orders.

In the months following her death, the Fund became far more than a simple charity, the offices operating as a conduit for much hurt and unresolved anguish. The foundling charity was flooded with poems, poignant letters and tearful phone calls. One touching note read: 'I hope you are OK in heaven and dad'll look after you.' It was accompanied by a note from the sender's teacher explaining that the little boy's father had died on the same day as Diana.

From the moment of its conception there were those who sneered and sniped at its work, eager to smother the infant charity. 'Certainly St James's Palace [Prince Charles's London base] wanted the Diana Memorial Fund wrapped up as quickly as possible,' recalled Vivienne Parry, one of the charity's first trustees.

Besides the negative remarks of its naysayers, the nascent charity was also beset by problems almost before it had taken its first steps. A decision to sue Franklin Mint, an American company that was producing Diana dolls without the Fund's approval with regard to Diana's image rights, was manna from heaven for the critics. Not only did the Fund lose the case but the bitter legal wrangle cost millions of pounds in fees. The court case, together with the decision to license the use of Diana's name on tubs of margarine, even had Diana's brother on the warpath, describing the deal as 'tasteless'. Prince Charles's supporters gleefully released Earl Spencer's confidential letter to the Fund asking for it to be closed down at the earliest opportunity. 'Their motive is clear,' noted Vivienne Parry, 'the fund had filled a media vacuum left by Diana's death and the quicker we were shut down the quicker she will go away.'

The royal family's focus, however, was not on the dead but on the living, particularly Camilla Parker Bowles, the third wheel in the royal marriage. Prince Charles, who considered her presence in his future as 'non negotiable', instructed his advisers to introduce his partner to the public in a way that was unobtrusive and discreet. While Camilla kept a low profile, the Prince's new press spokesman, Mark Bolland, known by William and Harry as Blackadder, after the scheming nobleman in the eponymous TV comedy, devised ways to achieve his master's bidding. He used a meeting at St James's Palace between Prince William, seen as the living legacy of the late Princess, and

Camilla to signal her acceptance by Diana's children. Royal correspondents were briefed on the meeting, Bolland helpfully adding that Camilla needed a cigarette and a stiff gin and tonic after the fateful encounter. When William eventually realized that he had been played like a fish in order to enhance Camilla's standing, he was understandably furious that a very private and intimate family moment had been used in such a manner. Little wonder that Prince Charles's biographer Catherine Meyer described the atmosphere in the office of Prince Charles as akin to Wolf Hall, the treacherous and opportunistic world of Henry VIII brilliantly evoked by the novelist Hilary Mantel.

None the less the strategy worked: the Prince of Wales and his partner were able to fly to Greece for their first ever family holiday together without attracting negative headlines. The fact that William had been instrumental in inviting Camilla to join the party — as was conveniently leaked at the time — was interpreted as forgiveness for past transgressions, a latter-day version of the laying-on of hands. The subtext for the public to absorb was obvious: if William could forgive, so could the rest of the world.

Their holiday was followed by a carefully

choreographed photocall at the Ritz hotel in January 1999 where banks of photographers flashed away as the couple entered the building. Later that year, Bolland was on hand to guide Camilla through her launch into New York society, a brief trip that was to all intents and purposes a royal visit with people calling her 'ma'am'. When she was invited to join the Queen for the Golden Jubilee service in Westminster Abbey in June 2002, her acceptance inside royal circles appeared to be complete.

Their marriage in April 2005 was the culmination of a considered process, one that had been severely delayed, initially because of the unforeseen death of the Princess, and then by a cascade of curious and scurrilous headline-making incidents surrounding the French and then the unexpected British investigations into Diana's tragic accident.

Add to that the trial at the Old Bailey of Diana's former butler Paul Burrell on charges of stealing her property, of which he was acquitted. Then there were false allegations of male rape involving a member of the Prince's staff, which culminated in a formal investigation by the Prince's then private secretary Michael Peat. Topping off the lurid stories was a letter, purportedly written by Diana in October 1996 or 1995, where she wrote about her suspicions that there was a plot, organized by her ex-husband, to have her killed by engineering a car accident. Inevitably, the Prince became the subject of headlines such as: 'Charles: How much more can I take'.

The extraordinary decision to have a second British investigation into Diana's death, even after the French, who employed 30 detectives and interviewed 300 witnesses, had concluded that the crash was an accident, pleased no one — not the insulted French authorities, nor the Prince of Wales, nor Earl Spencer and his family. The only man delighted by the decision of the official coroner Michael Burgess to instruct Sir John Stevens, the Metropolitan Palace Commissioner, to open his own inquiry rather than rubber-stamp the findings of the exhaustive two-year French effort was Mohamed al-Fayed. He had already spent five million pounds and hundreds of thousands of man-hours attempting to prove that his son and Diana were murdered. 'Absolute black and white, horrendous murder,' he stated. It was a view that resonated in the Arab world where it was widely believed that the couple were killed because the shadowy Establishment did not want a Muslim to marry a princess. *Who Killed Diana? Order from the Palace* was a best-seller in Egypt while the then Libyan leader Colonel Gaddafi broadcast his view that French and English secret service agents had arranged the assassination.

As Fayed piled conjecture upon allegation upon accusation, many went along with his conspiracy theories. Secret services, the royal family, Prince Philip — all were viewed as potential murderers. Most popular among the 36,000 conspiracy theory websites were those stories concerning the involvement of Britain's spooks. Extra weight was added by the testimony of former British intelligence agents Richard Tomlinson and David Shayler when they cited an earlier unrelated plan to kill the former Serbian President Slobodan Milosevic in a faked car accident when he was due to visit Geneva in Switzerland. Not all were convinced, however. An agent from the KGB, Russia's spy service, even told espionage writer Philip Knightley: 'It takes a genius to make murder by car look like an accident.'

There were other runners and riders in the great conspiracy theory race, including that she was killed by international arms dealers due to her support for a landmine ban, that Osama bin Laden had her murdered as she was a poor role model for Muslim women, and that she was killed by the deeply strange Babylonian Brotherhood (believers in this group claim that members are in fact reptile humanoids who control humanity) as she was named after the moon goddess and the Pont de l'Alma, where the accident occurred, means passage of the moon goddess.

As was regularly pointed out, if Diana had genuinely believed that she could be killed in a premeditated car accident, as she had supposedly written, why was she not wearing a seat belt that fateful night. The conclusion of the British criminal investigation, published in December 2006, was virtually the same as the French report, stating that every conspiracy theory was without foundation and that all the evidence pointed to the deaths being the result of a tragic accident. A few months later, in April 2007, a jury at the coroner's inquest gave the verdict that Diana and Dodi were unlawfully killed as a result of the gross negligence of Mercedes driver Henri Paul and the paparazzi. 'When it is all over,' commented the former royal coroner Dr John Burton, '95 per cent of the people will still disregard the facts and want to go back to their conspiracies.'

The truth is that at heart the public find it difficult to believe that a modern-day goddess could meet her maker in the banality of a car accident with a drunk driver who was driving too fast. We need conspiracy theories to somehow rationalize, make ordered and bearable that which is chaotic and inexplicable. As Dr Patrick Leman of Royal Holloway College, University of London, who has conducted research into conspiracy theories, observed: 'When a big event happens we prefer to have a big cause. It upsets our worldview if there isn't a significant powerful explanation.' As a result, major world events, such as the assassination of John F. Kennedy, the death of Elvis Presley and the attack on the World Trade Center, are all surrounded by competing conspiracy theories.

These lurid allegations, endless conspiracy theories and nasty speculations did little to enhance the reputation of either the Prince or Princess of Wales. Diana's letter of foreboding, which was both pathetic and comic, made her seem, as *The Times* noted, like 'a drama queen or a tragic princess'. The witty, self-deprecating, courageous, caring and humane woman remembered by Diana's friends, and to whom the world responded when she died, was rapidly receding in the rear-view mirror. In life she feared that she would be dismissed as mentally unstable, in death she was increasingly being described as at best flawed and sometimes even mad, a woman who had preserved her reputation by dying young.

With the passing years there was a wholesale reassessment of her personality as her critics felt more able to speak out. 'I think she was out of control and it would have got worse,' the Queen's biographer Robert Lacey told talk-show host Larry King, while respected royal writer Hugo Vickers believed that she was 'spiralling into chaos'. 'It might have been a very sad middle age for her,' he opined. Prince Charles's biographer Penny Junor, who was helped in her profile of Diana by royal courtiers, stated that the Princess had threatened to have Camilla killed and was the first in the marriage to stray. Even friends of the Queen got in on the act, Lady Penn, a lady-in-waiting, telling the Queen Mother's official biographer, William Shawcross: 'The Queen found Diana's ill health or mental instability very hard to understand because she's a very matter-of-fact person.'

The fact that there were only ever a handful of bouquets outside Kensington Palace in the years following her death was seized upon as a sign of Diana's wilting reputation and the public's fading memory. It was more ammunition for those who felt that the outpouring of grief at her death was a hysterical overreaction, a temporary aberration before society once more embraced good sense and reason. Diana worship was simply a craze, like Pokémon.

Grandiose plans to honour her death had petered out. In the immediate aftermath of her death senior politicians suggested renaming Heathrow Airport and the August bank holiday in her name. These plans were quietly shelved and even those schemes that went ahead were bogged down in controversy. A £3 million water feature in Kensington Gardens to commemorate her life was awash with indecision and argument. The Diana Memorial Committee, chaired by the strong-minded Rosa Monckton, couldn't decide between a design offered by American landscape artist Kathryn Gustafson and one from the Indian-born British sculptor Anish Kapoor. In the end the then Culture Secretary, Tessa Jowell, was called in to make the final decision, plumping for the American entry. Since it was opened by the Queen in 2004 it has been dogged by complaints as to the high running costs, estimated at more than £1 million since it was completed, frequent closures for maintenance, and health and safety issues.

A children's playground and a memorial Diana walkway in Kensington Gardens fared better and are both still enjoyed by the public. Noticeably no member of the royal family, not even William or Harry, was present when the projects were opened by Earl Spencer and the then Chancellor, Gordon Brown, respectively. The royal family seemed all too happy to let Diana rest in peace, her memory unobserved, her life and achievements forgotten. They were conspicuous in their absence at any event relating to the late Princess. So it was that a hospice outside Cardiff, a hospital in Grimsby, a community nursing home for sick children and other projects, all named after the late Princess, were dedicated without remark or appearance from the House of Windsor.

The huge public turnout for the Queen Mother's funeral in March 2002 and the warm response to the Queen's Golden Jubilee later that year demonstrated that the Queen still enjoyed the affection of the nation in spite of the friction during the week of Diana's funeral. At a parade which formed the centrepiece of the Golden Jubilee celebrations Diana was relegated to a drive-on part, appearing as a cut-out figure on one of the convoy of floats that paraded down the Mall past the royal party, which included Camilla Parker Bowles. As novelist Robert Harris observed: 'Not since Trotsky was expelled from the Soviet Union in 1929 has a prominent public figure been so comprehensively airbrushed out of the nation's public life.'

What then of her living legacy, Princes William and Harry? Their interventions during the great Diana debate had been sporadic, in 1998 urging the public to stop grieving and move on and then accusing their mother's butler Paul Burrell of a 'cold and overt' betrayal when he published his memoirs. There were other reasons for their considered silence. Their father had been buoyed and gratified by a huge surge of sympathy as he was now viewed as a single parent bringing up two teenage sons on his own. Instinctively the boys didn't want to do anything that would rock the family boat and so they tiptoed around the whole issue of what to say and how to remember their mother.

There was also the Camilla issue to contend with. Though William was unhappy about being used to help rehabilitate her in the public mind, his alternative options were limited. Put simply, he didn't want to upset his dad. As the Prince's biographer Penny Junor remarked: 'While they love their father he is a complex man who is difficult to be the son of. They are very careful of his sensitivities and dance around them a lot.'

Nor were they at all comfortable about giving vent to private grief in public. Of the two brothers, it was William in particular who had a visceral loathing of the media for their perceived role in his mother's death. He was certainly not willing to reflect on his loss in public. In what became a mini crisis for the monarchy, in the immediate aftermath of Diana's death William even considered withdrawing from public life altogether. He needed much convincing to stay on course and recommit to his lifelong destiny. Prince Philip was the guiding hand here. In the week of Diana's death, William's grandfather was deeply concerned about the emotional state of the future king. During a conference call between Balmoral and Downing Street he butted in and told the shocked listeners: 'Our worry at the moment is William. He's run away up the hill and we can't find him.' He was eventually coaxed down by his sympathetic grandfather. As the then Prime Minister, Tony Blair, later commented in his memoir: 'He knew now if he didn't before what being a prince and a king meant. For all the sense of duty, the prison walls of hereditary tradition must have seemed too high a price to pay.'

Worse still, the two princes seemed to have no privacy even when they were off duty. Uncannily, their every movement and plan was monitored by the media. Personal arrangements, plans for birthday presents and even medical visits were all known by one newspaper in particular, the *News of the World,* and its royal correspondent Clive Goodman. It appeared to William and Harry that there were numerous so-called friends inside their different circles tipping off the media about their movements. For a young man who likes to be in control of his life, William felt under siege. It became all-consuming, the brothers distrusting everyone, a feeling that communicated itself to William's then girlfriend, Catherine Middleton, who doubtless worried that her family and friends could be thought to be leaking information. In November 2005, by a stroke of luck, they discovered that their telephone messages were being intercepted by Goodman and others. Their story would go on to become a key thread in the infamous phone tapping scandal, eventually leading to the closure of the *News of the World,* the jailing of Goodman and others, as well as the Leveson inquiry into press freedom and ethics.

Though the public implications were considerable, in personal terms the realization that their friends were not routinely betraying their confidences was both a release and a revelation for the young princes. 'It was a transformative moment in their dealings with the outside world,' comments a friend who was present during the original police investigation. 'From then on they were able to relax; at last they were able to distinguish between their private and public lives.'

Brothers grim no longer, they emerged as jaunty and jovial impresarios, organizing a pop concert held in July 2007 at Wembley Stadium in memory of their mother to mark the tenth anniversary of her death. William's sunny mood may have had something to do with his reconciliation with Catherine following a brief break-up. Fondly remembering their mother dancing barefoot to Michael Jackson in her sitting room, the princes wanted to convey her love of life, sense of fun and passion for dance and musicals. Not only did the concert raise £1.2 million for charities supported by Diana, it marked a major public step change: from then on, the princes would actively and consistently honour her legacy.

As boys they had toed the royal family line and had spoken, if at all, in hushed tones about their mother. As mature young men they made their own decisions, defying perhaps the wishes of the Queen and certainly their father, to honour their mother in the way that they felt she should be remembered. Their careful tiptoeing through the minefield that is Diana's legacy would have amused their mother. When she died she was no longer part of the royal family but her values had resonated with modern Britain and beyond. Her boys, now young men, wished to honour that. None more so than Prince Harry.

During a service of remembrance held at London's Guards' Chapel in the presence of the Queen and the Spencer family, Harry spoke movingly about his mother. It was a tribute from the heart, the Prince saying that their lives were divided into two parts — when their mother was alive and the ten years since her tragic death. When she was alive they took for granted 'her love of life, laughter, fun and folly. She was our guardian, friend and protector.' Rescuing her from the mire of controversy, her memory in danger of being forgotten or misrepresented, Harry wanted the world to remember the mother he lost and thought of every day. It was a positive message about an extraordinary human being, 'fun-loving, generous, down to earth, entirely genuine', who had made them and many others happy. This is how he wanted his mother to be remembered. Years later Harry confessed that he wished that he had spoken about her much, much sooner. He admitted: 'I never really dealt with what had happened. It was a lot of buried emotion. For a huge part of my life I didn't really want to think about it.'

Perhaps the moment that truly cemented Diana at the heart of the monarchy for generations to come took place in the Entrée Room at St James's Palace on 16 November 2010, when Catherine Middleton and Prince William confronted the world on their engagement day. Comparisons between Diana, the woman who said she would never ascend the throne, and the girl who will one day be crowned Queen were inevitable — and plentiful. It was all eerily similar to Diana's big day in 1981: the blue dress, the nervous voices, the hesitant body language. Taking pride of place was Catherine's engagement ring, the same sapphire and diamond worn by William's mother. It was the clearest signal yet that while Diana might be gone she was not forgotten. 'This was my way of keeping her close to it all,' William explained.

Left unsaid was the fact that the failure of his parents' marriage had given William the latitude to spend plenty of time finding a partner who would be a lover, companion and supporter no matter her social class. Catherine became the first commoner in 400 years to marry into the royal family. The days when Prince Charles was under pressure to marry a white Anglo-Saxon Protestant aristocratic virgin, such as Diana, are gone for good. At the time of writing Harry is in a serious relationship with Meghan Markle, a divorced activist Hollywood actress three years his senior and with a black mother who lives in a down-at-heel Los Angeles community. Whether or not it ends in wedding bells, it is a sign of how far the royal family have come. Not so long ago Prince Andrew was discouraged from pursuing his suit with another American actress, Koo Stark, because of her appearance in a movie where clothing was an optional extra.

If William's engagement ensured that Diana stayed at the heart of his family, the wedding of the Prince and Catherine Middleton at Westminster Abbey on 29 April 2011 marked a genuine transition for the royal family and the public. While the memory of Diana was in the minds of many — one woman spectator remarked: 'When the sun came out just as Kate reached the altar we knew it was Diana' — the wedding marked a new chapter in the unfolding royal story. The memories of that September day in 1997 when William and Harry walked solemnly behind their mother's funeral cortege were now overlaid by the sight of the smiling prince and his enchanting bride ready to begin a new life together. That he and Catherine named their second child Princess Charlotte Elizabeth Diana was an unmistakable gesture to the two women in William's life whom he respected and loved above all others.

William, Harry and now Catherine have all picked up the baton of charity work for which Diana is most admired. During its 16-year history, the Memorial Fund, in spite of its rocky inception, gave away a staggering £138 million to over 400 deserving charities, mainly to disadvantaged people on the margins of society, the very groups Diana had championed in her life. 'Her probable effect on charity,' according to one senior fund raiser, 'is more significant than any other person's in the twentieth century.' As Andrew Purkis, the former chief executive, recalls: 'I do think that the Princess was understood by many to be willing to reach out to stigmatized, marginalized groups like people who are dying, lepers, those suffering from HIV/Aids and so on.'

Though the Fund closed in 2013, in March that year the Royal Foundation of the Duke and Duchess of Cambridge and Prince Harry took over legal ownership of the charity. More importantly, the trio have continued and developed her work; a new generation with new ideas but the same ethos. Thus, Harry visited minefields in Mozambique in 2010 and Angola in 2013 to see the work of HALO, the landmine clearance organization passionately backed by the late Princess. The image of her walking alone through a recently cleared minefield is one of the most vivid representations of her humanitarian mission. For Harry the trip was very much a chance to follow in his mother's footsteps. His support of the National Aids Trust, and the Sentebale charity in Lesotho that helps orphan children, many suffering from AIDS, is testimony to his determination to keep his mother's flame alive.

Just as his mother reached out to those at the margins, so William has focused attention on the cyberbullying of young people on social media, especially those who are gay, lesbian, bisexual or transgender. He hosted a meeting of LGBT youngsters at Kensington Palace and even appeared on the cover of the gay magazine *Attitude*. Harry, who served in the Army for a decade, undertaking two tours of duty in Afghanistan, has enthusiastically embraced the Help for Heroes charity, which supports wounded soldiers as they try to rebuild their lives. He has taken a leaf out of his mother's playbook and spends time on private visits to the recovery unit at Headley Court where he meets wounded servicemen face to face on fact-finding missions. 'It's important to do stuff behind the scenes,' he says. 'It's something that our mother did a lot of and that's the time that you really get to learn and you actually get the honest truth out of people.' The Prince is also the founder of the Invictus Games, an international multi-sport event in which wounded, injured or sick armed services personnel take part in a variety of competitive sports, including wheelchair basketball and indoor rowing. In 2017 the games take place in Toronto, Canada, where Harry first met his current flame, Meghan Markle.

Like their mother, the two princes are willing to take on taboo or unpopular issues in order to provoke discussion and awareness. William, Harry and the Duchess of Cambridge joined together to found the Heads Together charity to help tackle the stigma of those suffering from depression and other unresolved mental illnesses. Their own willingness to speak out about their feelings towards their mother, their regrets and their memories has helped them engage and emotionally connect with others suffering from loss, bereavement and trauma.

In the popular imagination, William and Harry are considered their mother's rather than their father's sons, continuing her work in a way that reflects her essence, young men who, like their mother, are open, frank and human. There are none of the strangled feelings of their father — 'Whatever love means' — or the impassive stoicism of the Queen, who is frequently described as 'tightly wrapped'. In that regard Diana's determination to raise her boys so that they weren't afraid to express their feelings or show that they are human has paid off handsomely. Her friend Julia Samuel, co-founder of the Child Bereavement Trust, witnessed this at first hand, recalling being 'incredibly moved and touched' by William's honesty about his own feelings when, in support of the charity, he wrote a few words about his mother: 'Life has altered as you know it and not a day goes past without you thinking about the one you have lost. I know that over time it is possible to learn to live with what has happened and, with the passing of the years, to retain or rediscover cherished memories.'

All the evidence suggests that Diana's size-nine heels, what she called her 'tart's trotters', will be firmly imprinted on the monarchy for several generations to come. When the Queen dies, Prince Charles's reign will be something of an interregnum, rather like the brief reign of Edward VII. He has had a lifetime to ponder on how to project the image and work of the monarchy. Given his constitutional interests, particularly in influencing politicians and his focus on architecture, the environment and organic farming, it will be very different in style and substance to the monarchy imagined by the late humanitarian Princess. Her impact will be with King William and through him, his heirs, Prince George and Princess Charlotte.

In spite of the continuation of her work by her children, there are those, like Pulitzer prize–winning writer Anne Applebaum among others, who have argued that the Princess's legacy is pea sized and her impact transitory. In a historical comparison she is often viewed as a latter-day Princess Caroline of Brunswick, who was married to the Prince of Wales, later King George IV. Like Diana she was cast out of court and even barred from the Coronation of her husband in 1821, a victim of the devious royal family. Like Diana she was wildly popular, this first 'People's princess' becoming a rallying point for dissent. When she died three weeks after the coronation, thousands lined the route of her funeral cortege. Now she is but an entertaining footnote in history. Unlike Diana, though, she left no living legacy to continue her work. Diana most surely did. Even when they were part-time royals — Harry as an Apache helicopter pilot, William an air ambulance pilot — it was evident that Diana's legacy would be at the very heart of their charity work. Now that both princes have pledged themselves to work for the monarchy fulltime, that commitment will only expand.

While it is true that her death did not change the country, it was a jolting wake-up call for the monarchy, forcing the Sovereign and her family to recognize that the country was changing and that the Windsors were not representing that transformation. It was clear that many, particularly those in the shadows of society, felt that they were represented more by Diana than by the House of Windsor. Many felt themselves excluded from the traditional model of monarchy which, as historian Professor John Taylor has argued, is defined by household and family.

If, as French sociologist Émile Durkheim reasons, society has a shared sense of values known as the collective conscience, then it could be said that Diana played a role in expanding it, or in Diana's case the idea might be better phrased as the collective constituency. During her lifetime, and certainly after her death, she broadened what could be said and done and by whom. In the process she made the monarchy, or at least her version of that venerable institution, feel more inclusive.

Psychotherapist Dr Nicole Gehl observed: 'Her impact on the world has a lot to do with how people identified with her. They saw her as a rebel and a victim at the same time and she shook up the monarchy. In her fragility there was a lot of strength.' During the historic and unruly funeral week Diana was remembered as embracing and approachable, the royal family viewed as exclusive, distant and aloof. In short Diana was seen as a noble outsider, the House of Windsor as ignoble insiders.

The failure to fly the Union flag at half mast, the decision by the Queen to stay at Balmoral rather than heading to the nation's capital, and the royal family's failure to make any substantive statement about the Princess, had outraged many. At a time when leadership was needed, the House of Windsor dropped the baton, leaving others such as Prime Minister Tony Blair to articulate the nation's profound sense of loss.

The Queen's intervention later in the funeral week, when she spoke to the nation as both Sovereign and grandmother from the Chinese Room at Buckingham Palace, calmed the doubts in many hearts. None the less the damage was done, the enduring and deep-rooted compact between the monarchy and the people fractured and splintered. At least for a time. Her speech was, in part, atonement for standing on the sidelines, for failing to console the grieving population quickly enough. It was the Queen who led the tributes and who, most importantly, recognized the need for the ancient institution she heads to learn from the young Princess whom it had so recently banished.

Rather like a lovers' tiff, both parties,

public and monarch, were reconciled, though there was a recognition that things would never be quite the same again. It led to a much overdue re-evaluation of the relationship. As the Queen's private secretary Mary Francis later admitted, some 'harsh lessons' were absorbed by the House of Windsor. The institution was jolted out of its complacency and forced to look at itself with a very much more critical eye. Subtle changes in style and approach were brought forward with greater speed than might otherwise have been the case. As for the people, it was argued that they kept their respect for the Queen but put aside old-style deference. They became loyal citizens instead of loyal subjects, mindless worship replaced by clear-eyed respect.

In many ways the public were well ahead of the monarchy in appreciating Diana's humanitarian mission. It is ironic that as the royal family have become, in historian Frank Prochaska's telling phrase, a 'welfare monarchy', defined more by their civic and charitable work than by their symbolic or constitutional significance, it was the Princess who instinctively embraced and developed that ethos.

The feminization of the monarchy — women have dominated the House of Windsor for nearly two centuries — together with the emphasis on charity work dusted with the glamour of celebrity, found its apogee in the Princess. She was the only member of the royal family to be able to project that elusive combination on to a global stage. The fact that Prince Harry could convince the Queen as well as President Barack Obama and First Lady Michelle to take part in a promotional video for his brainchild, the Invictus Games, in Florida in 2016, shows that Diana's unique magic has rubbed off on her youngest son.

A far cry from her childhood, when she sensed that she might be the wife of an ambassador, or her early days inside the royal family, when Diana was genuinely shy and feared meeting her adoring crowds. By the end Diana became what might be termed a 'President Princess', both part of and independent from the royal family, a woman on her own who had found her public role on the world stage. As Diana's biographer Sarah Bradford says: 'She represented an all-important side of the monarchy, the ability to do good for the people, to promote their welfare and good causes and make them feel good about themselves.'

As an outsider she was able to accomplish many of her professional goals, though personal happiness seemed to elude her. She wanted to get married again and have more children. Family meant so much to her and, had she lived, she would be relishing her role as the world's most glamorous grandmother. But that was not to be.

In January 2017, the princes chose to commemorate their mother's life by commissioning a statue to stand in the public gardens of Kensington Palace. As they said: 'It has been 20 years since our mother's death and the time is right to recognize her positive impact in the UK and around the world with a permanent statue. Our mother touched so many lives. We hope the statue will help all those who visit Kensington Palace to reflect on her life and her legacy.'

While her life was brief she left an indelible mark on the royal family, the monarchy and the nation. Diana, Princess of Wales, lives on not just in our memories but in the lives and work of Princes William and Harry. As Prince Harry says: 'I hope she is looking down with tears in her eyes being incredibly proud of what we've established.' Diana may be gone but her sons will make certain that she will never be forgotten.

ABOUT THE AUTHOR

Andrew Morton is a leading authority on modern celebrity and royalty. Since his groundbreaking biography of Diana, Princess of Wales, he has gone on to write *New York Times* and *Sunday Times* (UK) bestsellers on Monica Lewinsky, Madonna, David and Victoria Beckham, Tom Cruise, Angelina Jolie, and the Duke and Duchess of Cambridge. The winner of numerous literary awards, he divides his time between London and Los Angeles.